Business Strategies for Information Technology Management

Kalle Kangas
Turku School of Economics and Business Administration, Finland

IRM Press
Publisher of innovative scholarly and professional
information technology titles in the cyberage

Hershey • London • Melbourne • Singapore • Beijing

Acquisitions Editor:	Mehdi Khosrow-Pour
Senior Managing Editor:	Jan Travers
Managing Editor:	Amanda Appicello
Development Editor:	Michele Rossi
Copy Editor:	Sharon Gable, Julie Randall, Angela Britcher & Bernard Kieklak, Jr.
Typesetter:	Amanda Appicello
Cover Design:	Korey Gongloff
Printed at:	Integrated Book Technology

Published in the United States of America by
    IRM Press (an imprint of Idea Group Inc.)
    1331 E. Chocolate Avenue, Suite 200
    Hershey PA 17033-1117
    Tel: 717-533-8845
    Fax: 717-533-8661
    E-mail: cust@idea-group.com
    Web site: http://www.irm-press.com

and in the United Kingdom by
    IRM Press (an imprint of Idea Group Inc.)
    3 Henrietta Street
    Covent Garden
    London WC2E 8LU
    Tel: 44 20 7240 0856
    Fax: 44 20 7379 3313
    Web site: http://www.eurospan.co.uk

Copyright © 2003 by IRM Press. All rights reserved. No part of this book may be reproduced in any form or by any means, electronic or mechanical, including photocopying, without written permission from the publisher.

Library of Congress Cataloging-in-Publication Data

Kangas, Kalle.
   Business strategies for information technology management / Kalle Kangas.
      p. cm.
   Issued also in electronic form.
   Includes bibliographical references and index.
     ISBN 1-931777-45-4 (soft cover) -- ISBN 1-931777-61-6 (ebook)
   1. Information technology--Management. 2. Information technology--Management--Case studies. 3. Business--Data processing. I. Title.
    HD30.2.K354 2003
    004'.068--dc21
                                                      2002156231

British Cataloguing in Publication Data
A Cataloguing in Publication record for this book is available from the British Library.

New Releases from IRM Press

- **Multimedia and Interactive Digital TV: Managing the Opportunities Created by Digital Convergence**/Margherita Pagani
  ISBN: 1-931777-38-1; eISBN: 1-931777-54-3 / US$59.95 / © 2003
- **Virtual Education: Cases in Learning & Teaching Technologies**/ Fawzi Albalooshi (Ed.), ISBN: 1-931777-39-X; eISBN: 1-931777-55-1 / US$59.95 / © 2003
- **Managing IT in Government, Business & Communities**/Gerry Gingrich (Ed.)
  ISBN: 1-931777-40-3; eISBN: 1-931777-56-X / US$59.95 / © 2003
- **Information Management: Support Systems & Multimedia Technology**/ George Ditsa (Ed.), ISBN: 1-931777-41-1; eISBN: 1-931777-57-8 / US$59.95 / © 2003
- **Managing Globally with Information Technology**/Sherif Kamel (Ed.)
  ISBN: 42-X; eISBN: 1-931777-58-6 / US$59.95 / © 2003
- **Current Security Management & Ethical Issues of Information Technology**/Rasool Azari (Ed.), ISBN: 1-931777-43-8; eISBN: 1-931777-59-4 / US$59.95 / © 2003
- **UML and the Unified Process**/Liliana Favre (Ed.)
  ISBN: 1-931777-44-6; eISBN: 1-931777-60-8 / US$59.95 / © 2003
- **Business Strategies for Information Technology Management**/Kalle Kangas (Ed.)
  ISBN: 1-931777-45-4; eISBN: 1-931777-61-6 / US$59.95 / © 2003
- **Managing E-Commerce and Mobile Computing Technologies**/Julie Mariga (Ed.)
  ISBN: 1-931777-46-2; eISBN: 1-931777-62-4 / US$59.95 / © 2003
- **Effective Databases for Text & Document Management**/Shirley A. Becker (Ed.)
  ISBN: 1-931777-47-0; eISBN: 1-931777-63-2 / US$59.95 / © 2003
- **Technologies & Methodologies for Evaluating Information Technology in Business**/ Charles K. Davis (Ed.), ISBN: 1-931777-48-9; eISBN: 1-931777-64-0 / US$59.95 / © 2003
- **ERP & Data Warehousing in Organizations: Issues and Challenges**/Gerald Grant (Ed.), ISBN: 1-931777-49-7; eISBN: 1-931777-65-9 / US$59.95 / © 2003
- **Practicing Software Engineering in the 21st Century**/Joan Peckham (Ed.)
  ISBN: 1-931777-50-0; eISBN: 1-931777-66-7 / US$59.95 / © 2003
- **Knowledge Management: Current Issues and Challenges**/Elayne Coakes (Ed.)
  ISBN: 1-931777-51-9; eISBN: 1-931777-67-5 / US$59.95 / © 2003
- **Computing Information Technology: The Human Side**/Steven Gordon (Ed.)
  ISBN: 1-931777-52-7; eISBN: 1-931777-68-3 / US$59.95 / © 2003
- **Current Issues in IT Education**/Tanya McGill (Ed.)
  ISBN: 1-931777-53-5; eISBN: 1-931777-69-1 / US$59.95 / © 2003

Excellent additions to your institution's library!
Recommend these titles to your Librarian!

To receive a copy of the IRM Press catalog, please contact
1/717-533-8845 ext. 10, fax 1/717-533-8661,
or visit the IRM Press Online Bookstore at: [http://www.irm-press.com]!

Note: All IRM Press books are also available as ebooks on netlibrary.com as well as other ebook sources. Contact Ms. Carrie Skovrinskie at [cskovrinskie@idea-group.com] to receive a complete list of sources where you can obtain ebook information or IRM Press titles.

Dedication

To my wife, Kaija, and to my daughter, Laura –
the two most important ladies in my world.

Business Strategies for Information Technology Management

Table of Contents

Preface viii
    Kalle Kangas, Turku School of Economics and Business Administration, Finland

Chapter I. Telework Effectiveness: Task, Technology and Communication Fit Perspective 1
    Bongsik Shin, San Diego State University, USA

Chapter II. Redefining the Manufacturing Enterprise through Information Technology 14
    Qiang Tu, Rochester Institute of Technology, USA
    Wei Wang, Rochester Institute of Technology, USA

Chapter III. Model-Supported Alignment of Information Systems Architecture 28
    Andreas L. Opdahl, University of Bergen, Norway

Chapter IV. A Framework for Research into Business-IT Alignment: A Cognitive Emphasis 50
    Felix B. Tan, The University of Auckland, New Zealand
    R. Brent Gallupe, Queen's University, Canada

Chapter V. IT Architecture in Strategic Alliance Negotiations: A Case 74
    Purnendu Mandal, Marshall University, USA

Chapter VI. How to Prioritize Information Systems Selection Decisions Under Time Pressure 86
    D. C. McDermid, Edith Cowan University, Australia

Chapter VII. A Framework for Extending Potency and Reducing Competitive Risk in the IT Strategic Systems Portfolio 96
    James D. White, DePaul University, USA
    Theresa A. Steinbach, DePaul University, USA
    Linda V. Knight, DePaul University, USA
    Alan T. Burns, DePaul University, USA

Chapter VIII. Partnering for Success in Application Service Provision 115
    D. E. Sofiane Tebboune, Brunel University, UK
    Philip Seltsikas, University of Surrey, UK

Chapter IX. The Resource-Based Theory of the Firm: The New Paradigm for Information Resources Management? 129
    Kalle Kangas, Turku School of Economics and Business Administration, Finland

Chapter X. A Theoretical Framework for Measuring the Success of Customer Relationship Management Outsourcing 149
    Babita Gupta, California State University Monterey Bay, USA
    Lakshmi S. Iyer, University of North Carolina, USA

Chapter XI. Implementation of the ASP Organizing Vision: The Role of Participation and Trust 160
    Rajiv Kishore, The State University of New York at Buffalo, USA

Chapter XII. Measurement Issues in Decision Support Systems ... 168
    William K. Holstein, The College of William and Mary, USA
    Jakov Crnkovic, State University of New York at Albany, USA

Chapter XIII. Information Technology Strategic Alignment: Brazilian Cases 186
    Fernando José Barbin Laurindo, University of São Paolo, Brazil
    Marly Monteiro de Carvalho, University of São Paolo, Brazil
    Tamio Shimizu, University of São Paolo, Brazil

Chapter XIV. Technology Trust in B2B Electronic Commerce: Conceptual Foundations 200
    Paul A. Pavlou, University of Southern California, USA
    Pauline Ratnasingam, University of Vermont, USA

Chapter XV. The South African Online Consumer 216
    Kevin Johnston, University of Cape Town, South Africa

Chapter XVI. Explaining Information Systems Strategic Planning (ISSP) Behavior: An Empirical Study of the Effects of the Role of IS on ISSP 226
    Jason F. Cohen, University of Witwatersrand, South Africa

Chapter XVII. National Culture and the Meaning of Information Systems Success: A Framework for Research and its Implications for IS Standardization in Multinational Organizations 242
    Hafid Agourram, Bishop's University, Canada
    John Ingham, University of Sherbrooke, Canada

About the Authors 264

Index 272

Preface

Without going deep into the history of computing, one can say that modern electronic computing has played some part in business for the last half of the century. During all of this time, there has been an ongoing discussion on the strategic meaning of information technology and on the need for computers and computing power.

In the beginning, the notion of computing was connotatively near to its original meaning: calculating. Computers were used to help people in various tasks that required much mechanical calculation: ordering, storing data, etc. At that time computers were merely machines — like any other mechanical devices people had invented to ease their tasks.

Ever since the notion of computing started to relate to the data processing of information, the whole idea has become somewhat mystified. Humans have long talked about an electronic brain: an electronic machine that would have the intelligence to produce information. This discussion will not go into the semantics of words such as "data" and "information." Simply put, when one adds some reasonable use and direction to data, it becomes information.

The title of the book itself — "Business Strategies for Information Technology Management"— raises some semantic questions. Terminology in the field of information systems (IS) and in information technology management (ITM) appears to be manifold, overlapping, confusing, and even faltering. For the field to become disciplined, a thorough framework is needed to provide a common vocabulary: everyone would speak the same language. A brief review of the terminology, therefore, is necessary because there exists a somewhat confusing jargon from different quarters of IS. The terms information technology (IT); the newcomer, information and communications technology (ICT); information systems strategy (ISS); strategic information systems (SIS); information [systems] management [strategies] (IMS); management information systems (MIS); decision support systems (DSS); and even data processing (DP) are used to relate the phenomenon to the context. These acronyms mystify the field even more in laypeople's eyes. The scientific community should know better.

Sometime in the 1950's, data processing became information processing with computers which were, in the beginning, mere calculators. Computers began to form IT organizations when conjoined with the knowledgeable people who used them. Hirschheim's notion (1983) that computer-based IS has typically evolved in haphazard fashion — stemming from the 1960's and the 1970's, when people did not know the actual possibilities of IS — is pessimistic. The systems had grown over many years and had been products of numerous, unrelated user requests. The systems tended to originate individually and to develop independently of one another. Hirschheim wrote his article in the early 1980's — in the era of huge corporate mainframes, which were supposed to solve all information problems. In the latter half of the 1980's, there was much discussion of centralization vs. decentralization in the literature; but today in the age of [personal] microcomputers, networked organizations, wideband telecommunications, and the Internet this discussion seems to have diminished. Individuals work with their own personal computers, in which they store programs used daily and personal files. The remainder of information is gathered in various databases — data warehouses — with easy retrieval through intra- or interorganizational networks or through the internet.

In the 1980's, several authors praised IT: it had become the ultimate weapon with which to sustain competitive advantage amid constantly toughening competition. Subsequently doubts diminished the praise, and today many business managers regard IT as a commodity: as a non-core resource (such as law or accounting) that one can outsource, but that one cannot do without. I argue that IT is different: that it cannot be treated as are other functions; that it is more valuable; and that, in some cases, it makes a significant difference (for example, in organizations in which it has prevailed, IT is the link that holds the network together).

Corporate infrastructure — large corporate information systems — emerged as a concept in the 1980's. The systems were standardized and were run from huge mainframe central computers, which were located at several computer centers. The data was distributed to users through "dumb" terminals at each location. This created centralized IT departments on one hand, and distributed systems and applications on the other hand.

To support their organizational structures many traditional, multinational firms relied upon inter-linked networks of mainframe computers, which radiated from headquarters; with smaller, mid-sized systems in regional offices and data centers; culminating with minicomputers in smaller, subsidiary locations. Large firms had formerly used a multitude of data centers operating in a multitude of locations. A few data "super centers" were sustained in the field by many smaller supporting centers. This framework of computer technology was linked together over international borders to serve corporate communications and control systems.

Traditional conglomerates had a series of "nearly–separate" businesses known as divisions. Divisions could be described as "firms within a firm." Each division had separate functional offices for accounting, for purchasing, for production, for sales, etc. A division was sold or procured as a stand-alone business quite often, or a strategic alliance was formed. Its internal structure did not change much, usually, during such activity; and its IT function was linked and aligned to existing corporate systems as much as possible. (A good example of this kind of conglomerate is IBM in its late 1980's form. The traditional structure, however, drove IBM to the verge of bankruptcy and to survive, it had to change drastically.)

The strategy-structure-system trilogy described above was a revolutionary discovery in the 1920's. It was a wonderful way to define large companies; and it supplied an effective intellectual framework within which to govern and coordinate immense conglomerates. Times change, however: companies with clear strategy and structure became more systematic. Predictable and machine-like systems of control, of course, were not helpful (Ghoshal, Bartlett, & Moran, 1999). The shift to a new paradigm in the digital economy can only happen through organizational learning, which is only enabled through a dynamic view of the firm and of entrepreneurship.

Operators in international markets often perform with their business partners occasional, one-time transactions through electronic devices. In today's digital economy, extensions of the traditional, intra-firm "value chain" concept (Porter, 1985) are emerging. The value chain is a customer-centered "wheel of fortune" that emerges more by coincidence than by plan or by design. The result is a need to build a one-time value chain for almost every transaction. This chain is ephemeral and dissolves once the transaction has been conducted. Traditional value chain and industry cluster analyses (Porter, 1985), as well as most other recent firm theory approaches, appear obsolete in the new information economy. Discussions on centralization and decentralization seem to be purely academic, having no practical value in the new economy.

Mata (1995), in a resource-based analysis, found that out of four attributes of IT — capital requirements, proprietary technology, technical IT skills, and managerial IT skills — managerial IT skills is the only resource that can bring sustained competitive advantage. Keen (1991) comes to a similar conclusion, noting that while IT may be a commodity, *IT management* is not — it is the value-added element that *leads to* competitive advantage. Mata (1995) points out, of course, that we cannot consider the other three attributes unimportant, since they may still produce, admittedly, temporary competitive advantage. Mata's analysis (1995) suggests that IT managers should work closely with other managers within a firm to support information needs of the latter. It must be recognized that information needs of various stakeholders vary in different kinds of firms, depending upon industries, resources, and structures. It is, therefore, vital that firms develop business strategies that support IT management.

The chapters in this book form a series of good examples of this principle. A short description of each chapter is presented in the following.

Chapter 1 discusses inter- and intraorganizational telework in many different forms including distributive project teams, telecommuting, mobile work, business-to-employee e-business, and the virtual corporation. It reviews implications of chosen variables such as task characteristics, communication quality, and technology support on telework success from a fit theory perspective. The examination focuses upon the implications of two- and three-way alignments among task characteristics, communications quality, and technology support on the distributive work setting.

Chapter 2 identifies the profound impact of modern IT on the manufacturing industry. Advanced manufacturing technologies, coupled with organization-wide information system infrastructures, have offered manufacturing firms tremendous opportunities for sustainable competitive advantages. This chapter introduces some current research ideas in the areas of information technology and of manufacturing strategic management.

Chapter 3 presents an alignment model and a representation framework for IS architecture management. The alignment model explains and supports the grouping of IS architecture elements into IS architecture areas, thereby offering a systematic way to generate alternative high-level principles for an IS architecture evolution in the long term.

Chapter 4 proposes a framework with which to guide research into a business/IT alignment. It reviews alignment research and considers some of the cognitive theories and methodologies that may be appropriate for the study of alignment. Contemporary empirical research into business/IT alignment explores the alignment issue by examining ways in which organizations conduct themselves. Managerial cognition is an area of growing interest and importance in strategic management.

Chapter 5 describes, via case study, the development of IT architecture for the purpose of forming a strategic alliance between an ICT organization and its partners. It also addresses how benefits to the negotiation process emerge during development. A telecommunications organization (TEL) intends to enter into an alliance with an existing retail electricity distribution business, so that TEL can improve its market position. An IT architecture for the new market situation is developed to help understand future information requirements, as well as the extent of the dependence of partners upon one another.

Chapter 6 reports on an action research study that uses the Strategic Choice method. This method is used to inform the prioritization of IT with respect to enhancing systems within a public sector Health Department. Such decisions are notoriously complex, fuzzy, time-consuming, and political for stakeholders. The results of the study indicate that the Strategic Choice method offers potential to reduce time commitment for stakeholders and to do so in a satisfactory manner.

Chapter 7 proposes that, in addition to balancing risk in the total IT project portfolio, organizations should also balance risk in strategic IT portfolios. A framework is distilled from the literature. The framework's validity is assessed using four classic cases in the strategic use of technology. Results indicate that overall strategic IT risk may be reduced by evaluating an organization's strategic IT portfolio.

Chapter 8 shows that the concept of strategic alliances is highly relevant to the ASP model. The chapter illustrates this with two cases, one of which is a failure because of inappropriate partnership management. It highlights the importance of focusing upon the management of alliances — instead of upon alliance formation — using a life-cycle approach to alliances. It also relates the immaturity of the ASP market to the difficulties in measuring the success of strategic alliances formed in this context.

Chapter 9 explores the theoretical foundations of the digital economy. It discusses eight main theories of the 20th century firm. Drawing upon literary review, the chapter presents frameworks for the theories; and it demonstrates that the only theory suitable for the digital economy is a resource-based view of the firm. The chapter suggests that studies on the digital economy emerge more fruitful when conducted under resource-based theory than under any other modern theory of the firm.

Chapter 10 suggests that success of CRM implementations is critical to the survival of firms in the 21st century. CRM literature classifies CRM products into three categories: operational, analytical, and collaborative. The chapter proposes a theoretical framework that examines the CRM outsourcing success. Examining pertinent literature, it proposes that CRM outsourcing success is influenced by the degree of CRM outsourcing; by partnership quality between the outsourcing firm and the vendor; and by organizational factors of the outsourcing firm, as well as by the quality of service from the vendor.

Chapter 11 describes "know-what" uncertainty, which firms generally face as they implement any techno-organizational innovation. It discusses some specific know-what uncertainties associated with a client adoption of the ASP paradigm. The chapter also discusses the role that participation and trust in the ASP organizing vision play in mitigating client-side know-what uncertainties during the course of adoption and implementation of the new IT governance model. Recommendations for clients and vendors for making the new IT-services paradigm a successful reality are also provided.

Chapter 12 focuses on the use of metrics for justifying investment in IT and technology and for measuring business and management performance. With several examples drawn from contemporary practice it introduces implementation guidelines for DSS development, focusing on the incorporation of new metrics that goes beyond ROI and "Balanced Scorecard"-like measures. Suggested guidelines include simplicity, selectivity, focus on research and learning, and benchmarking.

Chapter 13 presents a study about the effectiveness of IT applications in Brazilian companies. Effectiveness evaluation makes possible strategic alignments between IT and company business visions and should be analyzed as a continual process. A comparative analysis of IT strategic impacts is performed using different theoretical models. The study is based upon multiple interview cases in financial services, telecommunications, and building materials companies.

Chapter 14 deals with "technology trust," which is the subjective belief by which an organization assesses that the underlying technology infrastructure and support mechanisms are capable of supporting interorganizational communications, transactions, and collaborations. It conceptualizes technology trust, drawing upon the notion of institutional trust, and particularly upon the dimension of situational normality. The chapter makes sense of conceptual foundations of technology trust by bridging the gaps among technological solutions from the perspectives of an institutional trust (technology trust), of an interorganizational trust, and of value creation in B2B electronic commerce.

Chapter 15 attempts to develop a profile of online consumers in South Africa based on various research sources. The chapter further focuses on what is wanted by online consumers in South Africa, as well as on the challenges facing web developers and organizations developing websites in South Africa.

Chapter 16 discusses the contingent nature of IT strategic planning (ISSP) practices and presents the results of an empirical study of ISSP and the role of IS within 90 leading companies in South Africa. It shows that the relationship between ISSP and IS functional performance is significantly higher for firms within the strategic IS environment.

Chapter 17 claims that IS success is still one of the most researched topics in the IS discipline, but that most research defining and measuring IS success is conducted in North America. Researchers within the international management discipline have assessed that culture may be a major factor in influencing organizational structures and management practices. The chapter discusses reasons that organizations intending to standardize IS within different cultures should consider culture an important factor in achieving success. It then proposes a comprehensive framework for future cross-national research on IS success in multinational organizations.

REFERENCES

Ghoshal, S., Bartlett, C. A, & Moran, P. (1999, Spring). A new manifesto for management. *Sloan Management Review*, 40 (3), 9-20.

Hirschheim, R. (1983). Database — A neglected corporate resource? *Long-Range Planning*, 16 (5), 79-88.

Keen, P. W. G. (1991). Shaping the future. Boston: Harvard Business School Press.

Mata, F., Fuerst, W. L. & Barney, J. B. (1995, December). Information technology and sustained competitive advantage: A resource-based analysis. *MIS Quarterly*, 19 (4).

Porter, M. E. (1985). Competitive advantage: Creating and sustaining superior performance. New York: Free Press.

Acknowledgments

I would like to acknowledge the help of all involved in the collaboration and review processes of this book: without their support, the project would not have been satisfactorily completed. Most of the authors of the chapters included here also served as referees for articles written by other authors. Thanks to all those who provided constructive and comprehensive reviews. A further special note of thanks to the staff at Idea Group, Inc., whose contributions throughout the whole process — from inception of the initial idea to final publication — have been invaluable.

Special thanks, also, to the publishing team at Idea Group, Inc.: particularly to Amanda Appicello, who continuously prodded me — via e-mail — to keep the project on schedule; and to Mehdi Khosrow-Pour, whose enthusiasm initially motivated me to accept his invitation for taking on the project.

In closing, I wish to thank all of the authors for their insights and excellent contributions to this book. I also want to thank all of the people who assisted me in the review process. In addition, this book would not have been possible without ongoing professional support from Amanda Appicello, Mehdi Khosrow-Pour, and Jan Travers at Idea Group, Inc. Finally, I want to thank my wife and daughter for their love and support throughout the project.

Kalle Kangas, Ph.D.
Editor
Turku, Finland
September 2002

Chapter I

Telework Effectiveness: Task, Technology and Communication Fit Perspective

Bongsik Shin
San Diego State University, USA

ABSTRACT

We are witnessing rapid growth of inter and intra-organizational telework in many different forms: distributive project teams, telecommuting, mobile work, business to-employee, employee e-business, and virtual corporations. Despite the increasing prevalence of distributive work and its importance in creating business value, our understanding of its success factors is limited. Among many prospective factors, task characteristics, communication quality, and technology support have been mentioned frequently as key components for successfully running telework. Communications quality and technology support seem the direct result of operational design in managing the virtual process; while task characteristics of workers are typically pre-determined, unless they are modified for telework. This paper discusses the implications of chosen variables on telework success from a fit theory perspective. It focuses on examining the implications of two- and

Copyright © 2003, Idea Group Inc. Copying or distributing in print or electronic forms without written permission of Idea Group Inc. is prohibited.

three-way alignments among task characteristics, communications quality, and technology support on in a distributive work setting.

INTRODUCTION

Organizations are witnessing rapid growth of teleworking. Telework is a distributed and virtual work arrangement that allows employees to perform their work away from the central office using information and communications technologies (ICTs) (Lindstrom *et. al.*, 1997). Distributive project teams, telecommuting, mobile work, business-to-employee e-business, and virtual corporations are popular forms of telework. It effectively copes with individual (quality of life), organizational (customer orientation and growth in knowledge jobs), and societal (urban) changes. Telework, therefore, emerges an administrative innovation intended to produce various strategic and non-strategic business values, which include cost reduction, improved customer support, productivity increases, and enhanced worker retention and satisfaction.

Despite the increasing prevalence and the importance of the concept, understanding on its effective design is limited. There are many organizational, individual, and technological factors that play a significant role in deciding its effectiveness. Among them task characteristics, communications quality, and technology support emerge key success factors. This chapter re-visits these variables and discusses their implications on telework effectiveness (i.e., quality, quantity, timeliness, and satisfaction) from a fit theory perspective. The roles of two- and three-way alignments—among task characteristics, communications quality, and technology support in the distributive work setting—receive close attention.

A GENERAL MODEL OF TELEWORK EFFECTIVENESS

In this section, a general model of telework effectiveness lays the groundwork. In general, the review of literature on telework and innovation (given that telework is a form of administrative innovation) reveals that the success of telework is largely affected by three main forces: (1) *organizational-level forces,* such as management support, organizational motivation, and other organizational features; (2) *worker characteristics,* such as demographics and task nature; and (3) *design features* of telework.

There may be heterogeneity among organizations in their motivations for introducing telework. From a competing values framework perspective (Cooper and Quinn, 1993; Quinn and Rohrbaugh, 1983), motivation should attempt to improve an organization's survival, economic performance (profit maximization, productivity, and efficiency), human relationships (employee morale, cohesion, and commitment), and internal process management (organizational stability, equilibrium, and control). Organization-unique motivation is expected to become a powerful driving force for telework adoption and for further diffusion.

Another organizational-level attribute, management support has been emphasized as an effective stimulus for organizational change in many studies (Daft, 1978; Kimberly and Evanisko, 1981). Management is the single force that can abolish existing structural inertia (Aldrich and Pfeffer, 1976) and direct organizational resources toward innovation (Gary et. al., 1993). Management styles that underscore management-by-objectives and trust-based management appear vital in successfully running a telework program (Martino and Wirth, 1990).

Additionally, there are structural- and resource-related organizational features that may constitute internal barriers against a telework program. For instance, low job specialization (professionalism), high centralization in decision-making, and lesser-formalized rules and job evaluation systems may constitute structural constraints for telework diffusion (Ruppel and Harrington, 1995). Availability of slack resources, which bear the cost of purchasing technology and other requirements, may pose other constraints (Damanpour, 1991; Olson, 1988).

Professionals whose tasks are well-defined, who are able to perform independent work, who are knowledge workers, and who are comfortable in adopting information technologies may fit better into a virtual setup (Ruppel and Harrington, 1995). In addition, there may be worker profiles—of personality, of work habits, of task characteristics, and of attitudinal features-that make distributed working more viable (Pratt, 1984; Tamrat et. al., 1996).

Attributes of telework design, along with worker and organizational characteristics, have considerable impact upon its ultimate success. Some of the main design issues of telework include its scope and scale; its temporal (i.e., synchronous versus asynchronous) and spatial (i.e., collective versus individual) structures; its measurement benchmark of effectiveness; its IT support; its organizational policy; its supervision scheme; and its communications and coordination structures.

Effectiveness is a multi-dimensional concept that applies both to workers and to organizations. Effectiveness is frequently measured in terms of worker, management, and customer satisfacton; of productivity changes; and by cost/benefit effects (Shin et. al., 2000). It is thought that variables from three categories—design features, worker characteristics, and organizational characteristics—affect the ultimate success of telework innovation. In essence, individual- and organizational-level forces are relatively more static than are design features. A generalized model of telework effectiveness, then, occurs both at individual and at organizational levels (Figure 1). In the next section, the

Figure 1: A general model of telework effectiveness

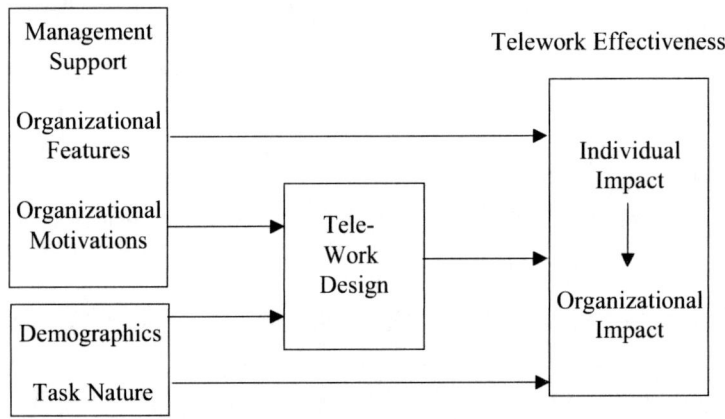

focus of discussion narrows to the relationship among three selected variables-task characteristics, communication quality, and technology support—as well as telework performance. It is repeatedly argued that these variables play the most significant roles in determining the performance of virtual work arrangements. Communication quality and technology support are affected, in general, by the details of telework design; task characteristics, however, are a worker-related variable. The main argument of this research is that two- and three-way *fits* among them become a determining factor in producing telework success.

FIT AS CONTINGENCY THEORY

Discussing the implications of selected variables on telework effectiveness, Venkatraman's (1989) and Van de Ven's and Drazin's (1985) work on the *fit* concept renders a solid theoretical foundation. Venkatraman (1989) defines fit from six different perspectives: *matching, moderation* (interaction), *mediation* (intervention), *gestalts* (internal congruence), *covariation* (internal consistency), and *profile deviation* (adherence to a specified profile).

Fit as matching is a "theoretically defined match between two related variables (Venkatraman, 1989)" without necessarily considering implications upon performance. For instance, we can think of fit between ideal specifications of an information system and those available in an existing information system. Matching, in this instance, is conceptually related to Van de Ven's and Drazin's (1985) *selection*, which views fit as the result of natural choice. In this paradigm, context engenders design. The fit of strategy at the organizational level, therefore, is the result of managerial choice (selection) to achieve congruence to organizational context. Venkatraman (1989) suggests that deviation scores and residual analysis are analytic approaches suitable for *fit as matching*.

As conceived by Van de Ven and Drazin (1985), *fit as moderation* is similar to *fit as interaction,* in which fit is the interaction of context and structure (design) on performance. From a contingency viewpoint, fit represents conformance to a linear relationship of context and design. Here, the impact of a predictor variable (design variable) on a dependent variable (performance variable) is moderated by—or dependent upon—the third variable (context variable), which we call a moderator (Venkatraman, 1989). The central point, here, is the relationship between measured performance and the interaction (fit) of the moderator and the predictor. The interaction effect of strategy as a predictor variable and of managerial characteristics as a moderator of organizational performance (Zigurs and Buckand, 1998) is one example.

Fit as mediation considers fit from the perspective of the intervention of the variable between an antecedent variable (strategy) and a consequent variable (performance). Within this scheme, the intervening variable has an indirect (intervening) effect on the antecedent variable and a direct effect on the consequent variable. The intervening effect becomes one dimension of fit: for example, the intervening effect of the national economy as a design variable and of organizational performance as a consequent variable. Fit as moderation and fit as mediation are typically applied to a situation with a single independent variable; a single moderator or mediator; and a single dependent variable (Zigurs and Buckand, 1998).

Fit as gestalts views the fit concept from a systems perspective, in which fit cannot be represented by the functional relationship of a few chosen variables; it should be understood, rather, from the dynamics of attribute (gestalts) clusters. It accordingly culminates in a multitudinous view: understanding fit requires an interpretive, rather than a functional, approach. This perspective corresponds to Van de Ven's and Drazin's (1985) "holistic patterns of interdependencies from the systems theory perspective." Here, fit requires an internal congruence of many contingencies, structures, and performance criteria.

Fit as covariation represents internal consistency among related variables or constituencies. It is conceptually similar to *fit as gestalts*, but Venkatraman (1989) uses an analogy to differentiate them: *fit as gestalts* can be regarded as a product of cluster analysis, in which a grouping of observations is made upon a set of attributes; covariation is the result of factor analysis, in which the grouping of attributes is also made from a set of observations. Covariation, therefore, indicates a logical linkage (alignment) among considered independent variables. Venkatraman (1989) suggests that first- or second-order factors from both exploratory and confirmatory (preferable) factor analyses could be utilized to identify the unobservable state of linkage (alignment).

Fit as profile deviation assumes the viability of profile specification for variables associated to a criterion variable. Fit represents the degree of adherence to a specified profile, and the level of fit is expected to affect performance. For instance, the contingency theory of *organization assessment* indicates that there are adequate organizational (unit) structures (systematized, discretionary, and developmental) for different task uncertainties (difficulty and variability) (Van de Ven and Drazin, 1985). The unit structures provides profiles against which to conduct a pattern analysis. Deviation from the profile implies a weakness of context and design fit. This is different from Gestalt or matching perspective because a specific profile is anchored to effectiveness (Venkatraman, 1989). Testing fit from this perspective demands the identification of distinct environments (tasks), determination of ideal resource allocation for each environment, and examination of context/design alignment effect (Venkatraman and Prescott, 1990).

TASK, COMMUNICATIONS, AND TECHNOLOGY FIT

A Research Model

This chapter discusses the effects of task characteristics, communications quality and technology support, and fit upon virtual work. Communications quality and technology support are either the direct results of program design or of telework policy; the task characteristics of a person, however, are typically pre-determined unless they are moderated for telework. Distributive work demands that team members rely on ICTs for communication, for coordination, and for collaboration in conducting business tasks. The effectiveness of these virtual processes are inevitably affected by the quality of technology support and communications management (Shin *et. al.*, 2000).

The success of the virtual process is better understood from the perspective of relationships among variables (Goodhue and Thomson, 1995). This contingency view is compelling in the sense that excess may be worse than adequacy. Providing the latest and greatest technologies, therefore, may not necessarily coincide with the improved performance of teleworkers when their tasks do not justify the use of technology in the first place. This lack of coordination may only result in over-spending and in wasted corporate resources without producing intended performance. The same line of reasoning applies to the relationships between technology support and communication quality and between task characteristics and communication quality. Accordingly, the degree of fit among the factors may prove important in attaining the effectiveness of virtual works. Figure 2 reflects the two- and three-way relationships among the involved variables.

Figure 2: A research model

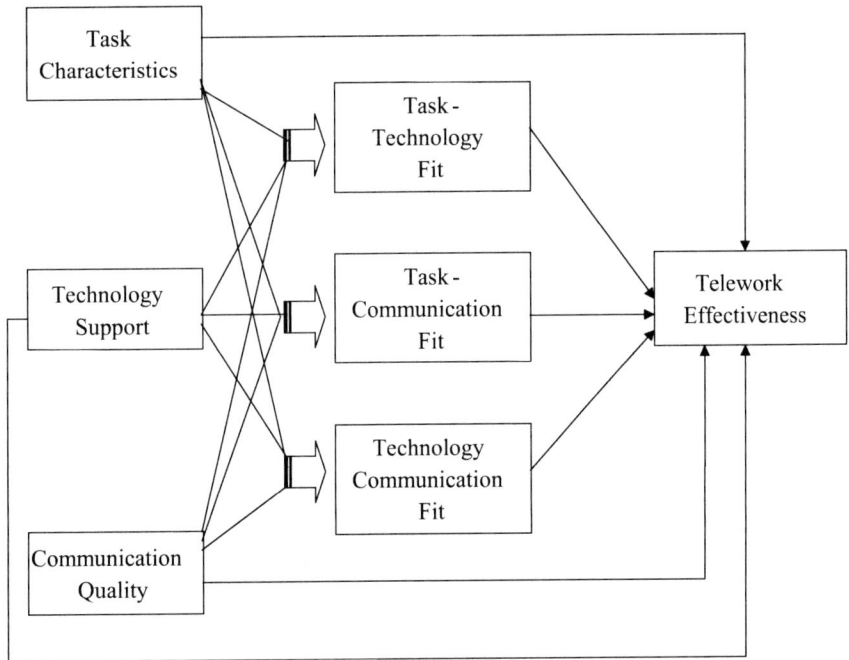

Research Propositions

Task characteristics differ in many ways, including job level, task interdependence, job discretion, skill variety, job pressure, closeness of supervision, and task significance (Kling, 1978; Turner and Karasek, 1984). From a slightly different angle, tasks can be characterized in terms of complexity, multiplicity, uncertainty (Campbell, 1988), portability (Venkatesh and Vitalari, 1992), and autonomy and responsibility (Kwon and Zmud, 1987).

Existing literature reveals inconsistencies regarding the impact of task characteristics on distributive work arrangements. Clustering responsibilities and assigning structured and repetitive tasks may make telework more productive in certain situations (Dubrin, 1991). Under other circumstances, enlarged jobs with high degrees of control, autonomy, and responsibility may result in both improved performance and worker satisfaction (Olson, 1988; Venkatesh and Vitalari, 1992). The relationship between task attributes and telework effectiveness may be primarily context-dependent and viewing it from a positive viewpoint may be difficult. Contingency factors include an organization's reward structure, measurement of effectiveness (i.e., productivity and satisfaction), telework motivations (i.e., strategy and labor cost control), and the level of electronic linkage (i.e., multi-channel communications, automated work-flow, and accessibility to an intranet) (Shin *et. al.*, 2000). Professionals whose tasks are well defined, who are able to work independently, and who are knowledge workers may find enlarged jobs more productive and satisfying (Devey and Risman, 1993). A survey of the literature derives the following:

Proposition 1: Tasks that are well defined and independent, regardless of complexity or routine nature, are better positioned for telework.

The potential role of ICTs in telework success has been pointed out repeatedly. Here, ICTs represent the tools available for undertaking assigned tasks in virtual settings. Some examples of ICTs are personal productivity tools (office software), communication tools (groupware), and others (infrastructure). These tools may weigh differently upon virtual work effectiveness. Communications technologies may be especially crucial: the degradation of communications and its coordination quality, during the adoption of telework within an organization, becomes a major concern (Shin *et. al.*, 2000).

Keller (1994) suggests that the fit between technology and information processing could predict project performance. Task and technology fit is "the degree to which a technology assists an individual in performing his or her portfolio of tasks (Goodhue and Thompson, 1995)." Technology is considered a static element: its role on a virtual process may be better understood from the *fit as mediation* perspective, in which teleworkers' productivity in conducting business tasks is affected by the design of ICT support. We derive, then:

Proposition 2: Task-technology fit is a positive indicator of teleworker performance, and its effect is realized through the intervening (facilitating) role of technology as tasks are assigned.

Task-technology fit may be further understood from the perspective of *matching* between task characteristics and corresponding requirements for technology support. Task characteristics, such as variability and analysis, may be highly correlated to the choice and use of ICTs (Ghani, 1992). Non-routine and complex tasks conducted within a virtual environment may demand advanced information processing and rich communications. On the other hand, repetitive and predictable tasks may not need the same degree of ICT support as do non-routine and complex tasks. Over-provisioning technologies may not contribute to corresponding performance improvement by teleworkers, resulting in poor return on investment (ROI). If we look at the task-technology relationship from a selection viewpoint (Van de Ven and Drazin, 1985), in which details of technology support are chosen based on task features, the following proposition becomes viable:

Proposition 3: The selection of ICTs affects the degree of telework effectiveness, and the optimal deployment of ICTs is achieved when they are adequately matched to a profile of task characteristics.

There is no need to emphasize the crucial role of communications in increasing worker productivity, and this becomes even more obvious when they are geographically scattered throughout the organization (Mohr and Sohi, 1995; O'Reilly and Roberts, 1977). An enhanced quality of internal processes in a virtual setup could also curtail unwanted outgrowths: worker social isolation, role conflict and ambiguity, and difficulties in coordination and supervision (Shin et. al., 2000). Adequate ICT provision, in the form of enhanced electronic linkage (Lucas and Baroudi, 1994), plays a vital role in telework success. Randolph and Finch (1977) empirically show that there is a significant association between technological certainty (e.g., routine vs. non-routine) and the frequency and direction (e.g., vertical vs. horizontal) of task-related communications.

Classical media richness theory posits that the information carrying capacity of a communications medium is determined by its feedback capability, by the kind of language used, and by the number of cues available (Daft and Lengel, 1984). Communications media also differ in supporting accessibility to information and data, in transportability of work (i.e., workflow management), and in collaboration support. Effectiveness of communications is achieved when the complexity of a communications task matches an appropriate medium. When a lean medium is used for complex communication processes, teleworkers' productivity suffers. We may assume, then:

Proposition 4: Communication quality is a positive indicator for telework effectiveness;

and

Proposition 5: The associative effect of the communication/technology fit on telework is realized when ICTs facilitate effective communication among distributed workers. In this case, ICT usage is optimized when teleworkers are able to choose adequately rich media for different levels of communication complexity.

Studies also indicate that the effectiveness of technology depends more upon how it is used than upon what is used (Markus, 1994; Schmitz and Fulk, 1991). Effective adoption of a lean medium may render distributed workers an information-rich tool that enhances productivity (Higa et. al., 2000). Accordingly, the social perception of technology capacity and the manner of its *utilization* (Goodhue and Thompson, 1995) may emerge a prevalent force, determining ICT value in supporting virtual work. It has also been suggested that technologies that are commonly available and that can be used spontaneously have a bigger impact on organizational processes (Mokhtarian and Sato, 1994). This emergent, non-deterministic perspective of technology is in line with the theoretical view of *fit as Gestalts*:

Proposition 6: The degree of communication/technology fit and its impact upon telework cannot be explained in a functional manner; rather, they are significantly affected by the social perception of available technologies and the manner in which these are used by distributed workers.

Binary relationships among task characteristics—communications quality and technology support—can be expanded into a three-way relationship. The three-way association represents a simultaneous fit of three variables, conceptually analogous to the additive effects of three binary fits. Telework success is a function of three-way fit:

Proposition 7: The degree of three-way fit among task characteristics, technology support, and communications quality is a positive indicator of telework effectiveness.

CONCLUSIONS

Task characteristics, communications quality, technology support, and commensurate two- and three-way alignments are indicators of telework effectiveness. One can assume that distributed work settings are significantly different from traditional, centralized work settings in various ways, including the management of communications and of task coordination. The fit concept emerges a theoretical foundation for telework performance and the selection of appropriate variables thereof. Theoretically, in addition to the independent roles of studied variables, joint relationships among them can become significant indicators of teleworker performance. Research can enrich this study by undertaking empirical investigations into the proposed impact of each variable and of its associative roles.

REFERENCES

Aldrich, H. E., & Pfeffer, J. (1976). Environments of organizations. *Annual Review of Sociology.* 2, 79-105.

Campbell, D. J. (1988). Task complexity: A review and analysis. *Academy of Management Review,* 13(1), 40-52.

Cooper, R. B., & Quinn, R. E. (1993). Implications of the competing values framework for management information systems. *Human Resource Management,* 32 (1), 175-201.

Daft, R. L. (1978). A dual-core model of organizational innovation. *Academy of Management Journal,* 21(2), 193-210.

Daft, R. L., & Lengel, R. H. (1984). Information richness: New approach to managerial behavior and organization design. *Research in Organizational Behavior,* 6, 191-233.

Damanpour, F. (1991). Organizational innovation: A meta-analysis of effects of determinants and moderators. *Academy of Management Journal,* 34(3), 555-590.

Devey, Y. & Risman, J. (1993). Telecommuting innovation and organization: A contingency theory of labor process change. 74(2), 367-385.

Dubrin, A. J. (1991). Comparison of job satisfaction and productivity of telecommuters versus in-house employees: A research note on work in progress. *Psychological Reports*, 68(3), 1223-1234.

Gary, M., Hodson, N., & Gordon, G. (1993). Teleworking explained. New York: John Wiley & Sons.

Ghani, J. A. (1992). Task uncertainty and the use of computer technology. *Information and Management,* 22(2), 69-76.

Goodhue D. L., & Thompson, R. L. (1995). Task-technology fit and individual performance. *MIS Quarterly,* 19(2), 213-236.

Higa, K., Sheng, O., Shin, B., & Figueredo, A. J. (2000). Software engineers' media use and their perception on the work productivity under telework environment. *IEEE Transactions on Engineering Management,* 47(2), 163-173.

Keller, R. T. (1994). Technology-information processing fit and the performance of R&D project groups: Test of contingency theory. *Academy of Management Journal,* 37(1), 167-179.

Kimberly, J. R., & Evanisko, M. J. (1981). Organizational innovation: he influence of individual, organizational, and contextual factors on hospital adoption of technological and administrative innovation. *Academy of Management Journal*, 24(4), 689-713.

Kling, R. (1978). The impacts of computing upon the work of managers, data analysts, and clerks. University of California, Irvine: Department of Information and Computing Science.

Kwon, T. H., & Zmud, R. W. (1987). Unifying the fragmented models of information systems implementation. *Critical Issues in Information Systems Research.* New York: John Wiley & Sons.

Lindstrom, J., Moberg, A., & Rapp, B. (1997). On the classification of telework. *European Journal of Information Systems,* 6(4), 243-255.

Lucas, H. C., & Baroudi, J. (1994). The role of information technology in organizational design. *Journal of Management Information Systems,* 10(4), 9-23.

Markus, M. L. (1994). Electronic mail as the medium of managerial choice. *Organization Science,* 5(4), 502-527.

Martino, V. D. & Wirth, L. (1990). Telework: A new way of working and living. *International Labor Review,* 129(5), 529-553.

Mohr, J. J. & Sohi, R. S. (1995). Communication flows in distribution channels: Impact on assessments of communication quality and satisfaction. *Journal of Retailing,* 71(4), 393-416.

Mokhtarian, P. L., & Sato, K. (1994). A comparison of the policy, social, and cultural contexts for telecommuting in Japan and the United States. *Social Science Computer Review,* 12(4), 641-658.

Olson, M. H. (1988). Organizational barriers to telework. In Werner, B. Korte, Robinson, S. & Steinle W. J. (Eds.), *Present Situation and Future Development of a New Form of Work Organization,* Elsevier: Science Publishers B. V.

O'Reilly, C. A., & Roberts, K. H. (1977). Task group structure, communication, and effectiveness in three organizations. *Journal of Applied Psychology.* 62(6), 674-681.

Pratt, J. H. (1984). Home teleworking: A study of its pioneers. *Technological Forecasting and Social Changes.* 25, 1-14.

Quinn, R. E., & Rohrbaugh, J. (1983). A spatial model of effectiveness criteria: Towards a competing values approach to organizational analysis. *Management Science,* 29(3), 363-377.

Randolph, W. A. & Finch, F. E. (1977). The relationship between organization technology and the direction and frequency dimensions of task communications. *Human Relations,* 30(12), 1131-1145.

Ruppel, C. P., & Harrington, S. J. (1995). Telework: An innovation where nobody is getting on the bandwagon. *Database,* 26(2-3), 87-104.

Schmitz, J. & Fulk, J. (1991). Organizational colleagues, media richness, and electronic mail. *Communications Research,* 18(4), 487-523.

Shin, B., Sheng, O., & Higa, K. (2000). Telework - existing research and future directions. *Journal of Organizational Computing and Electronic Commerce,* 10(2), 85-101.

Tamrat, E., Vilkinas, T., & W., J. R. (1996). Analysis of a telecommuting experience: A case study. *Proceedings of the 29th Annual Hawaii International Conference on Systems Sciences,* 376-385.

Turner, J. A., & Karasek, R. A. (1984). Software ergonomics: Effects of computer application design parameters on operator task performance and health. *Ergonomics,* 27(6), 663-690.

Van de Ven, A. H. & Drazin, R. (1985). The concept of fit in contingency theory. *Research in Organization Behavior.* 7, 333-365.

Venkatesh, A., & Vitalari, N. P. (1992). An emerging distributed work arrangement: An investigation of computer-based supplemental work at home. *Management Science,* 38(12), 1687-1706.

Venkatraman, N. (1989). The concept of fit in strategy research: Toward verbal and statistical correspondence. *Academy of Management Review,* 14(3), 423-444.

Venkatraman, N. & Prescott, J. E. (1990). Environment-Strategy Coalignment: An Empirical Test of its Performance Implications. *Strategic Management Journal,* 11(1), 1-23.

Zigurs, I. & Buckland, B. (1998). A theory of task/technology fit and group support systems effectiveness. *MIS Quarterly,* 22(3), 313-334.

Chapter II

Redefining the Manufacturing Enterprise through Information Technology

Qiang Tu
Rochester Institute of Technology, USA

Wei Wang
Rochester Institute of Technology, USA

ABSTRACT

This chapter identifies the profound impact of modern information technology on the manufacturing industry. Advanced manufacturing technologies, coupled with organization-wide information systems infrastructures, have offered manufacturing firms tremendous opportunities for sustainable competitive advantages. To fully realize the new technologies' strategic benefits, however, manufacturing management must both abandon traditional industrial mindsets and redesign manufacturing systems for maximum enterprise integration. Technology is, after all, merely an enabling factor. It requires other corresponding organizational changes to reach its full potential. We, the authors, also introduce current research ideas in the areas of information technology and of manufacturing strategic management.

INTRODUCTION

A much talked about topic in recent years is the emergence of a "new economy," characterized by sustained economic growth in the late 1990s (Gordon, 2000). Many researchers attribute the accelerated productivity growth to heavy investment and to rapid developments in information technology (IT) (Oliner & Sichel, 2000). A study by the Joint Economic Committee of the United States Congress (Feroli, 2001) concludes that information technology is an important factor in the recent acceleration of productivity growth and that both the production and the use of IT contribute to the productivity revival. Indeed, the new generation of IT, especially web-based electronic business technologies, have dramatically changed the nature of business competition and have altered the structure of markets in a number of industries (Segars & Grover, 1995; Stroeken, 2000).

Significant advances in the related technologies of computers, telecommunications, data access and storage devices, and software packages have created a wide spectrum of new opportunities for organizations. The speed, cost, size, and capabilities of the new IT continue to improve rapidly, and there appear to be unlimited applications that could be computer-enhanced. As the backbone of the U.S. economy, the manufacturing industry may well be the biggest beneficiary of all of these IT innovations (Shaw, Seidmann & Winston, 1997; Barua & Lee, 1997).

Manufacturing has traditionally been viewed merely as a functional area buffered from environment, but Skinner (1969) points out that some of the seemingly routine manufacturing decisions may, in fact, significantly influence corporate strategy. Wheelwright (1984) further defines the missing link between manufacturing strategy and corporate strategy. Subsequently, manufacturing is increasingly viewed as a strategic enterprise covering the entire value chain of new product development, materials purchasing, production, product distribution, and customer service (Doll & Vonderembse, 1991). The changing role of manufacturing is due, in large part, to rapid advances in both power and functionality within the new IT, especially with the help of highly-integrated and computerized supply chain management (SCM) systems (Keah, 2002). Interestingly, contemporaneous information systems (IS) literature discusses the changing role of IS from a back-office support function into a competitive weapon (Ives & Learmonth, 1984; Sethi & King, 1994). This is not mere coincidence. Researchers indicate that today's turbulent manufacturing environment is primarily customer-driven but, more importantly, that it is IT-enabled (O'Halloran & Wagner, 2001).

It is also necessary to clarify the scope of IT within this article. In a narrow sense, IS literature defines IT as information systems hardware and software used to organize, store, retrieve, and transfer data. It also facilitates communications such as office automation systems, management information systems, and decision support systems. In a broader sense, IT encompasses both IS and a wide variety of advanced manufacturing technologies (AMT) such as computer-aided design and manufacturing (CAD/CAM); computer-aided process planning (CAPP); computer numerically-controlled (CNC) machines; and flexible manufacturing systems (FMS) (Gerwin & Kolodny, 1992; Hill, 1994). A common characteristic of IS and AMT is the use of computers to manipulate data and to control operations. When islands of AMT integrate through IS, the result is a computer-integrated manufacturing (CIM) system, which is commonly regarded as the basis for the factory of the future (Rosenthal, 1984). Doll and Vonderembse (1987) define CIM as a computer automation system that blends recent developments both from manufacturing and from IT to achieve competitive advantage. In fact, Frohlich and Dixon (1999) find that IT adaptation during the course of AMT implementation is the most important action for systems success.

Both information systems literature and manufacturing management literature illustrate the profound impact of IT on manufacturing enterprises. The following sections will first present the competitive advantages created by using IT, both strategically and operationally. Various organizational requirements for realizing the full potential of new IT implementation are then explored. (In this chapter "IT" encompasses AMT, as well as the information systems infrastructures that connect them.)

COMPETITIVE ADVANTAGES OF IT IN MANUFACTURING

Researchers have been advocating IT's important role in creating sustainable competitive advantage for many years (Porter & Miller, 1985; King, Grover & Hufnagel, 1989). Earlier studies focused primarily on IT's direct operational benefits, such as cost reduction and productivity gains (Boddy & Buchanan, 1984). Later works introduced the strategic value of IT (Neumann, 1994). Strategic information systems (SIS) is one of the central themes in IS literature (Kettinger, Grover, Guha & Segars, 1994). Heavy investments in SIS, such as the extensive adoption of enterprise resource planning (ERP) systems, are thought to give manufacturers significant advantage over their competitors (Callaway, 1999). Evidence shows, however, that SIS technical advantages are difficult to sustain in today's highly dynamic business environment because proprietary technologies often become obsolete faster than expected (Mata, Fuerst & Barney, 1995). Recent empirical studies look into other strategic IT factors, such as IT systems integration (Truman, 2000) and IT infrastructure flexibility (Byrd & Turner, 2001). The new IT offers both operational and strategic benefits.

The Operational Benefits of IT

The most commonly noted operational benefits of IT include both efficiency and productivity increases, cost reduction, and quality improvement. An early empirical study by Boddy and Buchanan (1984) finds that IT produces significant productivity gains at the operational level. Parthasarthy and Sethi (1993) find that flexible manufacturing technology has significant impact upon a firm's cost and quality performance. Later, Kelley (1994) verifies that IT is positively related to production efficiency and productivity. Other studies confirm IT's positive influence upon aspects of corporate financial performance, such as return on investment (Mahmood & Mann, 1993; Byrd & Marshall, 1997). Oliner and Sichel (2000) attribute 43 percent of U.S. labor productivity growth in the late 1990s to increased investment in IT, and another 36 percent to efficiency gains in generating better and faster IT products and services. Both increased power and speed, as well as the reduced cost of microcomputers, make possible the migration of applications from mainframe architecture to smaller platforms for manufacturing firms. This has lead to IT downsizing. [Doll and Doll (1992) illustrate a case of significant cost savings through IT downsizing in a CBS/FOX video.]

The Strategic Benefits of IT

1. Enhanced competitive position

Porter and Miller (1985) state that information technology is transforming the nature of competition. According to Porter's competitive forces model, a firm's competitive position is determined by five forces: existing competition, potential entrants, substitute products, and bargaining power of buyers and suppliers. First, IT can increase the entry barriers and switching costs of new competitors with significant amounts of IT investment and higher levels of expertness in new technology. Second, IT can change the bargaining power of suppliers. Many auto manufacturers have been able to achieve JIT purchasing with suppliers through real-time connections of information systems. Third, IT can change the bargaining power of buyers. GM has been able to locate the best parts supplier through the successful implementation of an EDI system. Fourth, IT has created significant new business opportunities, such as the emerging area of electronic commerce. Finally, IT can change existing competition by restructuring the industry. Segars and Grover (1995), in a longitudinal study of the impact of IT on industry structure, found strong evidence that IT can restructure strategic groups, thus improving a firm's competitive position.

2. Improved strategic flexibility

Hayes and Pisano (1994) point out that in a turbulent environment, the primary strategic goal of a manufacturing firm should be strategic flexibility.

Skinner's (1974) notion of "focused factory" has dominated U.S. manufacturing for a long time. Skinner argued that firms can't achieve all objectives at the same time: they must focus, first, on one or two core competencies that fit their competitive strengths. Tradeoffs, then, are common: cost vs. quality, cost vs. variety, quality vs. delivery, and quality vs. productivity. Anderson, Cleveland and Schroeder (1989) suggest that tradeoffs are not necessary. World-class manufacturers are able to achieve competencies simultaneously (Oliver, Delbridge, Jones, & Lowe, 1994), but the key is proper utilization of information technology. Manufacturing management literature suggests that most manufacturing flexibility studies acknowledge the important enabling role of IT (Vokurka & O'Leary-Kelly, 2000), but that they focus primarily on AMT and often ignore another critical component of IT — the IS infrastructure of the firm. Byrd (2001) indicates that IS infrastructure flexibility (the ability of a firm's information systems to support and integrate a wide variety of hardware, software and other communications technologies) is the basis of a firm's overall strategic flexibility.

3. Facilitating manufacturing globalization

Manufacturing activities are becoming increasingly globalized (Miller, DeMeyer & Nakane, 1992). The global organizational scope has been proposed as a key dimension of generic manufacturing strategy (Kotha & Orne, 1989). By going global, firms may expect low cost production factors and improved delivery speed and flexibility via market proximity (Ferdows, 1989). Global information systems play a crucial role by connecting global customers and suppliers, by offering global product services, by sharing global information resources, and by reducing global risks (Ives & Jarvenpaa, 1991). Some practical issues in global IT management include language and cultural barriers, differing systems development standards, security and fraud concerns, and intellectual property and other legal issues (Edberg, Grupe & Keuchler, 2001). Another research topic of current interest is the effective management of the global human resource through global information systems (Niederman, 1999). With the rapid developments in broadband communications technologies, global virtual teams are increasing in popularity and considered the most effective decision-making mechanisms in new product development processes (Schmidt, Montoya-Weiss & Massey, 2001).

ORGANIZATIONAL REQUIREMENTS OF IT IN MANUFACTURING

Despite widely acclaimed strategic and operational advantages of IT, new technologies also place significant organizational requirements on manufacturing enterprises. Studies show that firms often experience short-term operational benefits (such as local productivity gains) from IT, but fail to explore long-term strategic opportunities (Boddy & Buchanan, 1984). Jaikumar (1986) argues that technology, itself, is usually not to blame. The problem lies in the management of technology planning, evaluation, and implementation. Many firms invest in new technologies out of external technological or competitive pressure, rather than out of strategic necessity. Decision makers often pay close attention to elaborate technical features; however, they are not sophisticated enough to explore the unquantifiable strategic benefits of new technology (Small & Chen, 1997). Many senior managers are stuck in an industrial paradigm of thinking, believing that technology will implement itself once installed. While in practice, the full institutionalization of a new technology requires many organizational issues to be properly addressed.

Some of the important organizational requirements that new IT places on the manufacturing enterprise include:

Strategic Justification of IT

Strategic justification ensures that the objectives of IT investment are properly aligned with those of manufacturing and corporate strategy. Traditional justification procedures tend to ignore strategic analysis and to focus on financial criteria (Small & Chen, 1997). Kaplan (1983) argues that simple financial criteria are not appropriate for the justification of new manufacturing technologies because strategic benefits and synergistic effects from systems integration are difficult to quantify. Powell (1992) also expresses concerns about the apparent lack of formal evaluation methods of IT investment returns and about the limited empirical research on this issue. Naik and Chakravarty (1992) advocate a QFD-based method, which uses matrices to relate strategic objectives to AMT characteristics.

IT strategic alignment is another process related to strategic justification. Henderson and Venkatraman (1993) argue that the inability to realize value from IT investment is sometimes due to the lack of alignment between business strategy and IT strategy. Reich and Benbasat (1996) build on the idea by proposing a methodology that measures the linkages between business and IT objectives. A comprehensive framework for IT investment evaluation within manufacturing firms, however, remains incomplete.

Organizational Structure Issues

The fit between information technologies and organizational structures has long been considered critical to the success of manufacturing firms (Louis, Guy & Francois, 1995). Zammuto and O'Connor (1992) state that flexible, organic structures are key to gaining the strategic flexibility benefits of AMT. Leifer (1988) studies the fit between a firm's information systems and its organizational structures, concluding that centralized systems need bureaucratic structures, while decentralized systems require team-based organic structures. Parthasarthy and Sethi (1993) empirically verify that flexible automation has significant positive impact upon business performance when the organizational structure is highly organic.

Results from a later study also indicate that decentralization interacts positively with AMT, whereas formalization and mechanistic structures interact negatively with AMT (Gupta, Chen & Chiang, 1997). The implementation of new technologies may force manufacturers to reconsider their organizational structures and business processes. A widespread research area is the implementation of ERP systems (Cliffe, 1999). Software must be customized and hardware may have to be upgraded to conform with specific firms. When the cost of customization and adaptation becomes unreasonably high, however, the new system may actually become a catalyst for re-engineering the whole organizational structure (Bingi, Sharma & Godla, 1999).

Work Design Issues

Zuboff (1988) points out that new "informating" technology requires workers to have higher "intellective skills" such as abstract thinking, problem solving, and inference capability. The traditional job specialization may limit workers' understanding of a new technology and hinder communication. Job enrichment then, such as cross-functional training, will be necessary. Similarly, Susman (1990) suggests that AMT increases task interdependences and skill requirements, thus demanding greater worker involvement and work group autonomy. Empirical evidence also shows that increased operator control improves worker performance and well-being where AMT systems are employed (Wall, Corbett, Martin, Clegg & Jackson, 1990).

New information technologies have also brought about significant changes to the jobs of information system users and managers. The increasing importance of end-user computing (Powell & Moore, 2002) and of user involvement is the direct result of highly distributed computing technologies. End users, however, often find professional technical support missing when they need it most; consequently, distributed systems and increasing user dominance are changing the jobs of IS managers, making them feel loss of power and control (McBride & Wood-Harper, 2002). Due to the high cost of recruiting and retraining information systems professionals, job enrichment methods are necessary to improve job satisfaction and raise levels of commitment within organizations (Raghunathan, Raghunathan & Tu, 1998).

Sophisticated new technologies also impose much higher demand upon users to continuously learn new systems and to update skills. There is no doubt that while advanced information technologies have brought many advantages to the workplace, they have also increased individual stress to significant levels (Mital & Pennathur, 2002). We are surrounded, and many times invaded, by modern technology and by information overload. This phenomenon is commonly labeled "technostress" (Sethi, Caro & Schuler, 1987): new computer technology redefines job descriptions, increases the possibility of job losses, and forces workers to cope with constant changes and updates of technology. Technostress, however, does not occur in the workplace alone. Worsening the situation, corporations expect employees to constantly monitor work at home or on vacation via email and wireless communications systems. Further empirical studies must explore effective ways of coping with technostress, the modern disease of adapting to advanced new technologies (Weil & Rosen, 1997).

Systems Integration Issues

The degree of system integration remains a central issue for manufacturing industries (Gorbach, 2001) — especially the integration of AMT sites with information systems. Researchers argue that to achieve expected technological benefits, manufacturing systems must be redesigned for integration prior to implementing flexible manufacturing technologies (Duimering, Safayeni, & Purdy, 1993). A major problem of CIM implementation today is the predominance of "bottom-up" approaches: individual components of a system grow through local adoption, resulting in "islands of automation" with localized benefits, while neglecting systems integration. A strategic "top-down" approach may prove more appropriate (Johansen, Karmarkar, Nanda & Seidmann, 1995). Vonderembse, Raghunathan, and Rao (1997) confirm in a series of recent case studies that, to achieve higher organizational performance in the highly uncertain post-industrial environment, firms must first focus on integration across the value chain before implementing automation projects.

Systems integration emerged a solution to the lack of integration between islands of automation. Companies quickly realized, however, that to run effective manufacturing businesses, integration had to extend beyond the confines of manufacturing floors to include non-manufacturing systems such as finance, marketing, accounting, sales, and personnel. This initiative resulted in ERP systems, which support linkage among cross-functional business units (Callaway, 1999). The cross-functional integration achieved by ERP is necessary for a systems approach to the design and manufacture of products. Such an approach utilizes up-to-date information from marketing, sales, accounting, finance and other non-manufacturing systems in the design and manufacture of products. Electronic business technologies also enable manufacturers to extend integration efforts from internal systems to external constituencies, covering the entire value chain. Recently, vendors of ERP software have responded to customer demands for enhanced technology to further support SCM, e-commerce, customer relationship management (CRM), and business intelligence (Callaway, 2000).

CONCLUSION

The new generation of cheaper, faster, and more powerful computer network-based information technology is revolutionizing almost every aspect of our society. Most of our daily tasks may now be computerized to attain greater efficiency. Broadband and high speed wireless network technologies have virtually shortened the physical distance and eliminated time differences in real-time communications. Studies find that widespread adoption of new technology accounts for almost 80 percent of U.S. labor productivity growth in the late 1990s. Besides the commonly recognized productivity and cost benefits, a carefully implemented IT project may give manufacturers significant longer-term strategic benefits such as enhanced competitive position, improved strategic flexibility, and more effectual global operations.

To fully realize these strategic benefits, however, senior manufacturing managers must first abandon the traditional "technology-will-implement-itself" mindset and, also, address a series of organizational issues before implementing new technologies. Some of the more prominent issues include formal investment justification, organizational structure choices, work system design, and systems integration. A much higher level of internal system integration and external enterprise integration throughout the supply chain may prove to be the most fundamental change that new IT brings to manufacturing industries. The issues discussed in this article should present some interesting research ideas in the fields of IT and of manufacturing strategic management.

REFERENCES

Anderson, J. C., Cleveland, G., & Schroeder, R. G. (1989). Operations strategy: A literature review. *Journal of Operations Management,* 8(2), 133-158.

Barua, A., & Lee, B. (1997). The information technology productivity paradox revisited: A theoretical and empirical investigation in the manufacturing sector. *International Journal of Flexible Manufacturing Systems,* 9(2), 145-166.

Bingi, P., Sharma, M. K., & Godla, J. (1999). Critical issues affecting an ERP implementation. *Information Systems Management,* 16(3), 7-14.

Boddy, D., & Buchanan, D. A. (1984). Information technology and productivity: Myths and realities. *Omega,* 12(3), 112-140.

Byrd, T. A. (2001). Information technology: Core competencies and sustained competitive advantage. *Information Resources Management Journal,* 14(2), 27-36.

Byrd, T. A. & Marshall, T. E. (1997). Relating information technology investment to organizational performance: A causal model analysis. *Omega,* 25(1), 43-56.

Byrd, T. A., & Turner, D. E. (2001). The exploratory examination of the relationship between flexible IT infrastructure and competitive advantage. *Information & Management,* 39(1), 41-52.

Callaway, E. (1999). *Enterprise resource planning: Integrating applications and business process across the enterprise.* Charleston, SC: Computer Technology Research Corp.

Callaway, E. (2000). *ERP - The next generation: ERP is web[-] enabled for e-business.* Charleston, SC: Computer Technology Research Corp.

Cliffe, S. (1999). ERP implementation. *Harvard Business Review,* 77(1), 16-17.

Doll, W. J., & Doll, M. W. (1992). Downsizing at CBS/FOX video. *Information & Management,* 23(3), 123-139.

Doll, W. J., & Vonderembse, M. A. (1987). Forging a partnership to achieve competitive advantage: The CIM challenge. *MIS Quarterly,* 11(2), 205-220.

Doll, W. J., & Vonderembse, M. A., (1991). The evolution of manufacturing systems: Towards the post-industrial enterprise. *Omega,* 19(5), 401-411.

Duimering, P. R., Safayeni, F., & Purdy, L. (1993). Integrated manufacturing: Redesign the organization before implementing flexible technology. *Sloan Management Review,* 34(4), 47-56.

Edberg, D., Grupe, F. H., & Kuechler, W. (2001). Practical issues in global IT management. *Information Systems Management,* 18(1), 34-46.

Ferdows, K. (1989). *Managing international manufacturing.* North Holland: Elsevier Science Publishers.

Feroli, M. (2001). *Information technology and the new economy.* Washington, DC: Joint Economic Committee of the United States Congress.

Frohlich, M. T., & Dixon, J. R. (1999). Information systems adaptation and the successful implementation of advanced manufacturing technologies. *Decision Sciences,* 30(4), 921-957.

Gerwin D., & Kolodny H. (1992). *Management of advanced manufacturing technology: Strategy, organization, and innovation.* New York: Wiley.

Gorbach, G. (2001). Integration: Key to collaborative manufacturing. *Msi,* 19(3), 30.

Gordon, R. J. (2000). Does the "new economy" measure up to the great inventions of the past? *The Journal of Economic Perspectives,* 14(4), 49-74.

Gupta, A., Chen, I. J., & Chiang, D. (1997). Determining organizational structure choices in advanced manufacturing technology management. *Omega,* 25(5), 511-521.

Hayes, R. H., & Pisano, G. P. (1994). Beyond world-class: The new manufacturing strategy. *Harvard Business Review,* 72(1), 77-84.

Henderson, J. C., & Venkatraman, N. (1993). Strategic alignment: Leveraging information technology for transforming organizations. *IBM Systems Journal,* 32(1), 4-16.

Hill, T. J. (1994). *Manufacturing strategy: Text and cases* (2nd ed.). Burr Ridge, IL: Irwin.

Ives, B., & Jarvenpaa, S. L. (1991). Applications of global information technology: key issues for management. *MIS Quarterly,* 15(1), 33-49.

Ives, B., & Learmonth, G. P. (1984). The information system as a competitive weapon. *Communications of the ACM,* 27(12), 1193-1201.

Jaikumar, R. (1986). Postindustrial Manufacturing. *Harvard Business Review,* 64(6), 69-76.

Johansen, J., Karmarkar, U. S., Nanda, D., & Seidmann, A. (1995). Computer integrated manufacturing: Empirical implications for industrial information systems. *Journal of Management Information Systems,* 12(2), 59-82.

Kaplan, R. S. (1983). Measuring manufacturing performance: A new challenge for managerial accounting research. *Accounting Review,* 58(4), 686-705.

Keah, C. T. (2002). Supply chain management: Practices, concerns, and performance issues. *Journal of Supply Chain Management,* 38(1), 42-53.

Kelley, M. R. (1994). Productivity and information technology: The elusive connection. *Management Science,* 40(11), 1406-1425.

Kettinger, W. J., Grover, V., Guha, S., & Segars, A. H. (1994). Strategic information systems revisited: A study in sustainability and performance. *MIS Quarterly,* 18(1), 31-58.

King, W. R., Grover, V., & Hufnagel, E. H. (1989). Using information and information technology for sustainable competitive advantage: Some empirical evidence. *Information & Management,* 17(2), 87-93.

Kotha, S., & Orne, D. (1989). Generic manufacturing strategies: A conceptual system. *Strategic Management Journal,* (10)3, 211-231.

Leifer, R. (1988). Matching computer-based information systems with organizational structures. *MIS Quarterly,* 12(1), 63-73.

Louis, R., Guy, P., & Francois, B. (1995). Matching information technology and organizational structure: An empirical study with implications for performance. *European Journal of Information Systems,* 4(1), 3-16.

Mahmood, M. A., & Mann, G. J. (1993). Measuring the organizational impact of information technology investment: An exploratory study. *Journal of Management Information Systems,* 10(1), 97-122.

Mata, F. J., Fuerst, W. L., & Barney, J. B. (1995). Information technology and sustained competitive advantage: A resource-based analysis. *MIS Quarterly,* 19(4), 487-506.

McBride, N., & Wood-Harper, A. T. (2002). Towards user-oriented control of end-user computing in large organizations. *Journal of End User Computing,* 14(1), 33-41.

Miller, J.G., DeMeyer, A., & Nakane, J. (1992). Benchmarking global manufacturing. Homewood, IL: Business One Irwin.

Mital, A., & Pennathur, A. (2002). Getting the most out of advanced manufacturing technology (AMT)-based systems. Part II: Recognizing and managing human limitations. *International Journal of Manufacturing Technology and Management*, 4(1-2), 119-133.

Naik, B., & Chakravarty, A. K. (1992). Strategic acquisition of new manufacturing technology: a review and research framework. *International Journal of Production Research*, 30(7), 1575-1601.

Neumann, S. (1994). *Strategic information systems: Competition through information technologies.* New York: Macmillan College Publishing Co.

Niederman, F. (1999). Global information systems and human resource management: A research agenda. *Journal of Global Information Management*, 7(2), 33-39.

O'Halloran, J. P., & Wagner, T. R. (2001). The next frontier. *The Journal of Business Strategy*, 22(3), 28-33.

Oliner, S. D., & Sichel, D. E. (2000). The resurgence of growth in the late 1990s: Is information technology the story? *The Journal of Economic Perspectives*, 14(4), 3-22.

Oliver, N., Delbridge, R., Jones, D., & Lowe, J. (1994). World-class manufacturing: Further evidence in the lean production debate. *British Journal of Management*, 5 (Special Issue), S53-S63.

Parthasarthy, R., & Sethi, S. P. (1993). Relating strategy and structure to flexible automation: A test of fit and performance implications. *Strategic Management Journal*, 14(7), 529-549.

Porter, M. E., & Millar, V. E. (1985). How information gives you competitive advantage. *Harvard Business Review*, 63(4), 149-160.

Powell, A., & Moore, J. E. (2002). The focus of research in end user computing: Where have we come since the 1980s? *Journal of End User Computing*, 14(1), 3-22.

Powell, P. (1992). Information technology evaluation: Is it different? *The Journal of the Operational Research Society*, 43(1), 29-42.

Raghunathan, B., Raghunathan, T. S., & Tu, Q. (1998). An empirical analysis of the organizational commitment of information systems executives. *Omega*, 26(5), 569-580.

Reich, B. H., & Benbasat, I. (1996). Measuring the linkage between business and information technology objectives. *MIS Quarterly*, 20(1), 55-81.

Rosenthal, S. (1984). Progress toward the factory of the future. *Journal of Operations Management*, 4 (3), 203-229.

Schmidt, J. B., Montoya-Weiss, M. M., & Massey, A. P. (2001). New product development decision-making effectiveness: Comparing individuals, face-to-face teams, and virtual teams. *Decision Sciences*, 32(4), 575-600.

Segars, A. H., & Grover, V. (1995). The industry-level impact of information technology: An empirical analysis of three industries. *Decision Sciences,* 26(3), 337-368.

Sethi, A. S., Caro, D. H. J., & Schuler, R. S. (1987). *Strategic management of technostress in an information society.* Lewiston, NY: Hogrefe.

Sethi, V., & King, W. R. (1994). Development of measures to assess the extent to which an information technology application provides competitive advantage. *Management Science,* 40(12), 1601-1627.

Shaw, M. J., Seidmann, A., & Whinston, A. B. (1997). Information technology for automated manufacturing enterprises: Recent developments and current research issues. *International Journal of Flexible Manufacturing Systems,* 9(2), 115-120.

Skinner, W. (1969). Manufacturing—missing link in corporate strategy. *Harvard Business Review,* 47(3), 136-144.

Skinner, W. (1974). The focused factory. *Harvard Business Review,* 52(3), 113-121.

Small, M. H., & Chen, I. J. (1997). Economic and strategic justification of AMT - Inferences from industrial practices. *International Journal of Production Economics,* 49(1), 65-75.

Stroeken, J. H. M. (2000). Information technology, innovation and supply chain structure. *International Journal of Technology Management,* 20(1-2), 156-175.

Susman, G. I. (1990). Work groups: autonomy, technology, and choice. In P.S. Goodman, & L.S. Sproull (Eds.), *Technology and Organizations* (pp. 87-108). San Francisco: Josey-Bass Publishers.

Truman, G. E. (2000). Integration in electronic exchange environments. *Journal of Management Information Systems,* 17(1), 209-244.

Vokurka, R. J., & O'Leary-Kelly, S. W. (2000). A review of empirical research on manufacturing flexibility. *Journal of Operations Management,* 18(4), 485-501.

Vonderembse, M. A., Raghunathan, T. S. & Rao, S. S. (1997). A post-industrial paradigm: to integrate and automate manufacturing. International Journal of Production Research, 35(9), 2579-2599.

Wall, T. D., Corbett, J. M., Martin, R., Clegg, C. W., & Jackson, P. R. (1990). Advanced manufacturing technology, work design, and performance: A change study. *Journal of Applied Psychology,* 75(6), 691-697.

Weil, M. M., & Rosen, L. D. (1997). *TechnoStress: coping with technology @work @home @play.* New York: John Wiley.

Wheelwright, S. C. (1984). Manufacturing strategy: Defining the missing link. *Strategic Management Journal,* 5(1), 77-91.

Zammuto, R. F., & O'Connor, E. J. (1992). Gaining advanced manufacturing technologies' benefits: The roles of organization design and culture. *Academy of Management Review,* 17(4), 701-728.

Zuboff, S. (1988). *In the Age of the Smart Machine: The Future of Work and Power*. New York: Basic Books Inc.

Chapter III

Model-Supported Alignment of Information Systems Architecture

Andreas L. Opdahl
University of Bergen, Norway

ABSTRACT

The chapter presents an alignment framework and an associated representation framework for information systems (IS) architecture management. The alignment framework supports identification of high-level longer-term principles for evolution of IS architectures. The fundamental idea of the alignment framework is to generate alternative future IS architectures by grouping IS-architecture phenomena into IS-architecture areas in different ways. The representation framework supports the creation of IS-architecture models that can support IS-architecture alignment and other IS-architecture management tasks. In addition, the representation framework is a conceptual model for thinking about IS-architectures. Together, the alignment and representation frameworks constitute an early theory of IS architectures and IS-architecture work. They are part of a comprehensive methodology that results from several years of case and theory studies, tool developments, industrial projects and consulting.

INTRODUCTION

Contemporary enterprises have numerous computer-based information systems (ISs). Each IS consists of one or more applications and other software systems, which often include one or more databases. Related in several ways, ISs exchange data, store the same kinds of data, support the same kinds of operations and so on. When the entirety of information systems in an enterprise and the relationships between them are managed improperly, or altogether ignored, problems occur. IS architecture, therefore, must be recognised and managed as a singular phenomenon. Andersen and Opdahl (1996) define IS architecture as "the set of computerised ISs in an enterprise, as well as the computerised communication paths between them. In a wider sense, [IS architectures are] also related to human information systems and communication, as well as infrastructural and organisational issues." This chapter presents two important elements of a methodology for IS-architecture work: frameworks both for IS-architecture alignment and for representing IS architectures.

IS-architecture work seeks to realise a satisficing long-term IS architecture for an enterprise. On the one hand, to support the enterprise well, the IS architecture must align with the enterprise. On the other hand, to maintain flexibility, it must remain independent from the enterprise's most volatile aspects. The balance between alignment and independence depends on a large number of other IS-architectural considerations. Whereas "alignment" in IS-management literature is often synonymous with "strategic alignment"—alignment with business goals—this chapter takes a broader view of alignment: one that includes alignment with organisational elements such as organisation and process structures, in addition to strategic alignment.

IS architectures and IS-architecture work have been central topics in both IS practice and IS research for several decades. Earlier work include Zachmann's (1978) seminal paper on information architecture; Nolan's (1973, 1977, 1979) *Information Resource Management (IRM)*; industrial methodologies, such as IBM's *Business Systems Planning* (Gillenson & Goldberg, 1984, chapt. 5); Brancheau and Wetherbe (1986); Andersen Consulting's *Method/1* (Flaatten, 1986), as well as its academic methods by Wetherbe and Davis (1983); Vogel and Wetherbe (1984); Leifer (1988); Hugoson's (1986) *Function-Based Systems Structuring (VBS)*; Kiewiet and Stegwee's (1992) clustering approach; Magoulas and Pessi (1991); Petterson and Goldkuhl (1994); Axelsson's (1995) discussion and comparison of IRM and VBS; Axelsson's (1998) process, activity, and component-oriented IS-architecture structuring (PBS & PAKS); Päivärinta (2001); and Päivärinta and Tyrväinen's (2001) work on genres and genre systems in IS-architecture work. Hackney, Burn, and Dhillon (2000) have challenged many of the assumptions underlying current approaches to IS-architecture work.

This chapter presents an alignment framework (section 2) for IS-architecture work, as well as an associated representation framework (section 3). The alignment framework and the representation framework are part of a comprehensive methodology, which is also briefly outlined (section 4). The methodology and its components result from several years of case and theory studies, tools development, industrial projects, and consulting within the RAISA (Representation, Assessment and Improvement of IS Architectures) project.

FRAMEWORK FOR IS-ARCHITECTURE ALIGNMENT

The alignment framework targets IS-architecture workers, aiding them in identifying high-level long-term principles for an evolving IS architecture. Ultimately the framework offers a systematic way of conceptualising—and eventually even generating with tools—alternative IS architectures. Each alternative is conceptualised according to a grouping principle, which will become the enterprises' high-level long-term IS-architecture principle if selected. The alignment framework, however, currently offers little help in selecting an IS-architecture alternative, leaving incomplete the development of detailed heuristics for IS-architecture selection. The framework, nevertheless, offers a description of IS-architecture alignment: it thereby contributes to early theories of IS architectures and to methodologies for IS-architecture work.

The following section presents the framework's view of organisations, of IS architectures and of IS-architecture alignment. Two grouping principles arising from the model are then introduced. Finally, practical use of the alignment framework is discussed.

Organisations and IS Architectures

The alignment framework views an organisation and its IS architecture as a collection of related elements. The elements and their relationships are instances of different metatypes. Some of the metatypes are organisational, such as objectives and strategies, organisation units, functions, locations, products, and processes. Other metatypes are IS-architectural, such as development activities, low-level operations carried out by applications, physical information, and responsibility for applications.

Elements of the same organisational metatype form an organisational structure; elements of the same IS-architectural metatype form an IS-architectural structure. There are, of course, relationships between elements from different structures and between elements in the same structure. Many structures are hierarchical. (Metatypes and structures are detailed in the next section, based on prior surveys (Opdahl, 1996) of available literature: Allen and Boynton (1991); Brancheau and Wetherbe (1986); Gillenson and Goldberg (1984, chapt. 5); Davis and Olson (1984, chapt. 20); Earl (1993); Emery (1977); Goldkuhl and Pettersson (1994); Goodhue, Wybo, and Kirsch (1992); Hart (1994); Warne and

Hart (1996); Hugoson (1986); Iivari and Koskela (1987); Kiewiet and Stegwee (1992); Leifer (1988); Lundeberg; Goldkuhl and Nilsson (1978); Magoulas and Pessi (1991); Nolan (1973, 1977, 1979); Magoulas and Pessi (1991); Periasamy (1993); Sowa and Zachman (1992); Tardieu (1992); Vogel and Wetherbe (1984); Wetherbe and Davis (1983); and Zachman (1987).)

The IS-Architecture Alignment Problem

One specific IS-architecture alignment problem is that of grouping all disjunctive IS-architecture elements in an enterprise into IS-architecture areas (Kiewiet & Stegwee, 1992) that are satisficing in for the long term. An IS (as an architectural area) combines, for example, information systems operations and physical information. Other architectural areas—responsibility areas—group responsibilities for IS-architectural activities and resources.

The alignment model forms IS-architecture areas by systematically grouping together IS-architecture elements according to selected relationships to other organisational structures. Operations and information within an IS may be grouped according to the organisational function of which they are part and by which they are manipulated. (A responsibility area may be grouped according to the organisational unit responsible.) As a result, elements in an IS-architecture area belong together because they are related in the selected way to the same organisational element—the area's grouping element. Because all of the elements in the same IS-architectural structure are grouped according to the same relationship to another organisational structure, the resulting IS architecture is deemed well-structured. In this way, the alignment framework offers a systematic way to generate numerous alternative and well-structured IS architectures for manual or heuristic assessment.

Grouping Principles: Organisational Structure and Hierarchical Levels

Grouping elements must belong to the same organisational metatype at the same hierarchical level with the corresponding organisational structure. Together the organisational structure and the hierarchical level constitute a grouping principle:

1. *Organisational structure:* The elements of an IS-architectural structure may, in principle, be grouped with elements from any organisational structure—by objectives strategies, organisational units, functions, locations, products, or processes. For example, physical information may be grouped either with the organisational units to which it is available or with the products to which it contributes.

2. *Hierarchical level:* When an organisational structure for grouping has been selected, the elements of an IS-architectural structure may be grouped, in principle, with organisation elements at a higher or lower hierarchical level. For example, physical information can be grouped with low-level organisation units such as departments (individual employees may perform this function for some applications) or with high-level units such as divisions (completely centralised ownership, indeed, may act as the single top-level enterprise element).

In this way, the alignment framework unifies two previously separate lines of work. Kiewiet and Stegwee (1992) discuss grouping by different organisational structures such as entity types, information processes, organisational units, and physical locations. They neglect explicitly considering, however, degrees of centralisation.

In another vein, several authors discuss degrees of centralisation, but without explicitly considering organisational structures: Emery (1977); King (1983); Davis and Olson (1984, chapt. 20); Magoulas and Pessi (1991); and Pettersson and Goldkuhl (1994a).

The alignment framework unifies the two lines of work by combining organisational structures with centralisation degrees, where hierarchical levels correspond to degrees of centralisation. Opdahl (1996) offers the following example:

> [T]he processes are first grouped after which organisation units [...] are responsible for them. Then, entity types are assigned to the processes that create them. In the first case, we represent the organisational-unit structure as a single element only: the enterprise itself. As a result, all information processes and entity types end up in the same IS area, giving us a completely centralised IS architecture. In the second case, we represent the organisational-unit structure at the highest possible level of detail with as many small organisational units included as possible. The result this time is a 'maximally' decentral IS architecture. We can therefore regulate the centralisation degree of the IS architecture produced by choosing to represent the relevant organisational structure in more or less detail.

This is a key contribution of the alignment framework.

Figure 1 shows the resulting IS-architecture alignment petal. The figure illustrates that the elements in each IS-architectural structure may be grouped as a "petal" (organisational structure) with a particular centralisation degree (hierarchical level within the organisational structure). When the same grouping

Figure 1: The IS-architecture alignment petal: Each IS-architecture metatype can be grouped according to one of the petals (an organisational metatype) with a particular centralisation degree in the petal (a hierarchical level in that organisational metatype).

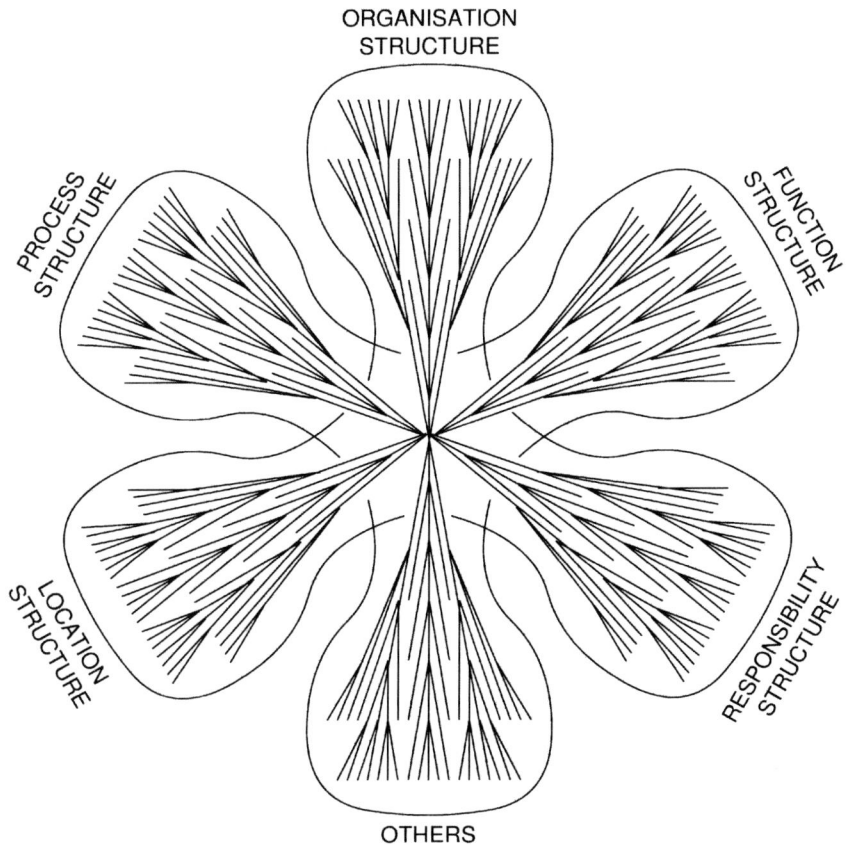

principle is used for several IS-architectural structures, the resulting IS-architecture areas will organize elements from all corresponding metatypes.

Using the Alignment Framework

IS-architecture work, according to the alignment framework, begins with an enterprise's existing organisation and IS architecture. The resulting IS-architecture solution comprises both blueprints for an acceptable IS architecture (a set of disjunctive, well-structured IS-architecture areas) and a set of high-level long-term principles (those used to conceptualise or to generate the selected IS architecture).

The framework explains precisely what it means to group IS-architecture phenomena into IS-architecture areas, offering a systematic way to conceptualise or to generate alternative future IS-architectures. This should aid both practical IS-architecture management today and offer possibilities for automated IS-architecture tool support in the future. The framework, however, offers little help in selecting future IS architectures. It aids selection to a limited extent by offering precise descriptions of IS architectures and of how they relate to organisations. (Further study of the framework is needed.) Compatibility and leveraging of current IS-architecture with ICT infrastructure are criteria for selecting new IS architecture principles.

FRAMEWORK FOR IS-ARCHITECTURE REPRESENTATION

The representation framework supports the creation of IS-architecture models that can support IS-architecture alignment and other IS-architecture management tasks. In other words, the representation framework can be used as a language for modelling enterprises. It identifies the information to collect and structures it in a way that suits the alignment framework and that facilitates tool-supported IS-architecture work. The representation framework can also be used as a conceptual model for thinking about IS architectures. It, thereby, emerges—along with the alignment framework—as part of an early theory of IS architectures. This section will first present the basic structure of the representation framework, along with its core metatypes. It then discusses practical use of the framework.

Basic Structure

The representation framework is a metamodel of organisations and their IS architectures. The most important part of the representation framework is the core metamodel—the starting point for IS-architecture improvement. Figure 2 shows the metatypes in the core metamodel. The boxes in this figure indicate model elements, whereas the arrows indicate model relationships. The representation framework also offers a number of extension metamodels (not shown in Figure 2), which describe, e.g., products and locations. Earlier versions of the framework were documented in extended ER (EER) notation (Elmasri & Navathe, 1994). Here a revised metamodel is documented using UML class diagrams (OMG, 2001).

Figure 2: The core of the IS-architecture representation framework: The core may be extended with metamodels that represent other metatypes, such as products and locations.

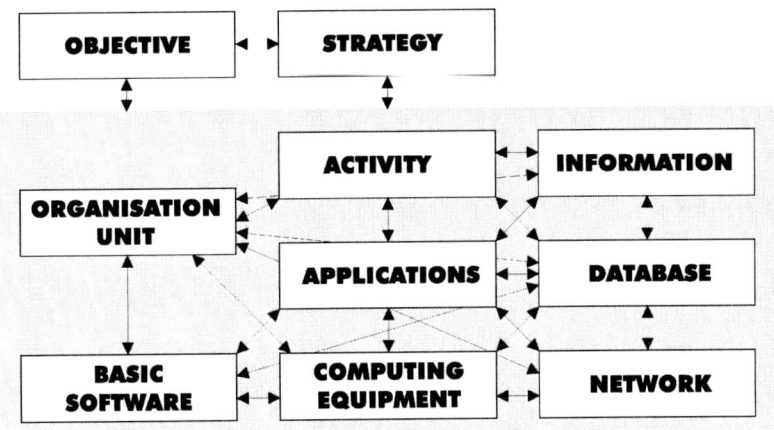

Objectives and strategies are realised by and, also, guide the operational enterprise (see Figure 2). The operational enterprise subdivides, then, into three levels. The highest (human) level comprises organisation units that implement activities which, in turn, manipulate information. The middle (IS) level incorporates applications and databases. The lowest (ICT infrastructure) level comprises basic software systems and the computers and networks on which they function. An element in an enterprise model is an instance of any of these metatypes: objective, strategy, organsation unit, activity, information, application, database, basic software, computing equipment, network, or an extensional metatype. In addition to metatypes, the representation framework also defines several sub-metatypes and types that are particularly important for IS-architecture management. Table 1 summarises the core metatypes. The criteria for inclusion of each metatype are theoretical or practical considerations and practical evaluations of the framework.

An element may be either a class, an object, or a group. (Classes and objects are defined by the UML [OMG 2001].) Groups are depicted (Figure 3) as aggregates of element objects. The need for groups has been identified in practical evaluation of the representation framework and is mirrored in the "multiobjects" of the OPEN Modelling Language (Firesmith, Henderson-Sellers, & Graham, 1997). The following section explains each core metatype in detail and mentions some of the extension metamodels.

Table 1: The core metatypes in the representation framework

Metatype (Subtype examples)	Description
Objective (Mission, business objectives, goals, etc.)	The motives/rationales for the activities carried out by the organisation units and for other phenomena. ***Objectives*** *can be either explicit statements or implicit ideas. They can be either shared or individual and either official or private.*
Strategy (Business strategies, principles, plans, and standards, etc.)	Guidelines for how organisation units carry out activities. ***Guidelines*** *can be either formal or informal.*
Organisation Unit (Divisions, business units, departments, work groups, employees, project groups, boards, committees, etc.)	One or more persons. *An **Organisation unit** may be either an individual or a group. It may be either permanent or temporary.* *Note that a **Role** is a subtype of an organisation **unit**, i.e., an individual unit at the type level. The **Role** subtype is so important in enterprise modelling that it should often have its own icon.*
Activity (Functions, processes, tasks, projects, etc.)	Actions or events that occur in the enterprise. ***Activities*** *can either be singular, continuous, or repeated.*
Information	A pattern of knowledge information or data that is used and/or produced in the enterprise. ***Information*** *exists in electronic or other formats, e.g., paper.*
Application	A software system that automates or supports an activity in order to let an organisation unit accomplish an objective.
Database (Electronic archives, libraries, etc.)	A collection of data or information within an enterprise. *A **Database** exists in electronic or other form.*
Basic Software (Operating systems, protocols, etc.)	A group of cooperating programs that are used by applications and by databases.
Computing Equipment (Computers, peripherals, etc.)	Hardware.
Network	A communications network which connects computers with other computers, peripherals and/or networks.
Phenomenon	Any of the above either an objetive, a strategy, an organisation unit, an activity, information, an application, a database, basic software, computing equipment, a network, or an instance of one of the extensional metatypes.

Figure 3: An element may either be a class, an object or a group. Groups are aggregates of element objects. All the elements in a particular group belong to the same class. Classes are also element-classifiers for groups.

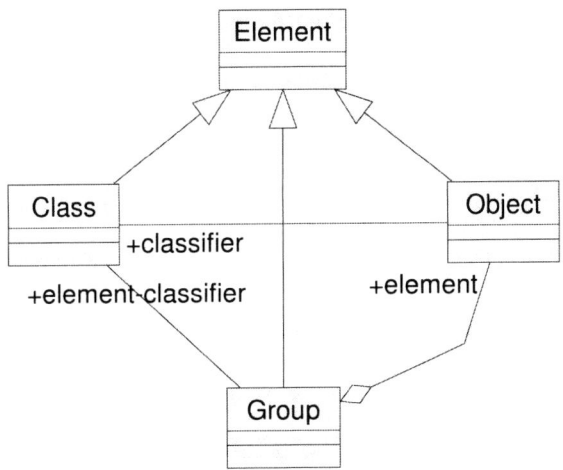

Objectives and Strategies

An objective represents motives or rationales for the activities carried out by organisation units and, sometimes, for other types of phenomena. Examples of objectives are missions, business objectives, goals, and critical success factors. Most of the objectives we have encountered in our study have been objects, rather than classes or groups. Objectives are operationalised by strategies and realised by activities. They can be either explicit statements or implicit ideas, either common or individual and either public or private. Objectives can be aggregates of more detailed objectives. Political extension metatypes introduce relationships that facilitate goal analysis in the tradition of Alexander (1970). Although they are not the most critical metatypes for IS-architecture work, objectives sometimes contribute to structuring parts of the IS architecture of a controlling and optimising enterprise, the information systems of which must provide information to monitor objectives.

A strategy represents a guideline for how an organisation unit carries out activities. Strategies may include general business strategies, principles, plans, job descriptions, and standards. Almost all of the strategies we have encountered in our study have been objects, although groups may be useful in some enterprise models (they preclude the need to represent each job description as a separate

Figure 4: Objectives are motives and rationales for activities and sometimes for other kinds of phenomena. Objectives are initiated by strategies and implemented by activities. Organisation units are responsible for objectives, and objectives may be aggregates of more detailed objectives. Strategies can be aggregates of more detailed strategies. They may be seen as high-level procedures that guide activities.

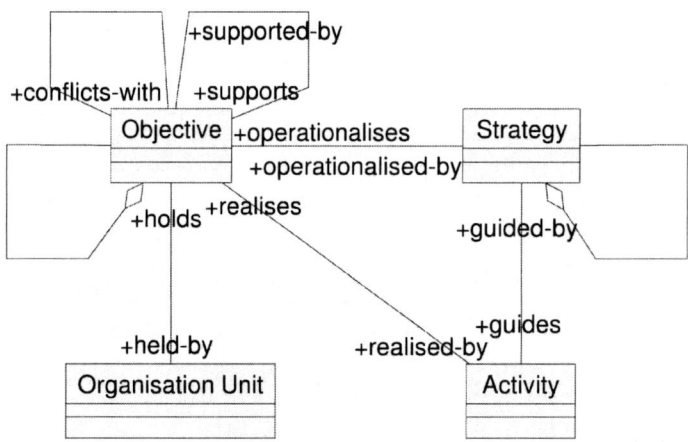

object). Strategies can be aggregates of more detailed strategies. More detailed strategies become procedures that guide activities. Strategies are either formal or informal. They are important in linking objectives to activities. (See Figure 4 for a representation framework at the metatype level.)

Organisation Units

Organisation units represent individuals or groups of individuals. Examples of organisation units are divisions, business units, departments, work groups, roles, employees, project groups, boards and committees. Roles are organisation units that represent discrete individuals at the class level. Roles are considered so important in enterprise modelling that they are identified explicitly in the representation framework, often meriting their own icons. Organisation units, furthermore, are either permanent or temporary. They implement activities, and they can be responsible for almost any other phenomena. Many uses of the representation framework define ownership as a distinct responsibility. Responsibility for an objective is different from merely holding that objective: responsibility is often pushed downward in the organisation. Organisation units also have available resources, including information, applications, databases, basic software, computing equipment and networks. Finally, organisation units can be aggregates of other organisation units. The representation framework allows

Figure 5: Organisation units represent individuals or groups of individuals. Organisation units implement activities and they can be responsible for almost any other phenomena. Organisation units also have available to themselves resources, including information, applications, databases, basic software, computing equipment and networks. Organisation units can be aggregates of other organisation units.

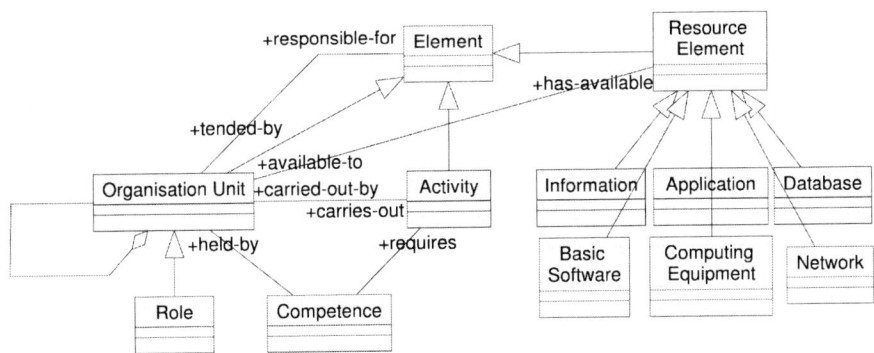

multiple top-level organisation units in the same model to represent suppliers to, customers of and partners of the enterprise being studied. Organisation units are important because IS-architecture work must consider which users and which groups of users are able to implement activities: they must have available applications, databases and information in the IS architecture.

Figure 5 illustrates this part of the representation framework at the metatype level.

Activities and Information

Activities represent actions or events that occur in an enterprise: processes, process steps, functions, low-level operations and projects. Unless they are extremely long-term, project objects are seldom represented in enterprise models, unlike project classes. Activities may be singular, continuous or repeated. They are important because IS-architecture studies must consider how activities are supported by applications. It is also essential to consider which activities manipulate which information. Finally, activities are important because they represent processes and functions, both important structuring principles (explained in the following text).

Information represents knowledge, information or data that is used and/or produced in an enterprise. The information we have represented in our study has always been at the class level—conventional for information and data modelling. Information formats may be electronic or other. Information is important because an IS-architecture study must consider how information is manipulated by activities, as well as which information is stored in which databases. Extension metatypes for relationships, properties and other are provided for more elaborate information modelling.

Figure 6 illustrates this part of the representation framework at the metatype level.

Three sub-metatypes of activities are so important in enterprise modelling that they are explicitly identified in the framework—processes, functions and operations:

- Processes are high-level activities composed of low-level activities called process steps. Process steps must be connected through exchange of informational or material resources, and they must contribute to the overall objective of the process. Delivering a product (horizontal processes), informing management (upwards vertical processes) or controlling operations (downwards vertical processes) are standard objectives. "Installing a set-top box," "reporting earnings" and "revising installation procedures" exemplify processes. Processes are important grouping principles in IS-architecture work. (Figure 7 builds upon Figure 6 with processes and process steps.)

Figure 6: Activities represent actions or events that occur in enterprises. Activities are supported by applications and manipulate information. Information comprises information or data that are used and/or produced in enterprises. Information is manipulated by activities and stored in databases.

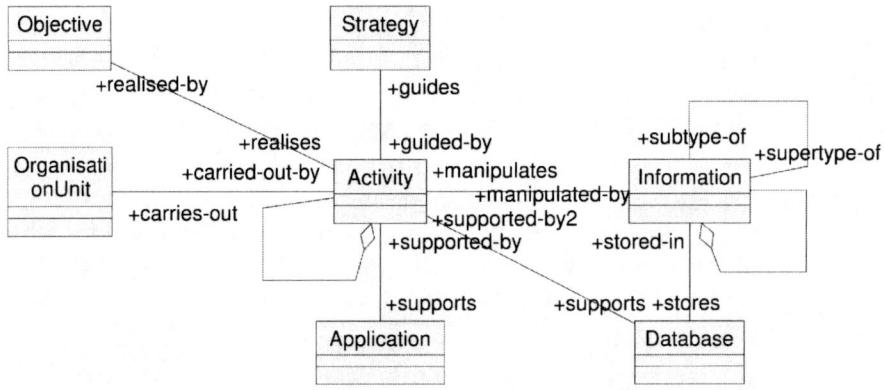

Figure 7: Processes are high-level activities that are composed of one or more lower-level activities called process steps. The steps must be connected through exchange of informational or material resources, and they must contribute to the overall objective of the process.

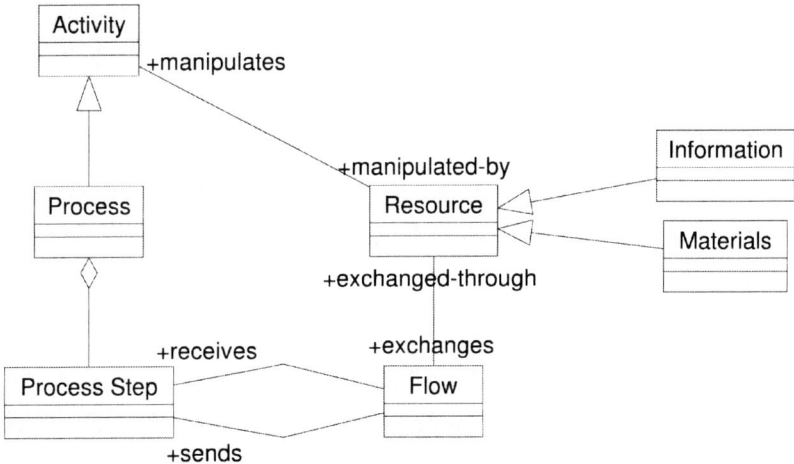

- Functions are high-level activities that comprise one or more low-level activities. Sub-functions require the same competencies and resources as the functions they compose. Examples of functions are accounting and ICT-support. Functions are also important in IS-architecture work as grouping principles.
- Operations are low-level activities: meaningful interactions between applications and users. The representation framework links activities to applications at the most detailed level. Activities carried out by organisation units and supported by applications may be classified as wholly manual (not supported by applications) or primarily computer-based (the activity is an operation). "Registering a customer," "group-authoring an annual report," and "checking the Internet for new competitors" are examples of operations. Operations are sometimes too low level to be represented explicitly in IS-architecture studies, but they have been used to suggest possible future allocations of operations to applications.

Applications and Databases

Applications represent software systems that directly support activities, furthering the objectives of organisation units. Applications may depend upon other applications and may manipulate databases. Databases hold enterprise information. Electronic databases, archives, and libraries exemplify the forms that databases may take. They store information and are manipulated by applications. Databases and applications depend upon basic software, applications, other databases and their interrelationships (the focus of IS-architecture work). Related applications and databases form information systems—an important outcome of IS-architecture work.

Figure 8 distinguishes this part of the representation framework at the metatype level. The illustration also includes ICT-infrastructure (discussed in the following section).

Computing Equipment, Networks and Basic Software

Computing equipment includes hardware such as computers and peripherals (printers and scanners). Networks connect computing equipment. Applications and databases depend upon basic software. Different from applications, basic software supports activities indirectly, although the distinction is not always crystal clear: a DBMS—usually considered basic software—often also provides an end-user report generation facility. Examples of basic software are operating systems and performance monitors. Basic software, computing equipment (in particular computers) and networks affect IS-architecture work in several ways. They indicate the ICT-platforms that are in place in the enterprise, as well as to what extent organisations depend upon particular platforms. They thereby

Figure 8: Applications are software systems that directly support activities. Applications may depend upon other applications and may manipulate databases. Applications are run on computing equipment and over networks. Databases store information and are manipulated by applications.

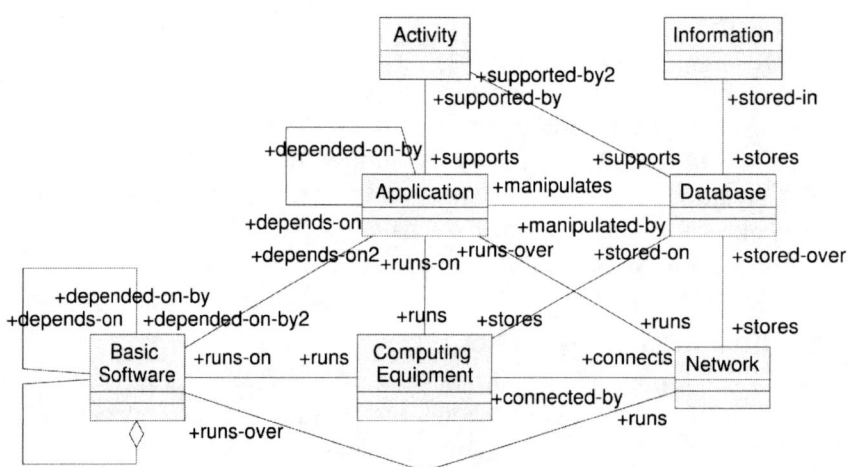

restrict, to an extent, the changes to existing applications and databases that can feasibly be made. They also indicate those elements in an ICT-infrastructure for which an organisation unit is responsible. Finally, they are a driver of change, because simplifying the ICT-infrastructure is an important concern in IS-architecture work.

Figure 8 depicts this part of the representation framework at the metatype level.

Extension Metamodels

The representation framework also offers extension metamodels (a few of which were previously mentioned and briefly outlined). The IS-architecture extension supports the modelling of IS-architecture areas, such as information systems and responsibility areas (as described in Section 2). Both conflicts and support among objectives and the organisations that work towards those objectives are captured by the political extension metatypes. The information modelling extension refers to the modelling of relationships and of properties in addition to the modelling of information. (See the process modelling extension in Figure 7.) Other extensions are provided for more detailed representation of communications, competencies, locations and products.

Using the Representation Framework

The representation framework is highly adaptable in several different ways. Metatypes, for example, are flexible in that they can be sub-metatyped to fit local enterprise terminology. Our studies have found that the strategy metatype has been refined into enterprise-specific terms such as "business strategy," "principle," "plan" and "standard." Visual presentations of enterprise models are adaptable because the representation framework is independent of particular diagram types and notations—they merely define metatypes; enterprises determine which diagram types they will use. In this sense, the representation framework is similar to, e.g., the UML metamodel rather than to the various diagram types of UML. This is important: most enterprises have particular sets of diagram notations currently in use and will resist changes. (The associated tool and methodology are also highly adaptable, as pointed out in the next section.)

METHODOLOGY FOR IS-ARCHITECTURE WORK

The alignment and representation frameworks are part of a comprehensive methodology that offers a position, a method and a modelling tool for representation, assessment and improvement of IS architectures. The position is the underlying view of IS architectures and IS-architecture work with emphasis on scalability, tailorability, adaptability, and participatory IS-architecture work. The method proposes a general way of thinking about and organising IS-architecture projects and is not a strictly prescribed way of working. It includes approximately 80 steps along two main paths: a general path that runs parallel to a modelling path, but that can also run alone. The *tool* is implemented by a template for Computas's generic enterprise modelling tool Metis (www.metis.no). Using a generic tool ensures that local adaptations are always possible. With some adoption effort, the Metis tool lets users visualise parts of enterprise models developed using the RAISA framework in a wide variety of ways. The largest enterprise models we have developed have used the visual notation of the Metis tool, where model elements are drawn as icons and relationships as arrows. Other applications of the framework have used a variety of notations, visualising relationships between model objects as matrices. The tool is also extendible and programmable, making it a starting point for further work on more elaborately tool-supported IS-architecture work.

Practical Experience

The methodology has been developed through several years of case and theory studies, tool development, industrial projects and consulting. Pettersvold (1996) focussed on the representation framework in her study of alignment at a regional Norwegian transport company. Lugenga (1997) used the framework and the information ward model (Hart, 1994; Warne & Hart, 1996) in a multi-case study of how to predict potential user-resistance towards new systems. Netteland (1999) focussed on data collection methods in her study of a regional Norwegian college. Recently, Steine (2002) has used the representation framework to represent, document, and evaluate a new e-procurement process in a major national oil company. Andersen (2002) has experimented with automatic extraction of personalised views on a complex industrial enterprise model based on the framework, whereas Gjesdal (2002) has used it in an investigation in which information types are used to learn about data warehouses and the opportunities they offer. In cooperation with IntraWeb AS, the author has studied how enterprise models can support IS-architecture evolution at Norway Post, resulting in a model of several thousand objects and links. The representation framework has been used in other commercial projects of similar size, one using the framework to understand the IS architecture of a telecommunications company and to propose paths for further evolution.

CONCLUSION AND FURTHER WORK

This chapter has presented alignment and representation frameworks for IS-architecture work. The frameworks are parts of an integrated IS-architecture methodology. A major benefit of the alignment framework is that its grouping principles can act as high-level long-term principles (Richardson, Jackson, & Dickson, 1990) for IS-architecture evolution. Providing principles of this kind is preferable to relying upon a blueprint of a future IS architecture alone: the principles are inherently general and will remain relevant longer, whereas the blueprint will gradually become outdated as the enterprise and its environment change. A major benefit of the representation framework is that it offers a model that is specific for conceptualising IS architectures and that supports the alignment framework. The framework thereby offers a path toward tool-supported IS-architecture work.

This chapter has presented a revised version of the representation framework illustrated by UML class diagrams rather than by EER diagrams. Using UML diagrams to define the syntax of the framework is an important difference from regarding the framework as an *extension* of the UML. (The UML diagrams presented in this chapter do not take UML semantics into account.) For the representation framework to become a proper extension of UML, e.g., activities should be defined as stereotyped UML activities and basic software might be considered stereotyped UML components. Aligning the representation framework more tightly with UML is left for further work, not least because UML semantics are currently unclear with respect to representing concrete problem domains (Opdahl & Henderson-Sellers, 2002.)

The RAISA alignment and representation frameworks are still being improved and extended. The most obvious path for further work is to extend the tool support and, in particular, to support automated generation of alternative future IS architectures using the alignment model. Developing heuristics for assessing alternative IS architectures is also a challenging task. Finally, extending the methodology with genres and genre systems (Päivärinta, 2001; Päivärinta & Tyrväinen, 2001) is another promising path for further work.

ACKNOWLEDGMENT

The author is indebted to Erling S. Andersen for his help with initiating the RAISA project; to Snorre Fossland for inspiring discussions and for his work on the RAISA template for the Computas-Metis tool; and to all the research students who have contributed to the project.

REFERENCES

Alexander, C.W. (1970). *Notes on the synthesis of form.* Harvard University Press.

Allen, B.R. & Boynton, A.C. (1991). Information architecture: In search of efficient flexibility. *MIS Quarterly*, December.

Andersen, E. S. & Opdahl, A. L. (1996). Supporting IS-architecture work: Progress reports from the RAISA project. In E. Eik, C. E. Moe and M. Sein (Eds.), *Proceedings of NOKOBIT'96*, Kristiansand, Norway, Agder University College.

Andersen, Ø. (2002). Individuelle perspektiver av komplekse virksomhetsmodeller (Individual perspectives on complex enterprise models), Bergen, Norway, University of Bergen, 2002.

Axelsson, K. (1995). Realization of a decentralized IS-strategy. In Sølvberg, A., Krogstie, J. & Seltveit, A.H. (eds.), *Information Systems Development for Decentralized Organizations*. New York: Chapman & Hall.

Brancheau, J.C. & Wetherbe, J.C. (1986). Information architectures: Methods and practice. *Information Processing and Management*, 22 (6), 453–463.

Davis, G.B. & Olson, M. (1984). Organization and management of the information resources function (pp. 629-657). *Management Information Systems—Conceptual Foundations, Structure and Development*. New York: McGraw-Hill.

Earl, M.J. (1993). Experiences in strategic information systems planning. *MIS Quarterly*, 17(1), 1–24.

Elmasri, R. & Navathe, S.B. (1994). *Fundamentals of database systems* (2nd. ed.). San Francisco: Benjamin Cummings.

Emery, J.C. (1977). Managerial and economic issues in distributed computing. In Gilchrist, B. (ed.), *Information Processing* (p. 77). North-Holland: IFIP.

Firesmith, D., Henderson-Sellers, B. & Graham, I. (1997). *OPEN Modelling Language—OML Reference Manual*. Cambridge: Cambridge University Press; SIGS Books.

Gillenson, M.L. & Goldberg, R. (1984). Business strategic planning: Concepts and needs. *Strategic Planning, Systems Analysis and Database Design* (pp. 57–65). New York: Wiley.

Gjesdal, O. (2002). Bruk av informasjon om virksomhetskontekst ved læring om bruk av datavarehus (Use of information about business context when learning about using a data warehouse.) Bergen, Norway, University of Bergen, 2002.

Goldkuhl, G. (1994). Några problem vid datadriven strukturering av informationssystem. (Some problems with data-driven structuring of information systems.) *Proceedings of LISS '94: Linköpings Informations System Seminarium*. Linköping, Sweden, Linköping University.

Goodhue, D.L., Wybo, M.D. & Kirsch, L.J. The impact of data integration on the costs and benefits of information systems. *MIS Quarterly* 16(3), 293–312.

Hackney, R., Burn, J. & Dhillon, G. (2000). Challenging assumptions for strategic information systems planning: Theoretical perspectives. *Communications of AIS* 3(9).

Hart, D.N. (1994). Information wards—A new conceptual tool for modelling the political implications of information systems development. *Technical Report CS01/94*, Australia: Australian Defence Force Academy; University of New South Wales.

Hugoson, M.-Å. (1986). Funktionell strukturering av informationssystem. (Functional structuring of information systems). *Nordisk DATAnytt*, 10.

Iivari, J. & Koskela, E. (1987). The PIOCO model for information systems design. *MIS Quarterly*, 401–419.

Kiewiet, D.J. & Stegwee, R.A. (1992). Conceptual modeling and cluster analysis: Design strategies for information architectures. *Proceedings of the Thirteenth International Conference on Information Systems (ICIS)*.

King, J.L. (1983). Centralized versus decentralized computing: Organizational considerations and management options. *ACM Computing Surveys* 15(4), 319–349.

Leifer, R. (1988). Matching computer-based information systems with organizational structures. *MIS Quarterly*.

Lugenga, N.G.P. (1997). Using the information ward model to defuse user resistance—Extending the role of information systems architecture work. Bergen, Norway, University of Bergen, 1997.

Lundeberg, M., Goldkuhl, G. & Nilsson, A. (1978). *Systemering* (Software engineering). Lund, Sweden.

Magoulas, T. & Pessi, K. (1991). En studie om informationssystemarkitekturer (A Study on Information System Architectures), Göteborg, Sweden, Gothenburg University, 1991.

Netteland, G. (1999). Bruk av gruppevise og individuelle intervju i en metode for IS-arkitekturarbeid-prioritering av forbedringsområder. En empirisk evaluering av RAISA-modellen for IS-arkitekturrepresentasjon (Use of group and individual interviews in a method for IS-architecture work—prioritisation of business areas [...]), Bergen, Norway, University of Bergen, 1999.

Nolan, R.L. (1973). Managing the computer resources: A stage hypothesis, *Communications of the ACM* 16(7), 399–405.

Nolan, R.L. (1977). Restructuring the data processing organization for data resource management. In Gilchrist, B. (Ed.), *Information Processing 77*, NorthHolland: IFIP.

Nolan, R.L. (1979). Managing the crisis in data processing, *Harvard Business Review*, March-April.

Object Management Group. (1999). OMG Unified Modeling Language Specification (Version 1.3).

Opdahl, A.L. (1996). A model of the IS-architecture alignment problem. In Lind, M., Axelsson, K. & Goldkuhl, G. (Eds.), *Proceedings of VITS Autumn Conference*. Sweden, Borås College.

Opdahl, A.L. & Henderson-Sellers, B. (2002). Understanding and improving the UML metamodel through ontological analysis. *Journal of Software and Systems Modelling,* 1(1).

Päivärinta, T. (2001). The concept of genre within the critical approach to information systems development. *Information and Organization* 11, 207–234.

Päivärinta, T. & Tyrväinen, P. (2001). Structuring information by genres to bridge the social and technological information resources management—Leavitt's framework revised. In Bjørnestad, S., Moe, R., Mørch, A. & Opdahl, A.L. (Eds.) *Proceedings of IRIS24*. Ulvik, Norway.

Periasamy, K.P. (1993). The state and status of information architecture: An empirical investigation. In DeGross, J.I., Bostrom, R.P. & Robey, D. (Eds.) *Proceedings of the Fourteenth International Conference on Information Systems.*

Pettersson, K. & Goldkuhl, G. (1994). A comparison between two strategies for information systems architectures. *Technical Report LiTH-IDA-R-94-08.* Linköping, Sweden: Linköping University.

Pettersvold, G. (1996). Representasjon av IS-arkitektur for å motivere IT-strategiarbeid (Representation of IS architecture to motivate IT-strategy work). Bergen, Norway, University of Bergen, 1996.

Richardson, G.L., Jackson, B.M. & Dickson, G.W. (1990). A principles-based architecture: Lessons from texaco and star enterprise. *MIS Quarterly.*

Sowa, J.F. & Zachman, J.A. (1992). Extending and formalizing the framework for information systems architecture. *IBM Systems Journal,* 31(3), 590–616.

Steine, S.B. (2002). Developing and evaluating hypermedia-based documentation from enterprise models. Bergen, Norway, University of Bergen, 2002.

Tardieu, H. (1992). Issues for dynamic modelling through recent developments in European methods. In Sol, H.G. & Crosslin, R.K. (eds.), *Dynamic Modelling of Information Systems II*, Elsevier.

Vogel, D.R. & Wetherbe, J.C. (1984). University planning: Developing a long-range information architecture. *Planning and Changing*, Fall.

Warne, L. & Hart, D. (1996). The impact of organizational politics on information systems projects failure — A case study. (pp. 191–201). In Nunamaker, J.F., Jr. & Sprague, R.H., Jr. (Eds.), *Proceedings of the 29th Annual International Conference on System Sciences*, IEEE Computer Society Press.

Wetherbe, J.C. & Davis, G.B. (1983). Developing a long-range information architecture. *Proceedings of the National Computer Conference.* Anaheim, CA.

Zachman, J.A. (1978). The information systems management system: A framework for planning. *Database.*

Zachman, J.A. (1987). A framework for information systems architecture. *IBM Systems Journal,* 26(3), 276–292.

Chapter IV

A Framework for Research into Business-IT Alignment: A Cognitive Emphasis

Felix B. Tan
The University of Auckland, New Zealand

R. Brent Gallupe
Queen's University, Canada

ABSTRACT

Contemporary empirical research into business-IT alignment is almost entirely behavioral in its focus. It explores the alignment issue by examining the ways in which organisations behave. In contrast, few studies have attempted to investigate the issue from a cognitive perspective. Managerial cognition is an area of growing interest and importance in strategic management. This chapter proposes a framework to guide research into business-IT alignment. It reviews alignment research and also considers some of the cognitive theories and methodologies that may be appropriate for the study of alignment.

INTRODUCTION

One of the top two concerns of business and information systems (IS) executives is the need to improve alignment between information technology (IT) and business strategy (Galliers, Merali, & Spearing, 1994; Watson &

Brancheau, 1991). Known as business-IT alignment, this issue is an important concern within the practitioner community.

The 1990s saw great strides in the conceptual development and in the empirical examination of different aspects of alignment. A frequently cited conceptual work on alignment is Henderson and Venkatraman's (1992) Strategic Alignment Model. This framework describes the interplay between IT and business domains. Bulk of the empirical investigations on this subject focuses on relationships between business strategy domains and IT strategy domains and their impact upon firm performance (Burn, 1996; Chan, Huff, Copeland, & Barclay, 1997; Tan, 1995, 1997). These studies agree that alignment is important to IS effectiveness and firm performance. Another aspect of alignment research concerns the conditions under which alignment may be achieved. Several studies have examined factors that influence alignment (Broadbent & Weill, 1993; Luftman, Papp, & Brier, 1999; Reich & Benbasat, 2000). All the above studies may be considered behavioral in nature and have largely ignored the impact of managerial cognition on organisational action.

Cognition in organisations is an area of growing interest and importance in strategic management and research (Huff, 1990; Walsh, 1995). The emergence of this research perspective in strategic management stems from a growing acceptance of the notion that organisations possess cognitive capabilities and that organisational development is dependent upon collective or shared managerial cognition (Stubbart, 1989). Other works on cognition within organisations have inferred that a link exists between managerial cognition and organisational action (Axelrod, 1976; Calori, Johnson, & Sarnin, 1992; Weick, 1984). Furthermore, there are those who contend that organisations consist of systems of interpretation with organisational members attempting to make sense of their constantly changing environments (Weick, 1995, 2001).

A relatively small but growing body of cognitive research can be found in the IS field. It primarily addresses the areas of development, implementation, and use of IT (DeSanctis & Poole, 1994; Griffith & Northcraft, 1996; Orlikowski & Gash, 1994). Despite increasing acceptance of cognition in IS research, it is not apparent that a cognitive stream exists within the discipline of business-IT alignment.

This chapter calls for increased cognitive emphasis in business-IT alignment research. It proposes a framework guiding business-IT alignment research. The framework takes into account the behavioral/cognitive contrast in strategic management and hopes to offer researchers in the field some guidance in the study of alignment from a cognitive approach.

The chapter begins with an introduction to business-IT alignment—a definition and a historical overview. A framework summarizing recent alignment research is then presented. Noteworthy literature is discussed using this framework: types of published alignment research are identified, and areas that need further attention are suggested. Next, we consider some of the cognitive theories and methodologies that may be appropriate for the study of alignment. The conclusion follows.

WHAT IS BUSINESS-IT ALIGNMENT?

Hofer and Schendel (1978) define the strategic management process as one in which general management seeks to align organisations with opportunities and constraints imposed by their respective environments. It is generally accepted that one of the key factors for successful strategic IS planning and implementation is the close link between business and IS strategic contexts (Boynton, R.W., & Jacobs, 1994; King & Sabherwal, 1992; Lederer & Sethi, 1988). This link may enable a firm to maximize IT investments and to coordinate with business strategies and plans. Commensurate increased profitability and competitive advantage usually follow. It is therefore not surprising that the need to improve alignment between IT and business strategy domains consistently ranks among the top two concerns in studies stemming from the US, the UK, Australia, and New Zealand (Galliers et al., 1994; Pervan, 1993; Davies, Menon, Munday, Thomson, & Young, 1995; Moynihan, 1988; Watson, Kelly, Galliers, & Brancheau, 1997). The term "alignment" has been used extensively in IS literature (Broadbent &Weill, 1993 #33; Baets, 1992 #26; Chan & Huff, 1993; Burn, 1996 #36; Henderson & Venkatraman, 1992). What exactly does business-IT alignment mean? Henderson and Venkatraman (1992) developed the theoretical construct of alignment. These authors argue that the concept of alignment is different from the traditional notion of linking IT to business strategy. The traditional view posits that IT activities are inextricably linked with business requirements. Alignment, however, goes beyond traditional linkage. Henderson and Venkatraman (1992) contend that alignment is based upon two building blocks—strategic fit and functional integration, which together coalesce four domains: business strategy, business infrastructure, IT strategy, and IT infrastructure. (This is discussed in detail in the section on frameworks.) Other researchers lend support to this argument. For instance, Chan and Huff (1993) posit that organisations typically achieve strategic alignment by passing through three stages—awareness, integration, and alignment. Awareness emerges when organisations become cognizant of the changing role of IT beyond traditional back-office support. Integration is marked by acceptance of the need to mesh IT and business operations. Alignment carries the idea of integration further by focusing on integrating IT with an organisation's fundamental strategies and core competencies. In a later publication, alignment is defined as the fit between the organisation's business strategic orientation and its IS strategic orientation (Chan et al., 1997). There are other more simplistic approaches to the concept, describing alignment as the extent to which business strategies are enabled, supported, and stimulated by information strategies (Broadbent & Weill, 1993).

To fully appreciate the concept of business-IT alignment, one needs to consider the historical context in which it has evolved. As suggested earlier, the alignment concept evolved within the area of strategic IS planning. Henderson et al. (1996) describe three eras of IS planning evolving from the traditional supporting view an emerging strategic perspective:

Era I—Resource Control: In the era of resource control, IS planning is focused upon internal functional perspectives. Automating internal business processes drives IS planning. The planning process employs a functional model of the business and identifies functional applications, associated resources, priorities, and timetables for development and implementation.

Era II—IS Architecture: The scope of the planning process is extended during the IS architecture stage. The enterprise becomes the context of the plan. The primary focus lies upon cross-functional integration and the development of infrastructures to enable it. The IS plan provides an enterprise-wide (and management-wide) view of IT, especially the linkage the IS plan to the business plan.

Era III—Strategic Alignment: During the strategic alignment phase, IT is viewed not only as a means of functional integration but as an opportunity to enhance the competitive capability of the firm. The context of IS planning is expanded to include the inter-organisational business network—it goes beyond the internal focus of the traditional IS planning process. The emphasis of IS planning concerns aiding senior executives in remaining competitive via technology.

It is therefore sensible and desirable for management to focus on aligning IT with the organisation's business strategy. This is a major management challenge as alignment is difficult to achieve. Complete alignment is usually unsustainable (Weill & Broadbent, 1998) because of the dynamic nature of strategic context, of characteristics of IT investment, and of developmental life cycles. Changes to one usually lead to changes in another.

In a further attempt to clarify the nature of the business-IT alignment construct, Reich and Benbasat (1996) contend that there are two dimensions to alignment—intellectual and social. The authors base their argument on a distinction Horovitz (1984) made between intellectual and social dimensions of the strategic business planning process. Reich and Benbasat assert that intellectual alignment is achieved when the content of business and IS plans are internally consistent and externally valid. To be internally consistent, an organisation's IS mission, objectives, and plans must reflect the stated business mission, objectives, and plans. To be externally valid, an organisation's business and IS plans must parallel external business and IS developments. For example, emergent technologies that can impact business strategy must be included with in IS strategy. According to these authors, social alignment occurs when IS and business executives understand and are committed to each other's mission, objectives, and plans.

A FRAMEWORK FOR BUSINESS-IT ALIGNMENT RESEARCH

A useful way of reviewing and organising research done on business-IT alignment is mapping the research onto a framework. Research frameworks can help identify the kinds of articles published in the field and suggest areas that require attention (Dickson, Senn, & Chervany, 1977; Gallupe & Tan, 1999; Gorry & Scott Morton, 1971; Ives, Hamilton, & Davis, 1980; Mason & Mitroff, 1973; Nolan & Wetherbe, 1981; Shaw, Gardner, & Thomas, 1997).

There have been two attempts thus far at developing a research framework for studying alignment, neither of which can be regarded as sufficiently expansive for reviewing work in the field. For instance, Reich and Benbasat's (1996) framework maps both intellectual and social dimensions of alignment against the cause (potential factors influencing alignment) and effect (the state of alignment itself) of alignment. Although the authors claim that the framework guides the study of alignment, most of the articles referenced in the model relate to IS planning rather than to alignment itself. In a book edited by Luftman (1996), Thomas and Dewitt present a framework for reviewing alignment research. This framework is based upon the work of Snow and Thomas (1993, #149). The framework describes two main types of alignment research—concept building and concept testing. Each category consists of descriptive research in addition to studies seeking both to predict and to explain IT alignment. Although the framework is excellent for evaluating the status of any research topic, Thomas and Dewitt (1996) primarily focus upon the works of scholars who had contributed to the book edited by Luftman. Consequently, a more comprehensive framework is necessary to systematically review business-IT alignment and to fully appreciate the knowledge that has been accumulated thus far. The resulting framework should not only take into account categories and dimensions published in earlier frameworks: it should also consider the behavioral/cognitive contrast recently emphasized in strategic management literature (Huff, 1990; Langfield-Smith, 1992).

This section and Figure 1 address this inadequacy.

Figure 1: A framework for reviewing business-IT alignment research

	Conceptual Level	Content Level	Process Level
Behavioral	Describes the concept of alignment and discusses the characteristics of the concept I – well researched	Tests and validates relationships between alignment and behavioral dimensions in organization context II – well published	Ascertains behavioral conditions under which alignment is enabled or inhibited III – emerging
Cognitive	Describes the concept of alignment based upon cognitive theories and associated characteristics IV – not published	Tests and validates the relationships between alignment and cognitive dimensions in a managerial context V – not researched	Provides explanations of cognitive profiles necessary for successful alignment VI – not researched

As with other fields of study, alignment research may be broadly categorized into conceptual and empirical work. Empirical research examines alignment at content and process levels. Content level research tests and validates relationships between alignment and other constructs in organisational and managerial contexts. Process level studies explore the circumstances under which relationships at content level research exist. Content and process levels of research are similar to the intellectual/social and to the cause-effect dimensions posited by Reich and Benbasat (1996) and to the explanation and prediction research proposed in Thomas and Dewitt's (1996) framework. Similarly, conceptual research defines and describes the alignment concept, placing it within the descriptive category (as Thomas and Dewitt's model does). The framework proposed here goes beyond conceptual/empirical domains to include behavioral/cognitive contrasts. Social science research has traditionally focused upon how organisations behave and think (Robey & Markus, 1998). Weick (1984) argues that "thinking is inseparably linked to action: 'managers behave thinkingly'…" (p.222). The inclusion of these dimensions of organisational behavior and managerial cognition within a research framework provide a richer, more thorough assessment of the business-IT alignment construct. The framework presented in Figure 1 purports to do just that.

Conceptual Research

Conceptual alignment research defines and describes the alignment construct as well as its dimensions and characteristics. It is highly descriptive in nature and is considered important to the early understanding of the alignment phenomenon (Butler & Fitzgerald, 1998; Thomas & Dewitt, 1996). Type I and IV categories within the research framework are conceptual in nature. All of the published literature conceptualising alignment presents models that describe the construct entirely from a behavioralist organisational perspective (Type I). There is nothing published that has attempted to take a cognitive or sociocognitive perspective (Type IV).

A number of Type I conceptual models have been proposed to assist organisations in developing business-IT alignment. As part of the Management in the 1990s (MIT90s) research program, Venkatraman (1989) argues that the new challenge for strategists is how best to reconceptualize the role of IT in business, how to identify the applications relevant to their particular strategic context, and how to reconfigure the business to not only fully exploit the available IT capabilities but also to differentiate their operations from competitors (pp. 126-127).

He proposes a hierarchical model that incorporates five levels of business reconfigurations along two basic dimensions—the degree of business transformation and the range of potential benefits from IT. For each level of transformation, Venkatraman identifies specific managerial implications. Synthesizing managerial challenges with evolving alignments between strategic contexts and IT is demonstrated in the Strategic Alignment Model (Henderson & Venkatraman, 1992, 1993; Henderson, Venkatraman, & Oldach, 1996). This model is regarded as the guiding framework in alignment research (Thomas & Dewitt, 1996). It describes the construct and its basic domains, having been used in a number of subsequent empirical works in the field. Henderson and Venkatraman developed the model to help practitioners conceptualize and direct the strategic management of IT. The model reflects the fact that, for many organisations, competitive advantage depends upon the harmonious interplay of business strategy, IT strategy, and IT and organisational infrastructures and processes

The Strategic Alignment Model specifically combines the notion of functional integration (between business and IT domains) with the concept of strategic fit (between internal and external contexts of the organisation), giving four key domains of strategic choice: business strategy, organisational infrastructure and processes, IT strategy, and IT infrastructure and processes. Henderson and Venkatraman contend that business-IT alignment involves simultaneous or concurrent attention to all four domains.

Based upon their extensive analysis of the phenomenon of strategic management, Henderson and Venkatraman propose four dominant strategic alignment perspectives—the first two are driven by business, while the third and fourth are enabled by IT strategy. The roles that business and IT managers play in each of the alignment perspectives are of particular interest, as are the performance criteria employed to evaluate the the contributions of IS. Henderson and Venkatraman argue that business strategy-driven domains provide the optimum route to successful alignment of IT and business strategy. While the perspectives are normative and appear simplistic they do (as Henderson and Venkatraman point out) draw managerial attention to the fact that IT itself is not a panacea for business ills; neither is it the sole consideration when attempting to achieve competitive advantage. Luftman, Lewis, and Oldbach (1993), following Henderson and Venkatraman, stress the need for managers to be aware of and to consider all four perspectives in order to fully comprehend the implications of IT usage in strategy formation. The Strategic Alignment Model provides a suitable framework for the investigation of IT-enabled transformation of organisations. It captures the complex web of conditions and factors that constitute domains and dimensions of the construct.

Other Type I publications have attempted to extend the Strategic Alignment Model. A noteworthy instance is MacDonald's (1991) Strategic Alignment Process, which highlights the supporting organisational and managerial processes required to exploit the earlier model. Based upon MacDonald's model (1991) and Parker, Benson, and Trainor's (1988) Enterprise-Wide Information Model, Baets (1992) describes a general process of aligning IS with corporate strategy, which takes into account broader information needs analysis. Baets argues that the process enables drawing a map of strategic IS planning in the banking sector. Other descriptive works have refined and extended the Strategic Alignment Model. Victor, Pine, and Boynton (1996) examine the potential role of IT capabilities within structural transformations in the market. Davidson and Movisso (1996) look at the role of organisational competencies.

In summary, the core of Type I alignment research is the Strategic Alignment Model. This model and its various extensions have enhanced the understanding of business-IT alignment and its dimensions. These models remain, however, largely theoretical and descriptive. In addition conceptual models, which account for cognitive dimensions that can lead to action within such behavioral models, is an area to which attention must be drawn (Type IV).

Empirical Research

As noted earlier, empirical alignment research can be categorized into content level (Types II and V) and process level (Types III and VI) studies. Behavioral content level (Type II) investigations focus upon the business strategy-IS relationship and how it affects firm performance and IS effectiveness. It is this category of alignment research that dominates the empirical literature.

Figure 2: Chan et al.'s (1997) conceptual model (adapted)

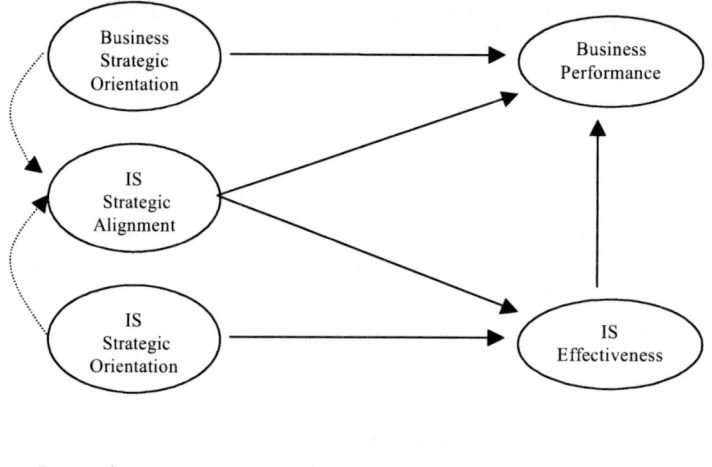

Legend
→ Path between research constructs
┅▶ Alignment Calculation

For instance, Chan et al. (1997) examine the fit between business strategic orientation, information systems strategic orientation, information systems strategic alignment, and their respective implications for perceived IS effectiveness and firm performance. The conceptual model developed by Chan et al. is presented in Figure 2. This research focuses upon developing multiple measures. Multiple measures are based upon different theoretical perspectives of the relationships between businesses and IS strategies (strategic orientations) in which each relationship requires different mathematical models. They provide insight into alternative methods of conceptualizing and measuring the constructs and their relationships.

Chan et al.'s work is one of several studies that also focuses upon measuring the alignment construct. Chan et al. discuss alternative ways of modelling alignment as conceptualized by Venkatraman (1989) and by Drazin and Van de Ven (1985). A basic matching model and a basic interaction model were used to calculate alignment. The findings offer modest support for the proposition linking alignment with performance, but they also show that alignment is consistently related positively to IS effectiveness. The authors employed both matching and interactional approaches to calculate alignment. The researchers contend that business strategic orientation, IS strategic orientation, and IS strategic alignment are best measured with holistic systems approaches instead of dimension-specific bivariate approaches. The results indicate that alignment is a better predictor of IS effectiveness than is an organisation's business strategic orientation.

Similarly, Reich and Benbasat (1996) contributed to the development of alignment measures by utilising multiple respondents and multiple methods in each of their 10 research cases. The authors focused solely upon the social dimension of alignment (the extent to which business and IS executives had developed mutual understanding of and commitment to business and IS missions, objectives, and plans). The objectives of the investigation focused upon clarifying the nature of the alignment construct and measuring the social dimension of alignment. The study examined written documents to determine the extent of cross references (of IS projects in business strategy and vice versa) and conducted interviews of IS and business executives. The authors proposed that there were two potential measures of the social dimension of alignment: understanding current objectives and sharing a vision for the usage of IT. The former measured short-term alignment, and the latter measured aspects of alignment in the long-term. This study shows the importance of multiple measures in examining the key dimensions of business-IT alignment.

In a recent study, a computer-based assessment tool was used to evaluate alignment (Luftman et al., 1999). The development of this tool drew upon the Strategic Alignment Model (SAM) (Henderson & Venkatraman, 1993). This instrument consisted of 36 items, 12 of which measured the four domains in the SAM model and 24 of which assessed "strategic fit" and "functional integration" relationships among these four domains. A 7-point Likert-type scale was used. Executives first familiarized themselves with the SAM model during a one-day workshop before completing the assessment. The authors found that more than half of the respondents believed that business and IT were properly aligned in their respective companies; 42 percent of the executives believed that business and IT were not properly aligned; and eight percent were unsure or had no opinion.

Another 7-point Likert-type instrument was used by Kearns and Lederer (1997) to measure alignment and its impact upon competitive advantage. The authors surveyed 153 CIOs using a structural equation model. Figure 3 illustrates the causal relationships in this study.

Figure 3: Kearns and Lederer's (1997) research model (Adapted)

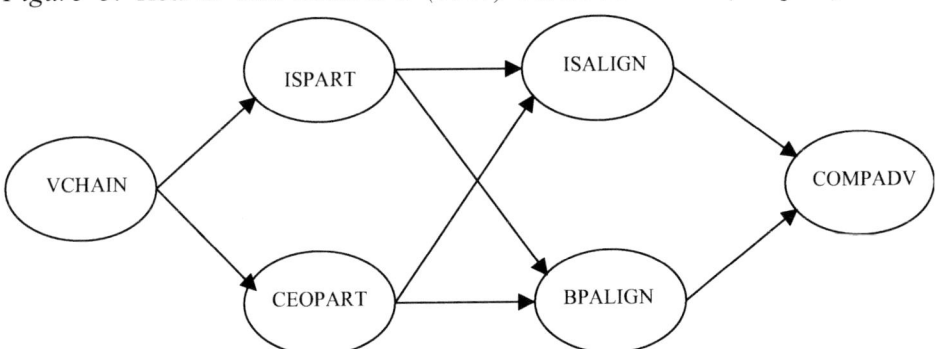

Kearns and Lederer measured alignment in accordance with two constructs: business plan aligned with IS plan (BPALIGN) and IS plan aligned business plan (ISALIGN). Average scores of both constructs across respondents determined the index of alignment. Alignment evaluation consisted of 12 items: six BPALIGN and six ISALIGN statements were scored on a 7-point scale. IS executive participation in business planning (ISPART) and CEO participation in IS planning (CEOPART) ascertained alignment. The authors used path coefficients derived from structural equation analysis to find support for all the relationships hypothesized in the research model.

A number of other Type II studies have been published. These explore the relationship between business and IS strategies and do not set out to specifically examine the business-IT alignment construct. Using path analysis to examine the relationships among competitive strategy, IT, and financial performance, Floyd and Wooldridge (1990) lend statistical support to the business-IT relationship. The results of a survey of both CEOs and CIOs of 131 organisations in Israel indicated that IS objectives are associated with organisational objectives and that for each IS objective there exists a corresponding organisational objective (Zviran, 1990). In a New Zealand study, Tan (1995) explains that variations in IT-strategy responsiveness are linked to an organisation's strategic orientation. Using Miles and Snow's strategic typology, Tan established that organisations with externally-focused aggressive approaches to product and market domains tended to use IS technology in a way different from organisations that were more conservative (internally-focused). Tan (1997) further concluded that despite this variation, both aggressive and conservative organisations reported highly favorable firm performance, suggesting that congruence between organisation strategic orientation and use of IS technology is more likely to lead to a desired level of firm performance. In a longitudinal study examining both business and IS strategies using the Strategic Alignment Model (mentioned earlier), Burn (1996) developed a "lead-lag" strategic alignment model that explains the dynamic nature of relationships between IS and business strategies. Burn argues that organisations not prepared to adopt the lead-lag model are likely to inhibit the innovative use of IS technology because of organisational "overstructure or lack of structure" (p. 10).

Type III alignment research is a process-level study that explores organisational contexts important for achieving business-IT alignment. Inquiry of this kind explores the characteristics of "well-aligned" enterprises, identifying critical organisational and managerial factors that lead to successful alignment. Comparatively few studies focus upon Type III research. IBM, however, researched the bench-marking of alignment in over 50 large companies (Prairie, 1996). Because it examines the organisational and managerial processes in companies that have achieved high levels of alignment, benchmarking can aid organisations in identifying reliable processes for implementation. The first stage of research was the American Express Benchmark study. It resulted in the identification of seven factors, one of which is business-IT alignment, that must be managed effectively to achieve IT transformation. These factors formed the basis of the second (ongoing) project, which is studying approximately 50 organisations. Results of the benchmarking study indicated that best-practice organisations are those that develop a synergy among planning, funding, and communications. Common among all three areas is the bringing together business and IS executives to jointly manage the challenge of aligning business and IS strategies.

Broadbent and Weill (1993) performed a notable study of the Australian banking industry. Through interviews and analysis of annual reports and other strategic planning documentation, the authors ascertained several organisational planning practices that contribute to and enhance alignment. Their results indicated that to achieve alignment, organisations need consistency within four areas: firm-wide strategy formation processes, organisational structures and accountabilities, IS responsibilities and policies, and IS technology strategy. Their study supported 15 specific propositions from among the four areas that appear to facilitate alignment. The key organisational practices and 15 propositions are presented in an alignment model illustrated in Figure 4.

Figure 4: Alignment model (Adapted from Broadbent & Weill, 1993)

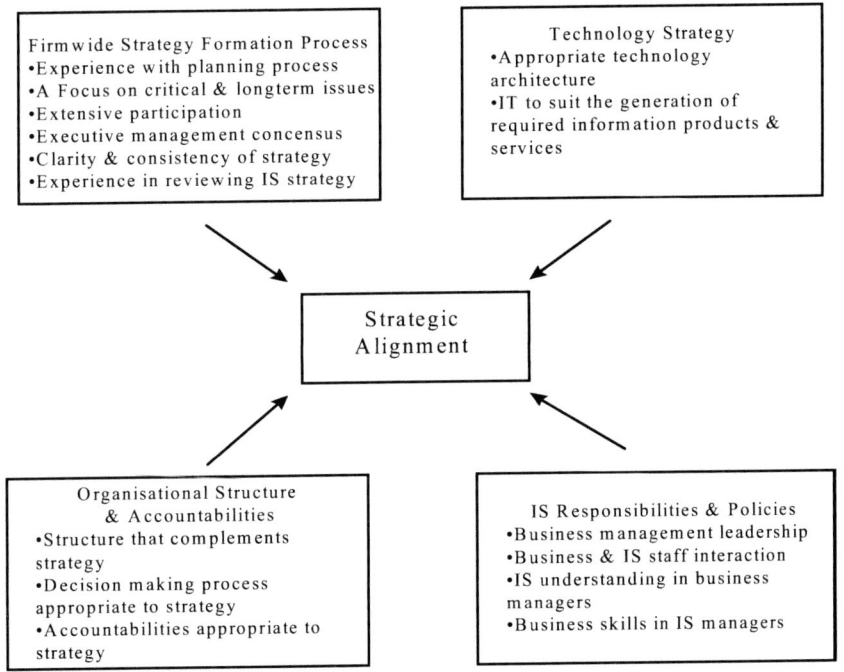

Similarly, a multi-year investigation into the enablers and inhibitors of alignment was conducted between 1993-1997 by Luftman et al. (1999). Results indicated that certain activities assist in achieving alignment while others clearly form barriers. Luftman et al. (1999) concluded that executives need to minimize activities that inhibit alignment and maximize activities that bolster it. The authors recommended that executives (a) improve the relationships between business and IS functional areas; (b) mutually cooperate and participate in strategy development; (c) communicate effectively in terms understood and appreciated by their business partners; (d) maintain executive support; and (e) prioritize projects more effectively.

Reich and Benbasat (2000) examined business—IS relationships by exploring the concepts of cooperation and mutual understanding between the two groups. Figure 5 depicts the conceptual model tested in their study. The model is based on the Theory of Absorptive Capacity and includes four factors that potentially influence the social dimension of alignment. These factors include shared domain knowledge between IS and business executives, successful IS implementation history, communications between IS and business executives, and connections between business and IS planning processes.

The results of the study lend support to all elements of the model. All four factors influenced both short- and long-term alignment. Communication between business and IS executives proved the strongest influence on the social dimension of alignment. Communication was influenced by shared domain knowledge and successful IS implementation history. Connections between business and IS

Figure 5: Factors influencing the social dimension of alignment (Adapted from Reich & Benbasat, 2000)

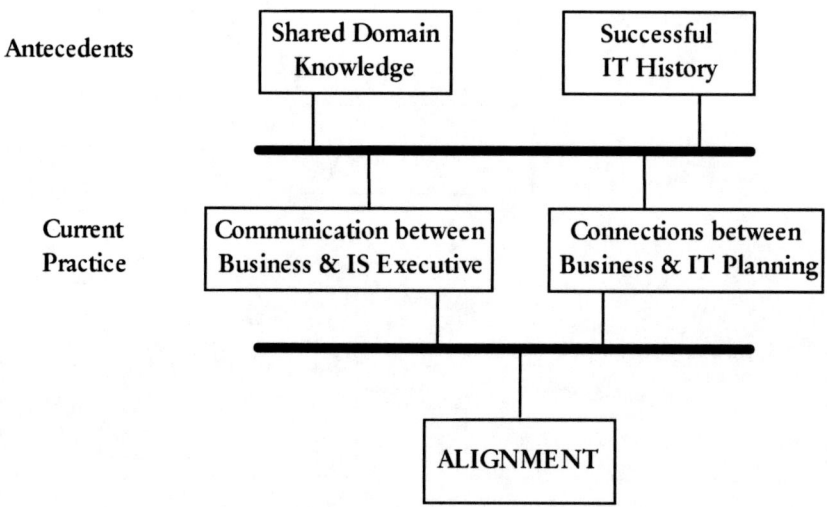

planning processes emerged influential. Reich and Benbasat concluded that both managers and researchers should direct significant attention towards communications and towards the creation of shared domain knowledge between business and IS executives.

The Type II and III empirical alignment research discussed so far are studies that examine how organisations behave. Type V and VI alignment research takes a cognitive approach to the field. A review of the literature revealed that nothing has been published from a cognitive perspective concerning content- and process-level alignment research.

In recent years, researchers in the field of organisational management have given increased attention to the cognition of managers (Daniels, de Chernatony, & Johnson, 1995; Dutton, Walton, & Abrahamson, 1989; Reger & Huff, 1993). Research into managerial cognition considers managers' mental models or systems of interpretation important determinants of key resource allocation decisions. It views managers both as interpreting strategic issues and as having the power necessary to implement choices derived from those interpretations (Hambrick & Mason, 1984). Managers perceive their environments through the systems of interpretation. Systems of interpretation must be shared by members of a management team if they are to achieve some form of common action (Langfield-Smith, 1992; Stubbart, 1989). Underlying the cognitive perspective of organisational management is a growing acceptance that "an organisation is a deliberately created and maintained social institution within which consciously coordinated behaviors by members aim to produce a limited set of intended outcomes" (Jelinek & Litterer, 1994, p. 12).

A cognitive thread also runs through IS research, especially in the areas of systems development, implementation, and usage. Bostrom and Heinen (1977) attribute many of the social problems associated with implementations of information systems to frames of reference (cognition) held by systems designers. Building upon this work, Dagwell and Weber (1983) and Kumar and Bjorn-Andersen (1990) examine the influences of systems designers' values as well as the views of users upon systems development. Orlikowski and Gash (1994) developed and tested a concept of technological frames, arguing that the frames offer an interesting and useful analytical perspective for explaining and anticipating actions.

Cognitive emphasis in business-IT alignment research appears lacking. One reason may be that dominant models of organisational theory give priority to economics-based assumptions of rationality (Walton, 1985). Consequently, the individuals' abilities to make sense and to give meaning to events are essentially ignored, leading to an inadequate understanding of the alignment phenomenon. This apparent gap has inhibited the development of collective and integrative theories in alignment research. A greater understanding of what constitutes subjective interpretations of individuals or of groups—and the impact of these interpretations upon organisational action and business-IT alignment outcomes, based upon established cognitive theories and methods—is necessary.

COGNITIVE THEORIES AND METHODOLOGIES

The cognitive approach to organisational studies takes for its foundation individuals (or, more particularly, their cognition and subjective understanding of conditions faced and outcomes desired). The paradigm implicit within this approach gives import to how organisations work and how people within organisations achieve shared action (Jelinek & Litterer, 1994). There is overwhelming evidence suggesting that individuals know their environments via mental or cognitive models (Kelly, 1955; Stubbart, 1989) and that these models are invariably linked to action (Axelrod, 1976; Weick, 1984).

Cognition entails the assumptions, expectations, values, and beliefs held by individuals in an organisational context (Orlikowski & Gash, 1994). It allows individuals to interpret and to make sense of events occurring around them (Weick, 1995, 2001).

The present section elaborates on cognitive theories and methods appropriate for the study of business-IT alignment.

Personal Construct Theory and Cognitive Mapping

Kelly (1955) argues that individuals use personal constructs to interpret and understand events that occur around them and that these constructs are tempered by an individual personal experiences. "Man looks at his world through transparent templets which he creates and then attempts to fit over the realities of which the world is composed" (pp. 8-9). Thus, individuals come to understand the world in which they live, erecting personally-organized systems of interpretation or constructs of experienced events. The system is rendered personal in that individuals interpretate their own respective experiences. Individuals, however, may share views and appreciate other individuals' interpretations or constructs of events. Kelly's supposition, known as Personal Construct Theory, is formally presented as a fundamental postulate with eleven corollaries.

Constructive Alternativism: Underlying Kelly's (1955) fundamental postulate and eleven corollaries is a philosophical assumption: the events an individual faces are subject to a great variety of constructions. He calls this philosophical position constructive alternativism, an assumption that all events are subject to as many alternative interpretations as an individual may conceive. Constructive alternativism stresses the importance of events and the meaning individuals

```
**********************************
        Lake Erie College
       10/15/2003 12:26:46 PM
**********************************

Business strategies for information technology management /
Kangas, Kalle
3035610030775
Due: 4/12/2004 11:59:00 PM

Web-powered databases
Taniar, David
```

assign to these events. Kelly's philosophy of constructive alternativism allows the individual to propose a reality, but contends that no interpretation of reality is absolute and irrevocable. All events may be construed in alternative ways.

Fundamental Postulate: Kelly (1995) fundamentally postulates that individual understanding is "psychologically channelized" (p. 46). by the ways in which events are anticipated. Constructive alternativism is embedded within this basic postulate. Accordingly, all individual representations are anticipatory in nature: individuals anticipate events via personal constructs. Individuals interpret their environments through a system of personal constructs, which provide frameworks for assessing events as they occur. Kelly further argues that individual constructs are not constant, but continually fluctuating as a result of experience. Individuals, then, both create and are created by the world within which they operate.

Corollaries: Eleven corollaries elaborate Kelly's theory. The Individuality Corollary renders individual constructs of the world as unique; the Range Corollary provides a context for constructs; the Experience Corollary has constructs evolve through social interaction; and the Commonality Corollary asserts that similarity of constructs within isolated groups of individuals implies similarity of cognition.

Cognitive Mapping: Personal Construct Theory provides a foundation for assessing individuals' systems of constructs. A number of techniques, such as unstructured interviews, have been used to elicit personal attributes, but cognitive mapping is generally recognized as superior. A cognitive approach to understanding how managers organize subjective experiences into patterns may be represented with a cognitive map. There are several categories of cognitive maps. Category 1 maps depict attention, associations, and importance of concepts; Category 2 maps categorize schema; and Category 3 maps evince influence and causality. Mapping techniques include content analysis, linguistic analysis, repertory grid technique, and causal mapping. Huff (1990) provides a comprehensive discussion of the different kinds of maps and mapping techniques.

Possible Research Questions: Personal Construct Theory, cognitive mapping techniques, and the resulting maps may be used to examine mutual understanding between business and IT executives (Reich & Benbasat, 2000) regarding strategic IS issues. Are there cognitive similarities or differences among executive groups? To what extent do similarities or differences influence the strategic IS decisions made and, hence, the alignment of business and IT? Another important issue is the user-analyst/developer relationship, which lends itself to requirements analysis. Can Personal Construct Theory and cognitive mapping help us better understand the cognitive profiles of users and analysts and their impact upon the alignment of IT to user needs?

Copyright © 2003, Idea Group Inc. Copying or distributing in print or electronic forms without written permission of Idea Group Inc. is prohibited.

Cognitive Categorization Theory and Visual Card Sort Technique

Cognitive Categorization Theory contends that the basis of mental activity is memory, which records previous experiences (Estes, 1994). Interest in how managers organize knowledge about their environments stem from research into strategic groups and competitive industry structures (Daniels et al., 1995). Initial conceptions of managerial categorization were based upon the hierarchical model of Mervis and Rosch (1981). Experimentally established principles of cognitive categorization are evident. Categorization is almost always probabilistic, with some members of a category being closer to the central tendency of a category than others (Smith & Medin, 1981). Category structures are context-dependent because personal experience leads to the objective categorization of events and of things (Barsalou, 1982). Finally, individuals may be categorized according to features in common with the group under examination (Medin, 1989).

Visual Card Sort Technique: A flexible method is required for maintaining consistency within categories, continually in flux. One method that is consistent with the psychology of categorization involves a visual card-sorting task that categorizes individuals within a particular domain according to concepts (Canter, Brown, & Groat, 1985). This method requires participants to name objects within the domain of investigation—in this example, the names of competitor companies. The company names are written on cards (Daniels et al., 1995). Participants are then asked to sort the cards into related groups. Next individuals are asked the rationales for their respective groupings of cards (companies). The card-sorting technique provides a quick and apparently valid way of representing the relationships among objects within the research domain. The arrangement of cards also provides descriptions of objects or of clusters of objects. A simple photograph of the arrangement is taken as record of the exercise. A map depicting the results as spatial relationships may then be constructed. Participants are asked if they wish to arrange the cards differently if given the opportunity to do so, which allows researchers to capture the context sensitivity of participants' mental models. Planned redundancy within the card-sorting technique leads to a fuller and more accurate depiction of participants' mental models.

Social Cognitive Theory

Social Cognitive Theory (Bandura, 1986) is a widely accepted, empirically validated model of individual behavior. It is based upon the premise that environmental influences such as societal pressures or unique situational characteristics; cognitive and other individual factors, including personality as well as demographic characteristics; and behavior are reciprocally determined.

Individuals choose the environments in which they exist while they are influenced by those same environments. Furthermore, behavior in a given situation is affected by environmental or situational characteristics, which are reciprocally affected by the same behavior. Finally, behavior both is influenced by cognitive and personal factors and affects those same factors.

Cognitive Influences: While Social Cognitive Theory has many dimensions, IS researchers should appropriately focus upon the role of cognitive factors in individual behavior within the business-IT alignment context. Bandura advances two sets of expectations as the major cognitive forces guiding behaviors (Compeau & Higgins, 1995). The first set of expectations relates to outcomes. Individuals are more likely to adopt behaviors that they believe will result in valued outcomes, rather than those that they expect will result in unfavorable outcomes. The second set of expectations encompasses what Bandura calls self-efficacy, or beliefs about one's ability to organize and to execute courses of action required to attain desired outcomes. Self-efficacy influences selection of behaviors; the efforts and persistence exerted in overcoming obstacles to executing those behaviors; and ultimately, mastery of selected behaviors.

Possible Research Questions: While Social Cognitive Theory has been useful to IS researchers in regarding technical computer skills and usage (Compeau, Higgins, & Huff, 1999; Hill, Smith, & Mann, 1987), it has not been adapted for usage in the study of business-IT alignment. Questions concerning the latter remain: To what extent does the self-efficacy of business and IT executives influence outcome expectations, thereby influencing business-IT alignment within organisations? What similarities or differences are evident among business and IT groups concerning self-efficacy and outcome expectations? Do these impact the achievement of alignment?

CONCLUSION

This chapter reviews the literature on business-IT alignment. The framework presented in Figure 1 systematically organizes published works. Conceptual and empirical research into business-IT alignment has focused on patterns of behavior in organisations. Most of the published empirical literature examines the relationships between business strategy and IS-performance, with lesser attention directed towards how organisations achieve successful alignment.

Cognitive emphasis in business-IT alignment research appears sparse. Dominant models of organisational theory give priority to economics-based assumptions of rationality (Walton, 1985). Individual imperatives to make sense of and to assign meaning to events have been largely ignored, consequently leaving a void in understanding the alignment phenomenon. The apparent gap has inhibited the development of distinct and integrative theories in alignment research. Cognitive perspectives of individuals or of groups of individuals (business and IT groups) and the impact of these on business-IT alignment are needed. This chapter presents cognitive theories and methods appropriate for advancing our understanding of business-IT alignment, and it suggests areas for future research through a cognitive lens.

REFERENCES

Axelrod, R. (1976). *Structure of decision: The cognitive maps of political elites*. Princeton, NJ: Princeton University Press.

Baets, W. (1992). Aligning information systems with business strategy. *The Journal of Strategic Information Systems, 1*(4), 205-213.

Bandura, A. (1986). *Social foundations of thought and action*. Englewood Cliffs, NJ: Prentice-Hall.

Barsalou, L. W. (1982). Context-independent and context-dependent information in concepts. *Memory and Cognition, 10*, 82-93.

Bostrom, R. P., & Heinen, J. S. (1977). MIS problems and failures: A socio-technical perspective, part I - the causes. *MIS Quarterly, 1*(3), 17-32.

Boynton, A. C., R.W., Z., & Jacobs, J. C. (1994). The influence of it management practice on IT use in large organisations. *MIS Quarterly, 18*(3), 299-318.

Broadbent, M., & Weill, P. (1993). Improving business and information strategy alignment: Learning from the banking industry. *IBM Systems Journal, 32*(1), 152-179.

Burn, J. M. (1996). IS innovation and organisational alignment - a professional juggling act. *Journal of Information Technology, 11*, 3-12.

Butler, T., & Fitzgerald, B. (1998). Enterprise transformation and the alignment of business and information technology strategies: Lessons from practice. In T. a. L. Larsen (Ed.), *Information Systems: Current Issues and Future Changes* (pp. 393-416.). Helsinki, Finland: Chapman & Hall.

Calori, R., Johnson, G., & Sarnin, P. (1992). French and British top managers' understanding of the structure and the dynamics of their industries: A cognitive analysis and comparison. *British Journal of Management, 3*, 61-92.

Canter, D., Brown, J., & Groat, L. (1985). *The research interview: Uses and approaches*. London: Academic Press.

Chan, Y. E., & Huff, S. L. (1993). Investigating information systems strategic alignment. *Proceedings of the Fourteenth International Conference on Information Systems*. Orlando, Florida.

Chan, Y. E., Huff, S. L., Copeland, D. G., & Barclay, D. W. (1997). Business strategic orientation, information systems strategic orientation[,] and strategic alignment. *Information Systems Research, 8*(2), 125-150.

Compeau, D., Higgins, C. A., & Huff, S. (1999). Social cognitive theory and individual reactions to computing technology: A longitudinal study. *MIS Quarterly, 23*(2), 145-158.

Compeau, D. R., & Higgins, C. A. (1995). Computer self-efficacy: Development of a measure and initial test. *MIS Quarterly, 19*(2), 189-211.

Dagwell, R., & Weber, R. (1983). Systems designers' user models: A comparative study and methodological critique. *Communications of the ACM, 26*(11), 987-997.

Daniels, K., de Chernatony, L., & Johnson, G. (1995). Validating a method for mapping manager's mental models of competitive industry structures. *Human Relations, 48*(9), 975-991.

Davidson, W. H., & Movisso, J. F. (1996). Managing the business transformation process. In J. N. Luftman (Ed.), *Competing in the Information Age: Strategic Alignment in Practice* (pp. 322-360). New York and Oxford: Oxford University Press.

Davies, J. G., Menon, R., Munday, S. R., Thomson, B. G., & Young, L. (1995). Key issues in information systems management: A New Zealand perspective. *New Zealand Journal of Computing, 6*(1a), 15-21.

DeSanctis, G., & Poole, M. S. (1994). Capturing the complexity in advanced technology use: Adaptive structuration theory. *Organization Science, 5*(2), 121-147.

Dickson, R. W., Senn, J. A., & Chervany, N. L. (1977). A program for research in MIS. *Management Science, 23*(9), 913-923.

Drazin, R., & Van de Ven, A. H. (1985). Alternative forms of fit in contingency theory. *Administrative Science Quarterly, 30*, 514-539.

Dutton, J. E., Walton, E. J., & Abrahamson, E. (1989). Important dimensions of strategic issues: Separating the wheat from the chaff. *Journal of Management Studies, 26*(4), 379-396.

Estes, W. K. (1994). *Classification and Cognition*. New York: Oxford University Press.

Floyd, S. W., & Wooldridge, B. (1990). Path analysis of the relationship between competitive strategy, information technology and financial performance. *Journal of Management Information Systems, 7*(1), 47-64.

Galliers, R. D., Merali, Y., & Spearing, L. (1994). Coping with information technology? How British executives perceive the key information systems management issues in the mid-1990s. *Journal of Information Technology, 9*, 223-238.

Gallupe, R. B., & Tan, F. B. (1999). A research manifesto for global information management. *Journal of Global Information Management, 7*(3), 5-18.

Gorry, G. A., & Scott Morton, M. S. (1971). A framework for management information systems. *Sloan Management Review, 13*(1), 55-70.

Griffith, T. L., & Northcraft, G. B. (1996). Cognitive elements in the implementation of new technology: Can less information provide more benefits? *MIS Quarterly, 20*, 99-110.

Hambrick, D. C., & Mason, P. A. (1984). Upper echelons: The organisation as a reflection of its top managers. *Academy of Management Review, 9*, 193-206.

Henderson, J. C., & Venkatraman, N. (1992). Strategic alignment: A model for organisational transformation through information technology. In T. A. Kochan & M. Useem (Eds.), *Transforming Organisations*. Oxford and New York: Oxford University Press.

Henderson, J. C., & Venkatraman, N. (1993). Strategic alignment: Leveraging information technology for transforming organisations. *IBM Systems Journal, 32*(1), 4-16.

Henderson, J. C., Venkatraman, N., & Oldach, S. (1996). Aligning business and IT strategies. In J. F. Luftman (Ed.). *Competing in the Information Age: Strategic Alignment in Practice* (pp. 21-42). New York: Oxford University Press.

Hill, T., Smith, N. D., & Mann, M. F. (1987). Role of efficacy expectations in predicting the decisions to use advance technologies: The case of computers. *Journal of Applied Psychology, 72*(2), 307-313.

Hofer, C. W., & Schendel, D. (1978). *Strategy Formulation: Analytical Concept*. St. Paul, MN: West Publishing.

Horovitz, J. (1984). New perspectives on strategic management. *Journal of Business Strategy, 4*(3), 19-33.

Huff, A. S. (1990). *Mapping Strategic Thought*. Chicester, UK: John Wiley & Sons Ltd.

Ives, B., Hamilton, S., & Davis, G. B. (1980). A framework for research in computer-based management information systems. *Management Science, 26*(9), 910-933.

Jelinek, M., & Litterer, J. A. (1994). Toward a cognitive theory of organizations. In C. Stubbar, J. R. Meindl, & J. F. Porac (Eds.). *Advances in Managerial Cognition and Organizational Information Processing* (pp. 3-41). Greenwich, Connecticut: JAI Press.

Kearns, G. S., & Lederer, A. L. (1997). Alignment of information systems plans with business plans: The impact on competitive advantage. *Paper presented at the 1997 Americas Conference on Information Systems*. Indianapolis, Indiana.

Kelly, G. A. (1955). *The Psychology Of Personal Constructs*. New York: W.W. Norton & Company Inc.

King, W. R., & Sabherwal, R. (1992). The factors affecting strategic information systems applications: An empirical assessment. *Information and Management, 23*, 217-235.

Kumar, K., & Bjorn-Andersen, N. (1990). A cross-cultural comparison of IS designer values. *Communications of the ACM, 33*(5), 528-538.

Langfield-Smith, K. (1992). Exploring the need for shared cognitive map. *Journal of Management Studies, 29*(3), 349-368.

Lederer, A. L., & Sethi, V. (1988). The implementation of strategic information systems planning methodologies. *MIS Quarterly, 12*(3), 445-461.

Luftman, J. N. (Ed.) (1996). *Competing in the information age: Strategic alignment in practice*. New York: Oxford University Press.

Luftman, J. N., Lewis, P. R., & Oldach, S. H. (1993). Transforming the enterprise: The alignment of business and information technology strategies. *IBM Systems Journal, 31*(1), 198-221.

Luftman, J. N., Papp, R., & Brier, T. (1999). Enablers and Inhibitors of Business-IT Alignment. *Communications f the Association for Information Systems, 1*.

MacDonald, H. (1991). Business strategy development, alignment and redesign. In M. S. Scott Morton (Ed.), *Corporation of the 1990s: Information Technology and Organisational Transformation*. Oxford and New York: Oxford University Press.

Mason, R. O., & Mitroff, I. I. (1973). A program for research in management information systems. *Management Science, 19*(5), 475-485.

Medin, D. L. (1989). Concepts and concept structure. *American Psychologist, 44*, 1469-1481.

Mervis, C. B., & Rosch, E. (1981). Categorization of natural objects. *Annual Review of Psychology, 32*, 89-115.

Moynihan, J. A. (1988). Current issues in introducing and managing information technology: The chief executive's perspective. In *Information Technology for Organisational Systems*. Brussels-Luxembourg: Elsevier Science.

Nolan, R. L., & Wetherbe, J. (1981). Toward a comprehensive framework for MIS research. *MIS Quarterly, 4*(2), 1-19.

Orlikowski, W. J., & Gash, D. C. (1994). Technological frames: Making sense of information technology in organizations. *ACM Transactions on Information Systems, 12*(2), 174-201.

Parker, M., Benson, R., & E., Trainer. (1988). *Information economics: Linking business performance to information technology*. Englewood Cliffs, New Jersey: Prentice Hall.

Pervan, G. P. (1993). Results from a study of key issues in Australian IS management. *Paper presented at the 4th Australian Conference on Information Systems*. Brisbane: University of Queensland.

Prairie, P. L. (1996). Benchmarking IT strategic alignment. In J. N. Luftman

(Ed.). *Competing in the Information Age: Strategic Alignment in Practice*. Oxford and New York: Oxford University Press.

Reger, R. K., & Huff, A. S. (1993). Strategic groups: A cognitive perspective. *Strategic Management Journal, 14*(2), 103-124.

Reich, B. H., & Benbasat, I. (1996). Measuring the linkage between business and information technology objectives. *MIS Quarterly, 20*(1), 55-81.

Reich, B. H., & Benbasat, I. (2000). Factors that influence the social dimension of alignment between business and information technology objectives. *MIS Quarterly, 24*(1), 81-114.

Robey, D., & Markus, M. L. (1998). Beyond rigor and relevance: Producing consumable research about information systems. *Information Resources Management Journal, 11*(1), 7-15.

Shaw, M. J., Gardner, D. M., & Thomas, H. (1997). Research opportunities in electronic commerce. *Decision Support Systems, 21*, 149-156.

Smith, E. E., & Medin, D. L. (1981). *Categories and concepts*. London: Harvard University Press.

Stubbart, C. I. (1989). Managerial cognition: A missing link in strategic management research. *Journal of Management Studies, 26*(4), 325-347.

Tan, F. B. (1995). The responsiveness of information technology to business strategy formulation: An empirical study. *Journal of Information Technology, 10*, 171-178.

Tan, F. B. (1997). Strategy types, information technology and performance: A study of executive perceptions. *Paper presented at the Proceedings of the Third AIS Americas Conference on Information Systems*. Indianapolis Indiana.

Thomas, J. B., & Dewitt, R. (1996). Strategic Alignment Research and Practice: A Review and Research Agenda. In J. N. Luftman (Ed.). *Competing in the Information Age: Strategic Alignment in Practice* (pp. 385-403). New York: Oxford University Press.

Venkatraman, N. (1989). The concept of fit in strategy research. *Academy of Management Research, 14*(3), 423-444.

Victor, B., Pine, B. J. I., & Boynton, A. C. (1996). Aligning IT with new competitive strategies. In J. N. Luftman (Ed.). *Competing in the Information Age: Strategic Alignment in Practice* (pp. 73-96). New York and Oxford: Oxford University Press.

Walsh, J. P. (1995). Managerial and organisational cognition: Notes from a trip down memory lane. *Organization Science, 6*(3), 280-321.

Walton, E. (1985). The relevance of Personal Construct Theory to Management. In F. Epting & A. W. Landfield (Eds.). *Anticipating Personal Construct Theory* (pp. 95-110). Lincoln and London: University of Nebraska Press.

Watson, R. T., & Brancheau, J. C. (1991). Key issues in information systems management: An international perspective. *Information and Management, 20,* 213-223.

Watson, R. T., Kelly, G. G., Galliers, R. D., & Brancheau, J. C. (1997). Key issues in information systems management: An international perspective. *Journal of Management Information Systems, 13*(4), 91-115.

Weick, K. E. (1984). Managerial thought in the context of action. In S. S. (Ed.), *The Executive Mind.* San Francisco, CA: Jossey-Bass.

Weick, K. E. (1995). *Sensemaking in organizations.* California: Sage Publications.

Weick, K. E. (2001). *Making sense of the organization.* Malden, MA: Blackwell Publishers.

Weill, P., & Broadbent, M. (1998). *Leveraging the new infrastructure: how market leaders capitalize on information technology.* Boston: Harvard University Press.

Zviran, M. (1990). Relationships between organisational and information systems objectives: Some empirical evidence. *Journal of Management Information Systems, 7*(1), 65-84.

Chapter V

IT Architecture in Strategic Alliance Negotiations: A Case

Purnendu Mandal
Marshall University, USA

ABSTRACT

In forming strategic alliances managers should consider information technological fit along with other business considerations among partners. The development of IT architecture for the new situation and its use in the negotiation process could potentially be rewarding for all the parties involved. This chapter uses a case study to describe the way in which the development of IT architecture for the proposed alliance between an information and communications technology (ICT) organisation and its partners helped in the negotiation process. A telecommunications organisation (TEL) intended to enter into the retail electricity distribution business in alliance with existing operators in the retail electricity industry so that TEL could improve its market position. An IT architecture for the new market situation was developed, which helped in understanding the future informational requirements and dependence of partners on each other.

INTRODUCTION

Competency of an appropriate IT architecture enables an organisation to reap the benefits of information technology (Feeny & Willcocks, 1998). Conceiving and implementing the architecture, however, has not been easy for CIOs. Whenever an organisation changes its business strategy and operating procedures, perhaps because of a BPR or a strategic alliance, new information systems are required. How would the exact form and components of the entire IT be determined for optimizing business goals? How and to what extent does the existing IT/IS infrastructure satisfy the new systems requirements? It is incumbent upon the CIO to play a role in answering these questions.

IT architecture is instrumental to the achievement of business goals (Hay & Munoz, 1997). IT design activities can lead to an optimally re-designed system. Three critical design activities direct systems design towards meeting business needs: (1) strengthening the existing architecture relative to internal process changes, (2) redesigning IT architecture when major shifts take place due to BPR or strategic alliances, and (3) designing IT architecture anew for business start-up. Good methodology currently supports two of the above-mentioned situations: strengthening existing architecture and designing new IT architecture (Laudon & Laudon, 2000). Redesigning IT architecture relative to BPR or strategic alliance is more challenging and contextual rather than procedural (Nissen, 1998). Independent of dealing with the broad scope of an organisation's IT systems, IT architecture planning must regard strategic considerations—particularly in the negotiation phases of new alliances.

The case of a telecommunications company highlights major considerations in IT architecture planning that result from strategic alliances with new business partners. The telecommunication company (TEL) identified a new market opportunity as a result of changed market conditions. Originally a traditional telecommunications and information services concern, it had identified a new market opportunity within retail electricity distribution—the apparent result of market deregulation within the electricity industry. The company's own strengths in IT areas, its strong market position, and its experience in forming alliances with other business partners from the electricity industry emerged main considerations for the strategic move.

The formation of a strategic alliance enabled the transformation; there remained, however, many considerations to address prior to the strategic alliance and its subsequent IS metamorphosis. The architecture of the IS become a high priority of management because it would guide negotiations through alliance formation stages. Discussions centered around key elements for the proposed structure and how they would interact with the existing telecommunications business.

This scenario is equally applicable to other business situations. As a model, it suggests specific guidelines to practitioners who face similar situations. The chapter, then, presents a brief account of strategic alliance concepts and their relevance to IT architecture planning. Subsequently, I highlight pertinent research. Descriptions of the telecommunications company's operations and of the business environment within the electricity industry follow. Three additional sections present the logical steps leading to IT architecture development.

STRATEGIC ALLIANCE CONCEPTS

Definitions of strategic alliances abound in the literature, with common threads among them: the establishment of inter-organisational relations and the encouragement of collaborative behaviour. Strategic alliances, alternatively, are mutual agreements between two or more independent firms for the purpose of serving common strategic business objectives (Bronder & Pritzel, 1992). Strategic alliances exist when the value chains between at least two organisations with compatible goals are combined for the purpose of sustaining and/or achieving significant competitive advantage (Bronder & Pritzel, 1992). Alliances may exist among any number of organisations. For example, telecommunications organisations might form alliances to facilitate international joint ventures. Alliances may be established between banking organisations and IT suppliers. Strategic alliances may significantly improve organisational performance through joint, mutually dependent actions. For strategic alliances to be successful, business partners must follow structured approaches in developing alliances, which may include:

- *strategic planning* – As a result of rapid advancements in technology, globalization, and increasing environmental complexity and uncertainty, strategic planning has emerged a business-critical capability of organisations, supporting the realization of long-term alliances;
- *communications* – It is essential that the organisations maintain established and proven business processes that can support effective and efficient inter- and intra-organisational communication alliance structures. Because the commitment of employees is also needed to realize successful alliances, the communications structure must have the capability to inform employees about changes that may occur in organisational/alliance goals and objectives;
- *efficient and effective decision making* – Senior managers must be capable of identifying and of assessing suitable partners. Preferred suppliers/partners are then integrated into business plans and appropriate performance measures are determined;
- *performance evaluation* – It is important to evaluate and to monitor the performance of partners. Total partnership commitment requires reasonable assurances that suppliers will be financially stable for the remainders of the relationships. Risk to alliances must be minimized;
- *relationship structure* – Organisations must determine relationship structures that appropriately correspond with organisational goals and objec-

tives. Alternatives such as outsourcing may be considered for new joint ventures: how much or how little of a business can or should be outsourced is a critical strategic decision;
- *education and training* – It is essential that necessary personnel are exposed to training and education that supports win-win relationships for both parties. In addition, it is important to differentiate between training and education, with the former relating to skills development and the latter to knowledge.

Strategists have often suggested that organisations consider entering into similar or somewhat related market sectors to broaden their product/service portfolios (Markides & Williamson, 1997; Henderson & Clark, 1990). Both customers and products within related markets should be identified with relative ease for formulating strategies. Organisations are able, then, to exploit their competencies and strategic assets for the generation of strategic competitive advantage (Markides & Williamson, 1997). Determining the design and the requirements of a new IS is relatively simple in this situation. In contrast, diversification into a significantly different market for an IT/IS organisation is extremely challenging, requiring considerable evaluation.

IT ARCHITECTURE AND STRATEGIC ALLIANCES

IT architecture is a high-level structuring of companies' informations systems. It is "the vision of an ultimate reality created in reaction to a defined strategy and known constraints" (Hay & Munoz, 1997). Strategic considerations, such as new alliances, require envisioning alternative IT architectures. Applegate, McFarlan and McKenney (1999) consider IT architectures as ranges of technical options as well as business options. "Just as the blueprint of a building's architecture indicates not only the structure's design but how everything—from plumbing and heating systems to the flow of traffic within the building—fits and works together, the blueprint of a firm's IT architecture defines the technical computing, information management and communications platform" (p. 209).

Figure 1 demonstrates the dynamic nature inherent in developing IT architecture. Technology—concerned with design, deployment, and usage—is denoted by the dotted oval. It forms the core of IT architectures, with unequaled IT professionals' time devoted to related activities. Considerations of business options, which feed into various technology options, are higher level activities within IT architecture. Business options, such as strategic alliances, outsourcing, diversification, and others are influenced by major internal as well as external

Figure 1: Forces affecting overall IT architecture

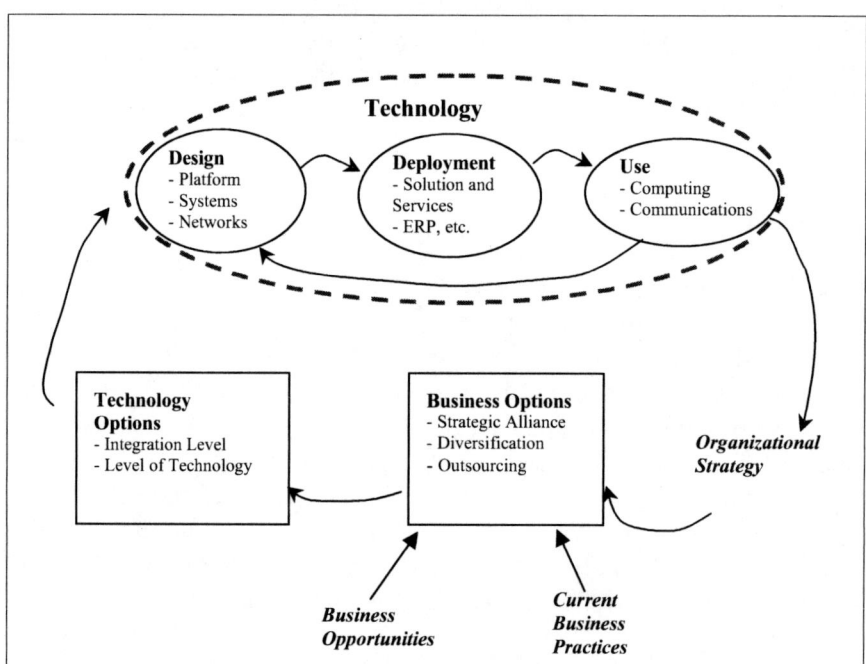

factors—current business practices, business opportunities, and organisational strategies. Technology links directly with organisational strategy. Technology (with its operational and technical settings) exerts strong influences upon organisations' future strategic directions. Thus, one can observe (as shown in Figure 1 through connecting lines) a close link between technical and other business factors: continually-changing business mirrors dynamically evolving IT architecture.

Traditionally, IT practitioners have viewed IT architectures as consisting of four components—data, function, hardware, and connectivity (Gifford, 1992). From managerial perspectives, however, IT architecture focuses upon achieving lasting competitiveness. According to Feeney and Willcocks (1998), companies today face three enduring challenges in achieving competitive advantage: focusing IS efforts to support business strategies, devising effective strategies for the delivery of low-cost and high-quality IS services, and choosing suitable technical platforms on which to mount IS services.

ROLES OF IT ARCHITECTURE

IT architecture serves three primary purposes in negotiating various terms and conditions of strategic alliances with partners:
1. Defining new environments for organisations and partners.
2. Determining project complexities and complements within alliances.
3. Providing the details of technical strengths and limitations within new alliances.

Planning new IT architectures first requires defining new organisational environments from an IT perspective. Strategic alliances, dictated by business needs, invariably pose new environments for organisations and their partners. A comprehensive understanding of the new environment is required before IT architecture development begins.

Understanding and projecting the complexities and complements within alliances forms the bases, rationales, procedures, and contents of envisioned information systems. Schematic presentations of informational links among partners greatly aides in appreciating the actual sizes and complexities of new IS implementations.

Enumerating details of technical strengths and limitations for new IT systems provides rationale for new systems: Why this particular IT architecture? Like architectural or engineering blueprints, IT architectural designs isolate components of IT and their interrelationships. Managers gain a great deal of knowledge from seeing these relationships: they analyze architectures, identify areas of potential conflicts, and make necessary contingency plan. For strategic alliance situations, managers may identify potential information-related problems that may be used as leverage in future negotiations with partners.

I presently describe the usefulness of preliminary IT architectures developed by a telecommunications organisation (TEL), exploring the possibility of strategic alliances within retail electricity organisations. The focus becomes pre-strategic alliance activities. My intention is not to present the technical details of a fully-developed IT system at TEL, but to provide an account of activities carried out in the pre-alliance stage.

THE NEW ENVIRONMENT: *WHICH SITUATION?*

Before designing a new IT architecture it is necessary to comprehend the environment in which the telecommunication organisation (TEL) operates. TEL provides services to its customers through its own telecommunications network and plans to increase its customer base by forming strategic alliances with retail electricity distribution organisations. While other large telecommunication organisations exhibit structural inertia, generating a competitive advantage in a new market poses an enormous challenge (Henderson & Clark, 1990). (Note: organisations must distinguish between new products and the means to producing new products.) The recent merger between America Online and Time-Warner Publishing demonstrates that it is possible for an IT organisation to offer new products in an existing market and be successful. This case models how strategic alliances and partnerships may provide entry into completely new product markets and how systems development that creates interfaces for existing IS or for newly integrated IS may result.

Retail distributors must make financial settlements with other suppliers within the electricity industry while contending with deregulation laws. The financial settlement should absorb the costs of electricity from the wholesale electricity market, tariffs for distribution of the same by transmissions and distributions service providers, and meter data from meter providers and meter data agents. The processes and systems required thereof must interface with retail energy distributors, with accounting and billing, and with service activation and service assurance processes and systems. Figure 2 illustrates the major revenue transactions between TEL and other parties within the supply chain.

Figure 2: Electricity retailing revenue flows

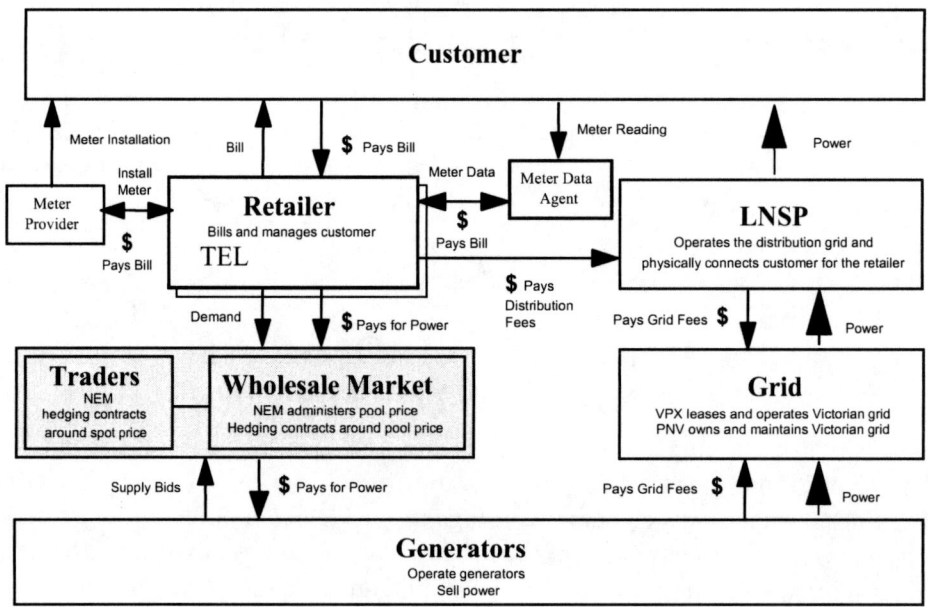

To conduct business as a legitimate market participant, TEL must purchase wholesale electricity and services for physical delivery and metering to customers. There are two clear options available to TEL for the purchase electricity:

- *Direct participation and trading in the national electricity market (NEM)*: TEL would perform all electricity trader functions, bid on and settle wholesale purchases within the national electricity market, and carry all market and prudential risks and responsibilities.
- *Engage energy trader specialists*: TEL must form close and long-term relationships with one or more traders. The energy trader specialist would operate all market trader functions and processes on TEL's behalf within an outsourcing arrangement.

COMPLEXITY IN IT ARCHITECTURE DEVELOPMENT: *WHAT IS THE CONTENT?*

TEL managers must be cognizant of the complexities and limitations of IT infrastructures before they venture into new business. TEL follows a standard procedure called PDOM (Product Development Operational Model) for all IT product development. IT architecture design also adheres to this procedure. PDOM is similar to standard SDLC (Systems Development Life Cycle) (Kendall & Kendall, 1995).

Figure 3 below represents the relationship that TEL must achieve with third parties.

Figure 3: Relationships between TEL and third parties

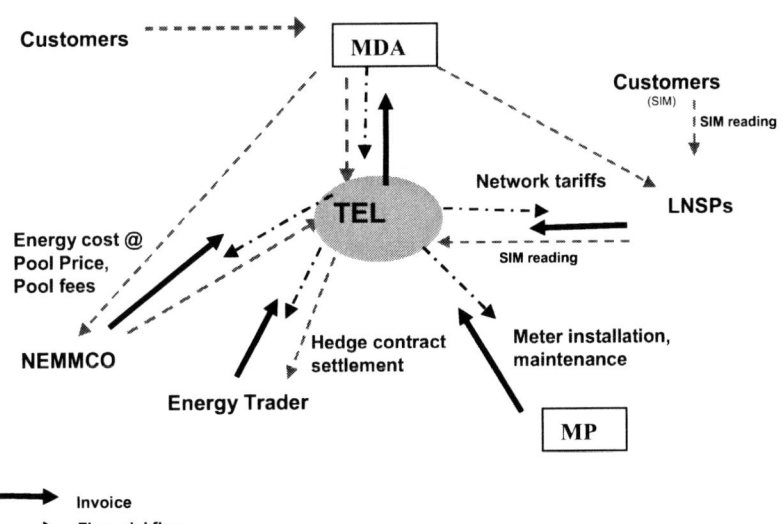

Figure 4: Market overview

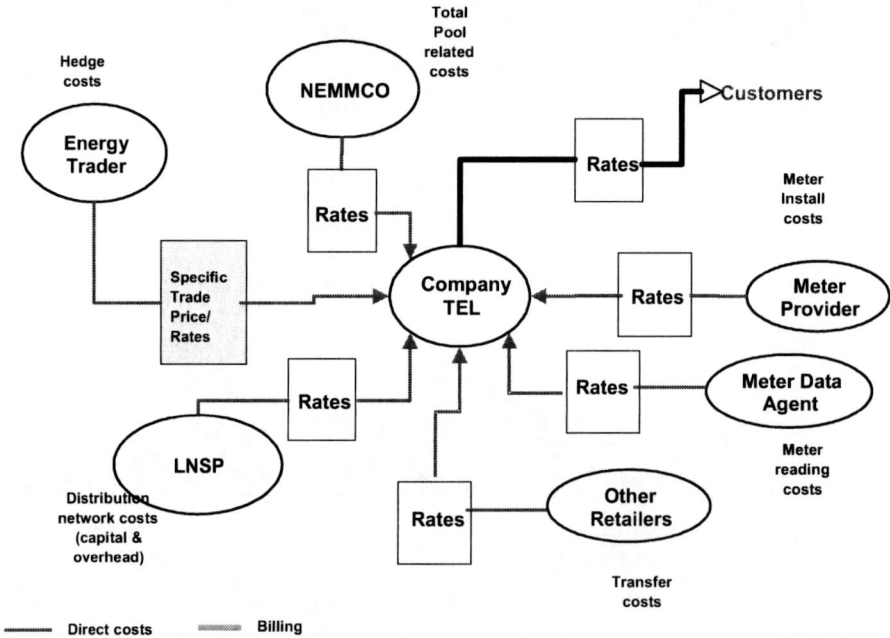

Integration with third parties is critical in assuring that customer charges are correct, that customer start and end dates are correct, and that rates, services rendered, customer usage, and losses are calculated correctly. Integration is also necessary to ensure and to document the details of customer accounts. TEL will be required to enter into binding agreements with NEMMCO (National Electricity Marketing and Management Company), LNSPs (Line Service Providers, who materially provide electricity via overhead lines), MDA (metering data agents), MP (meter providers), energy traders, and RP (retail providers).

Figure 4 indicates further details of third party relationships according to market rules. The diagram displays rates as related to the cost of energy on the left side; the right side of the figure relates rates to customer connection costs.

TEL's financial obligations to third parties within the electricity sector are on-going. Third party organisations include (*NECA*, 1998):

- *Electricity sourcing:* energy traders who purchase electricity from within the national electricity market.
- *NEMMCO:* provider of wholesale electricity; responsible for providing billing reconciliation data.
- *MDA:* NEMMCO accredited MDAs who collect and provide customer electricity usage data for billing purposes.

- *MP:* TEL, functioning as an RP, joins with MPs to provide and to maintain meter installations.
- *LNSP:* LNSPs distribute networks and connect and supply electricity.
- *NEMMCO and State Regulators:* issue operating licenses and collect all regulatory fees.
- *Generators:* fulfill outside-of-the-market long term energy requirements.
- *TEL Partner sales commissions:* payments and commissions to sales partners.

Figures 3 and 4 depict the complex relationships among TEL and its partners within the electricity market place. TEL must now investigate the relationships further.

DETAILS OF IT ARCHITECTURE FUNCTIONALITY

To forge meaningful alliances, TEL makes a number of major business decisions that depend upon the overall IT architecture. The decisions form the core of the IT system:

- The company will require customer-signed application forms prior to commencement of retail transfer processes.
- TEL will not enter into or conduct customer transfers under the BETS process.
- The company will negotiate contracts with LNSPs, ensuring that LNSPs will connect customers to their networks at customer-determined dates and times within reason. LNSPs will perform service location work.
- TEL will appoint only registered MDAs to read meters at start dates and times agreed upon by customers.
- MPs will install and remove electricity meters only upon instruction of company written documentation.
- MDAs provide all customer electricity usage data to the retailer for billing purposes. MDAs employ manual meter readers to read SIMs at minimum intervals of one month regardless of the billing cycle.
- TEL is obligated to MDAs, LNSPs, MPs, energy traders, and the Pool for electricity energy costs of goods sold.

TEL provides energy forecast data to energy traders. If these alliances eventuate, the existing processes and systems will generate reports of partner sales and commissions. TEL would provide most of the technical support to strategic partners. In general, partners in the electricity retail business do not have well-developed information systems—a conceivable limitation to full-scale systems integration. Electricity retailers currently have manual settlement systems and are either developing their own systems or are investigating installations of new systems applications.

IT systems architecture as presented above demonstrates how TEL could interact with other partners during the formation of strategic alliances. The IT architecture discussed here not only presents an overview of future challenges: it also demonstrates the nature of IT activities that would face CIOs when an alliance becomes a reality.

DISCUSSIONS AND FURTHER WORK

IT architecture can contribute greatly to negotiations in strategic alliance processes. In addition to presenting an overview of the information systems within an organisation, IS architecture becomes valuable during alliance negotiations by highlighting the major weaknesses and incompatibilities among various information systems. As demonstrated here, a telecommunications company may form strategic alliances with companies within the electricity distribution market, enabling the telecommunications organisation to enter into the electricity retail business. The settlement process presented here is a major component of business initiative carried out by TEL. The plan outlines business requirements for the construction of the system modeled and defines benchmarks for evaluation of third party settlement systems.

Businesses continually compete and evolve within an intensely competitive environment, and their evolution runs a continuum of newly-developed structures—from independence to interdependence. The developments of alliances and partnerships for competitive advantage initiate constant change. Business organisations are now re-thinking traditional business models and strategically planning for those that provide an edge. Strategic alliances are just one of many business models available to managers of organisations poised to improve performance.

Although this case study takes as its subject a telecommunications company, the concepts are applicable within any business sector and within any business entity. Developing fresh IT architectures, an inherently inquisitive process, potentially leads to systematic and practical gains.

REFERENCES

Applegate, L. M., McFarlan, F.W., & McKenney, J.L. (1999). *Corporate information systems management: Text and cases*. Irwin: McGraw-Hill.

Bronder, C., & Pritzl, R. (1992). Developing strategic alliances: A successful framework for co-operation. *European Management Journal*, *10*(4), pp. 412-420.

Feeny, D., & Willcocks, L. (1998). Core IS capabilities for exploiting information technology. *Sloan Management Review,* Spring 1998.

Gifford, R. (1992). Implementing the IS architecture. *Information Systems Management*, *9*(4).

Hay, G., & Munoz, R. (1997). Establishing an IT architecture strategy. *Information Systems Management*, *14*(3), p.67.

Henderson, R., & Clark, K (1990). Architectural innovation: the reconfiguration of existing product technologies and the failure of established firms. *Administrative Science Quarterly*, *35*, pp. 9-30.

Kendall, K.E, & Kendall, J.E. (1995). *Systems analysis and design* (3rd ed.), New Jersey: Prentice-Hall International.

Laudon, K., & Laudon, J. (2000). *Management Information Systems* (6th ed.), Upper Saddle River, New Jersey: Prentice Hall.

Markides, C.C., & Williamson, P.J. (1997). Related diversification, core competencies and corporate performance. In Cambell, A. and Sommer Luchs, K., (Eds.). *Core Competency-Based Strategy*, (pp. 96-122). London: International Thomson Business Press..

Nissen, M. (1998). Redesigning reengineering through measurement-driven inference. *MIS Quarterly*, *22*(4).

Chapter VI

How to Prioritize Information Systems Selection Decisions Under Time Pressure

D. C. McDermid
Edith Cowan University, Australia

ABSTRACT

This chapter reports on an action research study that used the Strategic Choice method. This method was used to support the prioritization of information systems with respect to enhancing these systems within a public sector health department. Such decisions are notoriously complex, fuzzy, time-consuming and political for stakeholders. The results of this study indicate that the Strategic Choice method offers the potential to reduce time commitment for stakeholders in a satisfactory manner.

INTRODUCTION

Currently, there are many occasions in which budget and constraints on personnel dictate that only a limited amount of development or systems enhancement is possible. This is becoming a more common problem as legacy systems and their ongoing need for maintenance continue to represent a growing proportion of an IT department's budget. In addition, the nature of the relationships between information systems is complex and often subtle in terms of their strategic contribution to the organization. Worse still, there is no single methodological approach which has been recognized as ideal for making this kind of decision (Gregory, 1995; Sikora et al., 1998), especially so when such decisions are often required to be made under severe time limitations.

The method used in this study was the Strategic Choice approach (Friend & Hickling, 1987). The approach is empirical rather than intellectual and explicitly recognizes some of the ways in which people, faced with complex decision problems in practice, cope with dilemmas at an intuitive level. It has been used in other decision domains (Stromberg & Khakee, 1993; Friend, 1989) but not in information systems selection. A particularly attractive feature of Strategic Choice was the potential for minimal involvement of the stakeholders, and so an action research study was set up to examine this question. As a consequence, only three two-hour sessions involving five stakeholders were required to arrive at a decision.

The study was set up on typical action research lines (Wood-Harper, 1985; Elden & Chisholm, 1993). All participants were qualified in terms of their agreement to participate in the research (Winter, 1998), in terms of the nature of the problem focus (Cook, 1998), and what their role would be within that. The chapter proceeds as follows. The next section provides a brief overview of the Strategic Choice method. This is followed by a section describing what actually occurred in each of the three sessions as well as some further detail of the method. The chapter closes with an evaluation of Strategic Choice in terms of the study's aims.

THE STRATEGIC CHOICE METHODOLOGY

Strategic Choice is best described as a framework involving four complementary phases (or modes) of decision-making activity. These are the shaping mode, the designing mode, the comparing mode and the choosing mode (Friend & Hickling, 1987). Researcher involvement is primarily facilitative, describing the process and assisting the workshop participants to work through all steps (modes).

In the **shaping** mode, decision-makers address concerns about the structure of the set of decision problems which they face. They may debate the way in which problems should be formulated and whether links exist between decision options. They may consider whether their current focus should be enlarged, or conversely broken down into more manageable parts.

In the **designing** mode, decision-makers address concerns about what courses of action are possible in relation to their current view of the problem shape. They may debate whether they have enough options in view, or whether design constraints of a technical or policy nature exist that restrict their ability to combine options to deal with different parts of the problem in a particular way.

In the **comparing** mode, decision-makers address concerns about the ways in which the consequences or other implications of different courses of action should be compared. Consequences based on economic, social and other criteria may be assessed.

In the **choosing** mode, decision-makers address concerns about incremental commitment to actions over time.

DESCRIPTION OF ACTION RESEARCH STUDY

The facilitator was an experienced business analyst who had worked for a number of years in a large health department in Australia. He was familiar with the systems and participants involved with this study. The need to make this decision had been identified as an important real-life decision. At the same time, the facilitator had been completing a masters degree and was looking for a topic in which to undertake his final project. He approached the senior management of the health department and obtained their approval to perform this study as part of his master's degree. His supervisor was an experienced action researcher and agreed to act as a methods advisor to this project provided there was a possible opportunity for later publication.

A standard and well-recognized approach to action research was followed using the model outlined by Susman and Evered (1978). The main steps in this approach are:
- Establish client system infrastructure;
- Diagnose step;
- Plan action;
- Take action;
- Evaluate; and
- Specify learning.

The development of a client-system infrastructure involved the facilitator negotiating the terms of the project with the client organization, briefing all participants about the goals and aims of the academic side of the study, ensuring that they were comfortable with this, and specifying the outcomes and deliverables of the study both in terms of the organization as well as the facilitator. The client-system infrastructure needs to be maintained throughout the life of the study and, therefore, may need to be reinforced in later phases, e.g., re-assuring or reminding participants of the initial agreement or goals.

The **diagnosing** step had to some extent already been completed in the sense that the organization had already identified the need to make a decision on information systems selection and that this decision had to be taken quickly. Previously, the organization and, indeed, some of the participants had exposure to the soft systems approach (Checkland, 1981; Checkland & Scholes, 1990). While this approach was recognized as a powerful tool for facilitating, decision-making was a considerable concern because the time available would clearly not allow this approach to be used.

At the outset, it was not clear just how many meetings would be required to meet the objective. However, at the **action planning** phase, a meeting was set for each of the four phases or modes of Strategic Choice, i.e., four meetings were planned. These were set up on the basis of allowing some time (roughly one week) between each meeting to allow for reflection and other tasks or information gathering that may have been found necessary.

The **action taking** phase was, of course, the running of the actual meetings themselves. These were run by the facilitator who led the group through the Strategic Choice method. Between each meeting, a meeting was held between the facilitator and methods advisor to discuss the success of the previous meeting and to amend if necessary any preparations for the next meeting. This constituted the **evaluation** phase. At the outset, this was seen as reflecting on the success or otherwise on following the Strategic Choice method, but as discussed in the next section, this turned out to be more complex than anticipated. The last phase of the cycle, i.e., the **specific learning** phase, was carried out after the project was completed and was an opportunity to evaluate the whole action research study.

In total, a series of only three workshops of about two hours each was necessary to resolve a real-world prioritization problem. Five (middle and senior) managers attended these sessions in addition to the facilitator and methods advisor.

Session 1 (Shaping Mode)

In this first session, all candidate information systems were identified. If two information systems were strongly coupled, for example, where data from one is input to the other, this was shown by a line connecting the two (Figure 1). The purpose of this was to show pictorially where systems have strong affinity with others and where they do not (Friend & Hickling, 1987).

While this took up a large part of Session One, there was no real disagreement concerning the systems or their coupling. The group was then asked to brainstorm issues, initiatives and pressures that they perceived to have an influence. These were listed and then summarized in terms of broad areas of interest. Three areas were found to be important, but there was no disagreement in the group about which one was the most important. Figure 1 was then updated

Figure 1: Health information systems

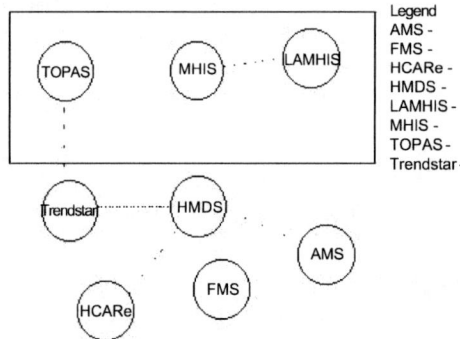

with a rectangle to indicate which information systems were considered the most important. The group was then asked to consider this set of related information systems. They were asked to identify strengths and weaknesses in relation to what was good about any of these systems and where gaps or improvements could be seen. The completion of this task ended the first session. Much of the information had been captured on electronic whiteboard and so the facilitator agreed to record the outcomes of the session and distribute these to stakeholders prior to the next meeting.

Session 2 (Designing and Comparing Mode)

The first session was considered to have identified the basic shape and territory of the problem. In the designing mode, the nature and number of options that are available are reviewed. It was here that a problem arose. In order to compare options, it is best if options can be expressed in a binary ("yes/no") fashion. However, some of the options were felt to represent different levels of modification rather than distinct options in themselves. This caused the team to reconsider the set of weaknesses identified previously with a view of reclassifying them as distinct options. The end result was the introduction of another system (HCARe) into the decision matrix. The effect of this decision was that there were now four main binary modification options, i.e., systems and thus 16 option permutations. However, seven of these were considered incompatible and so nine remained as viable (Table 1).

The construction of this table ended the second session. It was considered that the designing mode step had been completed and that the comparing mode

Table 1: Viable modification options

Row	MHIS	TOPAS	LAMHIS	HCARe
1	M	M	M	M
2	M	M	M	N
3	M	M	N	N
4	M	N	N	N
5	M	N	M	N
6	M	M	N	M
7	M	N	M	M
8	M	N	N	M
9	N	N	N	N

Legend: M = modify;   N = no change

had been started in this session but not completed. Further, the facilitator agreed to prepare cost, benefit and time estimates for the next meeting by consulting relevant stakeholders during the interim.

Session 3 (Comparing and Choosing Mode)

Estimates of costs, benefits and approximate development time were presented in Session Three. High cost was indicated as *****, low cost as *, high benefit as ***** and low benefit as *. For time estimates, a long development period was estimated at between five and 10 years, and a short development period at one to two years. Participants agreed to work with these measures because they felt that they were sufficient in being able to differentiate the decision options being compared. Time and benefit estimates were assigned for all eight decision options (rows one to eight), but, due to time limitations, there had been time only to agree on cost estimates for the decision options one, three and five (Table 2). The group was asked to indicate their preference from the nine available decision options. The ideal choice, if resources, funding and time were available, was agreed as decision option one, i.e., make required changes to all four systems to provide timely, good quality information. However, given cost constraint and the desirability of achieving benefit in the shorter term, decision option five was considered the best option.

Copyright © 2003, Idea Group Inc. Copying or distributing in print or electronic forms without written permission of Idea Group Inc. is prohibited.

Table 2: Viable modification options with costs, benefits and times

Row	MHIS	TOPAS	LAMHIS	HCARe	Cost	Benefit	Time
1	M	M	M	M	******	******	5-10yrs
2	M	M	M	N		****	3-5yrs
3	M	M	N	N	***	***	1-2yrs
4	M	N	N	N		***	1-2yrs
5	M	N	M	N	**	***	1-2yrs
6	M	M	N	M		****	3-5yrs
7	M	N	M	M		***	3-5yrs
8	M	N	N	M		**	1-2yrs
9	N	N	N	N			

EVALUATION

This section evaluates the action research approach taken as well as Strategic Choice as a method and is essentially in two parts. In the first part, a review of how the Susman and Evered model fitted the reality of the study is discussed, and then secondly the detail of what was learned about information systems selection is summarized.

While the Susman and Evered model was a useful template for this study, in practical terms, it was found that there were two places where learning took place. While the main formal evaluation took place at the completion of the study, surrounding each meeting, there was effectively a mini-learning cycle (McKay & Marshall, 2001). This involved **action planning** for the meeting, **action taking** (i.e., conducting the meeting) and **evaluation** of the meeting by the facilitator and methods advisor. Since the evaluation sometimes caused changes for the next meeting, this implied that the Susman and Evered template needed to be modified to show mini-learning cycles throughout the study. The kind of detail that was discussed during these mini-learning cycles and which was subsequently formalized in the specific learning phases is now summarized.

A key question in the **shaping** mode was "to what extent the nature of information systems selection problem is similar to strategic decision-making in general?" The stereotypical strategic decision model would allow related strategic options to be shown with cause-effect relationships as connections. In this study, related information systems were modelled and connections were added where (typically data) coupling existed. Clearly, cause-effect relationships are not the same as data couples. On the other hand, participants were comfortable with using the idea of coupling here and actively contributed to identifying connections between systems.

In the **designing** mode, the problem concerning binary ("yes/no") decisions was unanticipated and illustrated the flexibility of the approach. In both the design and maintenance of information systems, there is typically a broad range of options available, and many of these can be permutated with other options. At some point, the complexity becomes too much to deal with especially in groups and under severe time constraint. The interesting observation is that the group also sensed this and was prepared to compromise in order to make progress by simplifying the decision options to a structure that was more workable.

In the **comparing** mode a departure from the method took place in terms of content and process. Strategic Choice did not require participants to identify cost, benefit and time estimates.

Strictly speaking, Strategic Choice did not instruct participants to identify cost, benefit and time estimates. That was a decision initiated by the facilitator because it was felt that the full process in Strategic Choice was not particularly relevant to the problem on hand. Strategic Choice allows for the identification of three types of uncertainties (Figure 2). Uncertainties in the working environment (UE) can be dealt with by responses of a relatively technical nature (surveys, research investigations, cost estimates). The concern here is generally that not enough is known about the circumstances for this decision. Uncertainties in guiding values (UV) call for a more political response, for example, to clarify

Figure 2: Three types of uncertainty

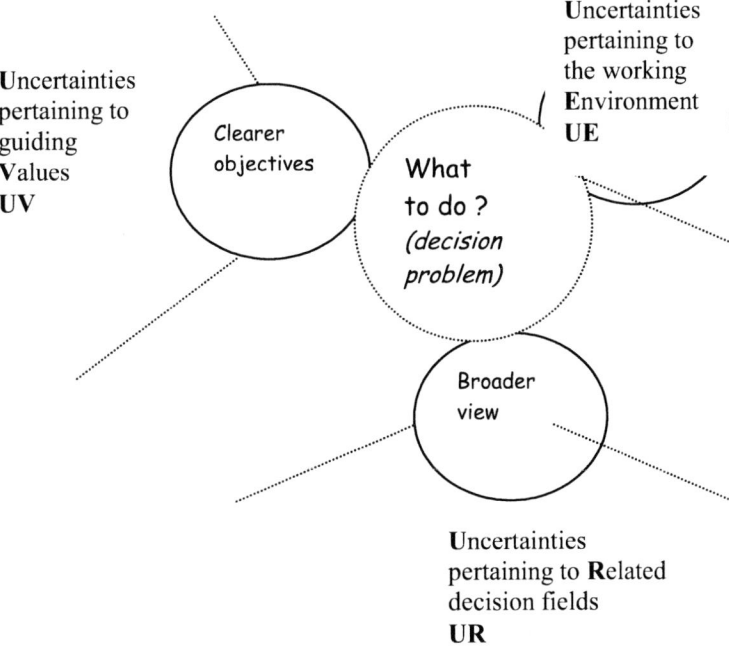

objectives, request more policy guidance from a higher authority. The concern for the decision-makers here is typically that because there are so many conflicting objectives, priorities and interests for this decision, the direction is not clear. Uncertainties in related decision fields (UR) call for a response in the form of exploration of the structural relationships between the decision currently in view and others with which it appears to be interconnected. The concern for the decision-makers here is that the decision is difficult because it has been viewed in a restricted way and that it shouldn't be treated in isolation.

That kind of problem was identified as an uncertainty in the environment, and, since classically information systems selection has relied on cost, benefit and time estimates in making decisions, this was seen as an acceptable proposed solution.

In retrospect, since it is generally considered that the shape and nature of a problem should determine the tools used in its solution, the borrowing of standard thinking from IS in terms of costs, benefits, and time estimates seemed a natural development, albeit that the group itself must have the power to make that final commitment to using those tools. Indeed, the group itself was quite comfortable with this compromise and created no disquiet with regard to this short-cut.

In reality, the **choosing** mode step was not completed. The Strategic Choice method puts considerable emphasis on this step particularly in managing and monitoring the uncertainties identified. This was not done within the confines of this study, because it was seen as the responsibility of whomever to assume the role of project manager for the option selected to follow through on these issues.

Overall, the Strategic Choice method was considered to have been successful as far as the participants were concerned. In a post-study interview, there was strong support for methods such as this which could facilitate group commitment to decisions under severe time constraints. However, there was recognition by participants that a more in-depth study would be necessary after initial selection was mandated (if only to confirm the decision) and that other information system selection decisions may not be as clear cut as this one. It was clear that this was a mature group in the sense that collectively they had skill, experience and understanding about decision-making processes generally; the role of facilitator and methods advisor might have been much tougher if this were not so.

Many tailoring and modification decisions were taken in applying the method which is noted from the above discussion. However, that is not perceived to be a weakness of the method. Rather, one important strength of the approach was the ease by which appropriate deviations from the stereotype were able to be employed without losing sight of the goals. With that said, more work is required in examining how the dynamics of these changes affect the suitability and efficacy of the method itself. Further work may also look at other kinds of problems where prioritization is required. For example, within a single project, there is often proliferation of requirements or "scope creep." The steps and philosophy of Strategic Choice may be found useful here in the prioritization of requirements.

REFERENCES

Checkland, P., & Scholes, J. (1990). *Soft Systems Methodology in Action.* Chichester, England: John Wiley and Son.

Checkland, P. B. (1981). *Systems Thinking, Systems Practice.* Chichester, England: John Wiley.

Cook, T. (1998). The importance of mess in action research, *Educational Action Research*, 6(1), pp. 93-109.

Elden, M., & Chisholm, R. F. (1993). Emerging varieties of action research: Introduction to the special issue, *Journal of Human Relations*, 46(2).

Friend, J. K. (1989). The strategic choice approach. In J. Rosenhead (Ed.), *Rational Analysis for a Problematic World.* John Wiley & Sons Ltd., pp. 121-157.

Friend, J. K. & Hickling, A. (1987) *Planning Under Pressure: The Strategic Choice Approach*, Pergamon, Oxford.

Gregory, F. H. (1995). Soft systems models for knowledge elicitation and representation, *Journal of the Operational Research Society*, 46(5), pp. 562-572.

McKay, J. & Marshall P. (2001). The dual imperatives of action research, *Journal of Information Technology and People*, 14(1), pp. 46-59

Sikora, R. & Shaw, M. J. (1998). A multi-agent framework for the coordination and integration of information systems, *Management Science*, 44(11), pp. 65-76.

Stromberg, K. & Khakee, A. (1993). Applying futures studies and the strategic choice approach to urban planning, *Journal of the Operational Research Society*, 44(3), pp. 213-224.

Susman, G. I. & Evered, R. (1978). An assessment of the scientific merits of action research. *Administrative Science Quarterly,* 25, pp. 582-603.

Winter, R. (1998). Finding a voice: Thinking with others: A conception of action research, *Educational Action Research*, 6(1), pp. 53-63.

Wood-Harper, T. (1985). Research methods in information systems: Using action research. In E. Mumford, Hirschheim, R., Fitzgerald, G. & Wood-Harper, T. (Eds.), *Research Methods in Information Systems* (pp. 169-191). North Holland: Elsevier Science.

Chapter VII

A Framework for Extending Potency and Reducing Competitive Risk in the IT Strategic Systems Portfolio

James D. White
DePaul University, USA

Theresa A. Steinbach
DePaul University, USA

Linda V. Knight
DePaul University, USA

Alan T. Burns
DePaul University, USA

ABSTRACT

This research proposes that, in addition to balancing risk in the total IT project portfolio as McFarlan suggested in 1981, organizations should also balance risk in their strategic IT portfolios. A framework is distilled from the literature that will both minimize the total risk of an organization's strategic project portfolio, and identify opportunities to extend the strategic life of its information systems. The framework's validity is assessed by using four classic cases in the strategic use of technology. Results indicate that overall strategic IT risk may be reduced by evaluating an organization's strategic IT portfolio against the five dimensions of the framework, and then seeking strategic IT projects and opportunities that would bring greater balance to the organization's efforts. In addition, by moving across boundaries in each of the five dimensions, strategic systems can adapt to competitive marketplace or technology changes, and thus maintain their strategic potency over extended time periods.

INTRODUCTION

In 1981, McFarlan proposed that organizations develop aggregate risk profiles for their IT project portfolios. This research builds upon that idea by suggesting that organizations construct and analyze a risk profile specific to their strategic IT initiative portfolio. As Clemons (1999) noted, risks are rising as traditional, technical, and financial, and project risks are being supplemented or replaced by new kinds of strategic project risk, including functionality risk and political risk. These additional risks have increased primarily due to the accelerated pace of change in the competitive environment. Despite such increased risks to strategic IT projects, little research has been directed at better managing competitive risk in strategic IT initiatives. This chapter addresses that void. It also builds upon the work of those who have noted the difficulties involved in sustaining competitive advantage, including Leininger (1992) and Mata et al. (1995), by providing a comprehensive framework that organizations can use to identify methods of extending the potency of their strategic systems.

BACKGROUND

This research proposes a five-dimensional framework that can be used to evaluate and balance risk in the strategic IT project portfolio and to extend the strategic life of IT systems. The Five Dimensions of IT Strategy, which were first presented at the 2002 Information Resources Management Association Conference (Knight et al.) built upon earlier work by White (2000). They are summarized in Figure 1. These dimensions are based upon the literature, as the following discussion of the five dimensions reveals.

Dimension 1: Primary Strategic Resource

An organization may strategically leverage either technology itself, or the information that IT systems track and analyze (King et al., 1989). One company, for example, may take advantage of technological advances in computing to provide a new way of relating to its customers, while another company may use the information created by its computer system processing, such as customer demographics or production and inventory status, as a key resource to support

Figure 1: Five dimensions of IT strategy

5	**COMPETITIVE IT ORIENTATION** (where?)	External			Internal	
4	**STRATEGIC MODE** (why?)	Offensive			Defensive	
3	**STRATEGIC TARGET** (who?)	Supplier		Customer		Competitor
2	**COMPETITIVE STRATEGY** (how?)	Differentiation	Cost	Innovation	Growth	Alliances
1	**PRIMARY STRATEGIC RESOURCE** (what?)	Technology			Information	

overall business strategy. Alternatively, information technology and information may be combined and used together to create competitive advantage. This ability to blend multiple aspects of a single dimension extends to all five dimensions of the framework.

Dimension 2: Competitive Strategy

Rackoff et al. (1985), building on the work of Porter (1980), identified five strategic thrusts: differentiation, cost, innovation, growth, and alliances. A company can adopt one or a combination of these five competitive strategies. A low-cost strategy reduces the cost of the company's products and services and information technology supports the low-cost producer strategy if it can lower labor costs, reduce fixed asset expenses, reduce interest and facilities, or otherwise lower overall costs. A differentiation strategy distinguishes the company's products and services from those of its rivals based on factors such as price, function, content, and service, or reduces the differentiation advantage of competitors. An innovation strategy seeks to serve a specialized market or introduce a product or process change that results in a fundamental transformation of the way in which business is conducted in the industry. A growth strategy achieves competitive advantage by sales volume or geographic expansion, backward or forward integration or product-line diversification. An alliance strategy seeks to gain competitive advantage via marketing agreements, joint ventures or acquisitions that promote the strategies of differentiation and growth.

Dimension 3: Strategic Targets

A strategic initiative may be aimed at relationships with three external strategic targets (Wiseman & MacMillan, 1984; Rackoff et al., 1985). These strategic targets include suppliers (organizations providing the materials, capital, labor or services that a firm needs to make its product), customers (end-users as well as middlemen who resell to end-users), and competitors (those who sell similar and potentially substitutable products).

Dimension 4: Strategic Mode

An offensive strategic mode is designed to achieve or increase competitive advantage, while a defensive strategic mode is designed to mitigate competitors' real or potential strategic advantages (Wiseman & MacMillan, 1984).

Dimension 5: Competitive IT Orientation

An information system may be oriented externally to directly support the company's external competitive strategy or internally toward improved efficiency and effectiveness which will, in turn, support the company's competitive strategy. This fifth, and final, dimension of the framework also has its roots in the literature. In particular, just as Porter and Millar (1985) offered both a view of the external competitive marketplace and a concept of the value chain, Benjamin et al. (1984) noted that IT could be used either externally in the competitive marketplace or internally to improve efficiency and effectiveness. Bakos and Treacy (1986) also addressed the internal vs. external orientation in their causal framework of competitive advantage.

METHODOLOGY

Four classic cases in the strategic use of IT, American Airlines, American Hospital Supply, Cisco Systems, and Amazon.com, are used to assess the framework presented above. This methodology is one recognized approach for model corroboration. For example, Grant (2002) in his exploration of business process engineering in the *Communications of the ACM*, mapped a series of illustrative cases to a framework.

APPLICATION OF THE FRAMEWORK

American Airlines

In its original strategic implementation, American Airlines' SABRE reservation system (Hopper, 1990; Fryxell, 1996) allowed travel agents direct access to flight booking information, without having to "phone" airline reservation centers. The system has since evolved to include travelocity.com, serving individual customers on the Web. It is now tied into a broad spectrum of other services and marketing programs, including hotels, car rentals, and frequent flier programs. On March 1, 2000, AMR Corporation, the parent company of American Airlines, sold its interest in SABRE, and an independent SABRE Holding Corporation was created.

Dimension 1: Primary Strategic Resource

In terms of the first level of the Five Dimensions Framework, SABRE began by primarily leveraging technology. American Airlines began working to computerize its reservation systems in the late 1950s, as volume outstripped manual processes that used index cards and chalkboards. SABRE began as an inventory-control system that monitored available seats and attached passenger names as bookings were completed. In 1976, the first SABRE terminal was installed making the same information available to travel agents as had been made available previously over the telephone. SABRE's online computer technology improved the way in which the information was distributed, closely identified travel agents with American's system through high switching costs, and created a formidable barrier to entry for competitors. Over time, as the marketing of complementary products and personal information was added, the system moved from primarily leveraging technology to primarily leveraging information, thus demonstrating how organizations can move systems across boundaries within one dimension of the framework to achieve greater strategic advantage.

Dimension 2: Competitive Strategy

Initially, SABRE's competitive strategy was primarily one of differentiation and innovation. This innovation triggered a process change for the airline industry, making it no longer possible for proprietary computer systems to bind customers to specific systems and products. As online reservations became the industry norm, SABRE's strategy evolved into one of growth through alliances with other travel industry providers. In addition to listing other airline schedules in SABRE, for a fee, American Airlines has formed joint ventures with Marriott and Hilton Hotels and Budget Rent-A-Car.

Dimension 3: Strategic Targets

SABRE's strategic target has always been the customer, although as the industry has evolved over time, the concept of the customer has changed focus, moving from travel agents to include individual travelers. At the time American installed its first reservation system at a travel agency, the bulk of travel arrangements were made via agents at American Airline reservation centers and less than 40 percent of bookings were handled by travel agents. By 1990,

SABRE operated at more than 14,500 locations in 45 countries, and travel agents accounted for more than 80 percent of all passenger tickets. Widespread use of online reservation systems accorded travel agents considerable power in the industry with the ability to directly influence passengers' choice of airlines. Emergence of the Internet offered airlines a method of bypassing the travel agent and directly targeting the individual traveler as the customer. Jupiter Communications, a New York-based media-research firm, reported that the number of travelers who used the Internet grew to 70 million in 1997 from 26 million in 1996 (Miller, 1999). Internet-based reservation systems eroded the power of the travel agents. In 1999, 65 percent of Travelocity's tickets were electronic, and United Airlines announced that for the first time more of its customers used e-tickets than paper tickets (Miller, 1999). In January of 2002, 94.3 million people visited travel sites like expedia.com, orbitz.com, travelocity.com, travelzoo.com, and priceline.com (NUA, 2002).

Dimension 4: Strategic Mode

SABRE was originally a defensive measure. Max D. Hopper, senior vice president for information systems at American Airlines, recalled "American began marketing SABRE to travel agents only after United pulled out of an industry consortium established to explore developing a shared reservation system to be financed by carriers and travel retailers, ... we would have lost market share in a biased reservation system controlled by a competitor" (Hopper, 1990). As online reservations systems expanded and ticket prices in the air travel industry were deregulated, SABRE evolved into an offensive competitive weapon.

Dimension 5: Competitive IT Orientation

Initially, airlines automated reservation systems in order to gain better control of their inventory and speed internal processing. When American extended its reservation system to serve travel agents directly, it became an externally centered competitive system that changed the nature of competition in the air travel industry.

Analysis

SABRE represents an externally-oriented strategic system, focused on the customer. However, SABRE's concept of the customer has evolved as individuals began making travel arrangements via the Internet, and the power of travel agents declined. Further, as SABRE's original innovation became the industry norm, the system's competitive strategy evolved into one of growth through alliances. At the same time, SABRE's defensive leveraging of technology became an offensive leveraging of information. Thus, the system was able to maintain its strategic value because as its external environment, including both the travel industry and supporting technologies, changed, the system itself also continued to adapt.

American Hospital Supply Corporation

At the time American Hospital Supply Corporation's (AHSC) Analytic Systems Automatic Purchasing (ASAP) order entry tracking and management system was developed, AHSC was one of several medium-sized regional hospital supply and distribution companies. Like its competitors, AHSC built its business around efficient purchasing, warehousing, and distribution of comparatively generic hospital supplies. American Hospital Supply's ASAP system can be traced back to 1957 when AHSC began to automate its internal order entry and billing procedures. What began as an internal move to automate the company's distribution function expanded in the 1960s and 1970s to become one of the first and most successful supplier-to-customer electronic linkages in the industry (Short & Venkatraman, 1992). The ASAP system was acquired by Baxter Travenol Laboratories when Baxter and AHSC merged in 1985, and by the Allegiance Corporation when it was created in 1996. The ASAP system is in operation today.

Dimension 1: Primary Strategic Resource

Initially, AHSC initiatives emphasized automation technology. Subsequently and incrementally, its strategy expanded to encompass both technology and information resources. Through the early 1960s, the typical ordering process between a hospital purchasing agent and the supply firm was the responsibility of the AHSC salesperson who either telephoned or mailed in a customer order to the firm's distribution center. AHSC adopted a strategy of selective automation through the deployment of IBM tab-card machines and, in 1963, included Dataphone technology that empowered customers to submit orders directly from their location (Short & Venkatraman, 1992). ASAP system enhancements continued to be driven by technology advances and in the early 1980s, AHSC used its ASAP system to help its customers automate their ordering and inventory control by placing order entry terminals in hospitals, effectively establishing a direct link between the distributor and its customers (Wiseman, 1988). When Baxter Travenol Laboratories acquired AHSC in 1985, the information potential of ASAP was recognized. Baxter's CEO viewed ASAP not only as an underutilized channel of distribution, but as a powerful asset that could provide an unmatched market intelligence opportunity similar to the market intelligence derived by United Airlines' Apollo and American Airlines' SABRE systems (Wiseman, 1988).

Dimension 2: Competitive Strategy

From an original emphasis on cost effectiveness, AHSC's competitive strategy matured to include differentiation, innovation, growth, and alliances. Although ASAP was developed to reduce order entry costs and solve AHSC problems with incomplete orders and late delivery, it also provided added value and distinguished AHSC from its competitors by enabling purchasing departments to coordinate purchasing, control inventory, check stock, and place and track orders easily (Neo, 1988). ASAP enabled AHSC to dominate the hospital supply industry by opening a direct link characterized by high customer switching costs between the customer and distributors. As a result, Johnson & Johnson, a major competitor, lost market share and other rivals were driven out of business (Wiseman, 1988). By the end of the 1980s, in the face of multiple competing systems, ASAP's director concluded, "...the life of vendor-discrete systems – at least those in health care – is limited. We are purposely following the successful example of American Airlines' moving into the all-vendor arena." Consequently, ASAP shifted away from a dedicated system with proprietary protocols toward a common electronic data interchange platform with gateways to third-party network providers (Short & Venkatraman, 1992).

Dimension 3: Strategic Targets

ASAP's strategic target has been and remains the customer. Over the life of the ASAP system, business focus has expanded from efficient distribution of products through automated order entry to delivery of integrated material management services and information-based logistical services (Short & Venkatraman, 1992).

Dimension 4: Strategic Mode

Although ASAP operates in an offensive strategic mode, it was not developed as a strategic system. Rather, it was intended to solve internal operating problems of incomplete orders and late delivery for one of its major customers, the Stanford Medical Center (Neo, 1988). After initial localized success, AHSC recognized the strategic potential of ASAP and, with senior management support, committed the financial resources needed to develop a nationwide system. By the late 1980s, 5,500 of the 6,900 hospitals nationwide were using ASAP (Short & Venkatraman, 1992).

Dimension 5: Competitive IT Orientation

Trying to solve internal problems with order processing and distribution, AHSC discovered a means of realizing external competitive advantage. Their major initiative in the marketplace became aggressive penetration of hospitals with ASAP. This allowed them to gain relative competitive advantage over other suppliers by achieving "prime vendor" status under which the customer agreed to volume purchases and the key purchasing decision shifted from price to service (Short & Venkatraman, 1992).

Analysis

ASAP is a customer-oriented offensive strategic system that incorporates both technology and information. ASAP is a classic strategic case not only because it represents a very early, perhaps the first, automation of a supply chain, but also because ASAP, like American Airlines, illustrates the need for ongoing investment in strategic systems and expansion of IT strategy across categories within the five dimensions. In response to customer requests and to thwart potential rivals, ASAP was the subject of eight major system enhancements between 1963, when Dataphone technology was introduced, and 1990 (Short & Venkatraman, 1992). Toward the end of the 1980s, advanced and pervasive microcomputer and network technology reduced barriers to entry and customer switching costs and created a declining relationship between the levels of investment in technology and realized competitive advantage. Initial advances in technology, such as the Dataphone, that led the movement of ASAP to an external, offensive, and customer-focused system from an internal and cost oriented system, subsequently reduced the strategic value of technology and contributed to ASAP's emphasis on information, growth and alliances.

Cisco Systems, Inc.

Cisco Systems, Inc. was forced to abandon their legacy environment in 1994 when an unauthorized method for accessing the core application database corrupted the central database. This provided Cisco with the opportunity to implement a large-scale, integrated information system that was driven by manufacturing capabilities but designed to meet all the business needs of the organization. Within two years, an ERP system replaced all IT applications and platforms worldwide. Next, Cisco's supply chain management initiative integrated suppliers into the ERP system. Finally, Cisco management decided to fuse Internet technology with their business processes, adding a Web-based front-end to the ERP/supply chain management system.

Dimension 1: Primary Strategic Resource

Initially, Cisco installed the ERP system to facilitate the flow of information between order entry, finance, and manufacturing. At the time, most manufacturing was outsourced to the point of final assembly and testing. Recognizing its strength in design and fulfillment, Cisco changed its business strategy to direct fulfillment from the contract manufacturers and the automation of the supply chain. The primary focus was the unimpeded flow of information that was critical to dynamic replenishment. Inclusion of technology as a primary strategic resource occurred when the widespread adoption of Internet usage allowed Cisco's customers to track order information through a Web-based front-end to the ERP system.

Dimension 2: Competitive Strategy

Cisco's first competitive strategy was cost savings. Upon implementation of the ERP system and the extension to the supply chain initiative, Cisco was able to realize an annual savings of $500-$800 million (Ansley, 2000). The current business strategy is to be a "one-stop shop" service provider for all customers, competing across the board with telecommunication carriers, Internet service providers, cable companies and wireless carriers. This is an innovative strategy since few other companies attempt to be a single resource for the customer.

Dimension 3: Strategic Targets

When Cisco's ERP system was implemented, there was no external target. As the system evolved to include supply chain management, the target became the supplier. Further enhancements of Web-enabling technology focused on the customer. Cisco has not focused on the competition as the target in the networking market. They measured progress against the best competitor in the world in each functional area (Nolan, 2001b).

Dimension 4: Strategic Mode

Cisco achieved competitive advantage in the networking market by capturing an approximate 80 percent share of the market for routers and switches used in local area networks and the Internet (Reinhardt, 1999). Management made a shift in business strategy to become a major player in the service provider market, of which the networking market where they had clear competitive advantage, is a segment. This represents a shift from an offensive mode in the networking market to one of defense in the service provider market, where Cisco competes against larger telecommunications players. The competition is now a concern, whereas in the past Cisco did not focus on the competitor as a strategic target.

Dimension 5: Competitive IT Orientation

The ERP system was originally implemented to integrate the internal order entry, finance, and manufacturing functions to improve efficiency and effectiveness. The supply chain initiative discussed earlier opened the system to external suppliers. Web-enabling these applications gave customers access to a more efficient way of doing business. While the competitive orientation began as internal with an ERP system, it expanded to include external elements as the supply chain and Web initiatives were added.

Analysis

The evolution of Cisco's strategic systems may be viewed in terms of three phases. Phase I may be seen as an ERP system leveraging internal information to provide cost savings. This system was initially developed during an era of relative technical stability that contrasts dramatically with the era of emerging technology that characterized American Airlines and American Hospital Supply's strategic initiatives. In this stable technological environment, the choice of technology providers for the ERP system was complex. Cisco's choice of vendors ultimately was based on strength and experience in manufacturing, long-term development plans for the functionality of the product, and close geographic proximity (Nolan, 2001a). Since Cisco was the clear market leader, its position may be characterized as offensive rather than defensive. Cisco's addition of a supply chain initiative to its ERP system may be seen as the trigger that began Phase II. Since the system now targeted suppliers, it added an external orientation. As the Internet became a "way of doing business," it became a keystone of Cisco's strategy. Since Cisco supplied 80 percent of the networking market powering the Internet, it became a logical extension for Cisco to incorporate that technology in their systems. Cisco's implementation of Web-based front-ends, which added an emphasis upon technology as a strategic resource, and extended its strategic target to include customers as well as suppliers, may be seen as triggering Phase III.

Amazon.com

Amazon.com opened its virtual doors in July 1995 with a mission of using the Internet to transform the book-buying process. Amazon initially concentrated on the business-to-consumer (B2C) marketspace, offering price-discounted books with relatively low shipping costs to customers anywhere, anytime. Amazon's original direct competitors were traditional brick-and-mortar storefronts such as Barnes & Noble or Borders, as well as higher education bookstores. In a relatively short timeframe, Amazon broadened its scope to include alliances with such companies as Toys 'R' Us, Expedia, and Hotwire. Some estimates indicate that Amazon may have accounted for roughly half of the Toys 'R' Us $225 million 2001 revenue (Wingfield, 2002).

Dimension 1: Primary Strategic Resource

Amazon's initial primary effort was to exploit technology, specifically the emergent World Wide Web, to offer consumers discounted books. Amazon continued to exploit technology by using its e-commerce platform reputation to build strategic alliances. In addition to technology, Amazon has also leveraged information as a strategic resource. It has accumulated voluminous information on individual as well as aggregate online buyer behavior. Knowing past purchasing habits of an individual allows Amazon to use "push" technologies to promote products through e-mail and a personalized front page. Further, the Amazon Website maintains extensive product information, beyond that found in traditional brick-and-mortar bookstores, including textual excerpts and book reviews by experts and consumers.

Dimension 2: Competitive Strategy

Amazon's competitive strategy can be characterized as a low-cost leadership strategy, where the company seeks to appeal to a broad spectrum of customers as the overall low-cost provider of online merchandise. Amazon differentiated itself from the competition by devising an innovative way for customers to purchase books quickly and easily online. As the Web and e-commerce matured, competitive retail establishments created online purchasing sites to complement their storefronts. The strength of sales in books led Amazon to expand its product lines to include CDs and videos. Again, online competitors emerged. Throughout, innovation has been a fundamental competitive strategy for Amazon. Its use of search engines, personalization techniques, and security has made the company a model, copied by other online retail sites. At the same time as it has emphasized innovation, Amazon has also sought growth through alliances with a variety of established companies, including Borders, Target, and Toys "R" Us.

Dimension 3: Strategic Targets

Amazon's IT efforts initially focused intensely on the customer, and the customer continues to be at the forefront of the company's IT efforts. Its front-end IT systems emphasize the customer's experience, with ease of use, ability to search, and personalization techniques, while its integrated back-end systems lower costs through volume purchasing and economies of scale (Hayes, 1999). Amazon's business practices and IT systems have expanded beyond the business-to-consumer (B2C) marketspace into the business-to-business (B2B) arena. It provides fulfillment and customer service functions for other organizations, has formed alliances with competitors and complementary service providers, and has addressed horizontal and backward integration. For example, Amazon has created a strategic alliance with Virgin Entertainment, a provider of entertainment content (Anonymous, 2002). Virginmega.com, powered by Amazon.com, provides users with news, reviews, and interviews plus information about Virgin Megastore locations and events. Amazon has an arrangement with Target.com, to oversee backend operations of fulfillment and customer service across all Target sites. In return, Target will pay both annual fixed fees and per-unit fees to Amazon (Prior, 2002). Amazon hired Excelon Corp. to build a private exchange with most of its suppliers (Konicki, 2000). Thus, Amazon is pursuing moves within the strategic target dimension by aligning itself with customers, suppliers, and competitors.

Dimension 4: Strategic Mode

Exploiting its first-mover advantage in the online marketspace, Amazon operated mostly in an offensive mode seeking competitive advantage in the early years. As Amazon's unique approach to retailing became more commonplace, it moved into new products and alliances as part of its quest for continued competitive advantage.

Dimension 5: Competitive IT Orientation

At its inception, Amazon had both an external and an internal competitive orientation. Externally, it emphasized building sales volume. Internally, it minimized costs through direct fulfillment of customer orders by publishers, and elimination of the need for brick-and-mortar stores. The emphasis upon both external and internal strategy has continued. Founder Jeff Bezos was quoted as saying that "we want to be the world's most customer-centric company, ... that we focus increasingly on trying to get the customer experience right. Within that, we want to build a place where people can come and discover anything they might want to buy online" (BusinessWeek, 1999).

Analysis

When Amazon.com is considered simultaneously with the other classic cases discussed here, substantial differences become apparent. Because Amazon emerged in the 1990s, it had the benefit of an existing body of knowledge concerning strategic IT systems. As a new company, its development efforts were not hindered by the need to integrate with existing legacy systems. The power of the Internet allowed Amazon to incorporate almost all categories in each of the five dimensions discussed here, and quickly gain competitive advantage. In the fast-paced Internet environment, first-mover advantage may be less effective if limited to a single dimension, because the competition can move quickly to copy any innovation. In such an environment, a new market entrant like Amazon does not have the luxury of time. "Because resources in e-commerce are immutable, imitators will erode any benefits accruing from a particular strategy or innovation unless new innovations are introduced. Amazon has been disrupting the status quo by developing new innovative ways to serve the customer online" (Mellahi & Johnson, 2000). Amazon.com's primary strategic resource emphasized both technology and information. Its comprehensive competitive strategy encompassed differentiation, cost, innovation, growth, and alliances. Although Amazon addressed all possible competitive strategies, it has consistently maintained a focus on one primary strategic target, the customer, relegating suppliers and competitors to secondary target status. The benefits (increased revenue at little expense) of adding suppliers and competitors to the system have been a welcome by-product of the emphasis upon serving the customer. As the competition copied Amazon's innovative ways and its competitive advantage was reduced, Amazon increased its product line and created alliances to better serve the online customer.

DISCUSSION

Comparison of the four classic cases presented here provides unique insights into the long-term characteristics of strategic information systems. In terms of *strategic resource*, whether an organization primarily exploits technology or information for strategic advantage is to some extent dependent upon historical technical context. Strategic initiatives begun during times when new technologies are spreading appear likely to leverage these technologies, and it is possible, if not likely, that the emergence of such technologies is in fact a trigger for the development of strategic information systems. American Airlines and American Hospital Supply initiated the strategic initiatives considered here at a time when online systems were emerging. Over time, the organizations involved became increasingly aware of the intelligence that these systems were providing, and they began to leverage information. Amazon.com followed a somewhat different approach. Although it began its strategic initiative by exploiting technology at a time when the Internet was an emerging technology, it also leveraged information, including using records of purchasing habits to "push" products through personalized Web pages and targeted email. If Amazon follows the pattern, then as its technology becomes more and more commonplace, it will, like American Airlines and American Hospital Supply before it, increasingly emphasize leveraging the information it gathers, information that is richer because of Amazon's growing network of alliances. While the American Airlines, AHSC, and Amazon initiatives were based in technological advances, the Cisco case discussed here originates during an era of stable technology, with the leveraging of information through an ERP system. Later, as the World Wide Web's competitive potential emerged, Cisco began leveraging this new technology. Overall, consideration of all four classic cases leads to the conclusion that technological advancement may be a primary trigger for many, or even most, strategic systems. When such advances are absent, a primary trigger must come from other arenas. In Cisco's case, this was a catastrophic corruption of its main database.

The cases considered here suggest that differentiation and cost are the *competitive strategies* for early strategic systems, while growth and alliances are more mature strategies. Innovation can be part of early strategies that support differentiation and cost or part of the more mature strategies of growth and alliance. American Airlines' initial competitive strategy was one of differentiation and innovation. After its innovation triggered process changes throughout the airline industry, its competitive strategy evolved into one of growth through alliances with other travel service providers. American Hospital

Supply's competitive strategy originally emphasized cost effectiveness, then innovation, and then as multiple competing systems evolved, matured to one of growth and alliances. Cisco's competitive strategy started with cost savings, and moved through innovation, supplemented by growth through acquisition. Amazon's competitive strategy began with a combination of innovation, cost, and differentiation. As the changes it brought to the bookselling industry spread, Amazon sought growth through alliances when it established relationships with both competitors and complementary service providers.

In all four of the classic cases discussed here, the customer is a major *strategic target*. For American Airlines, the customer has always been the target, although the nature of the customer has changed over time from travel agents to individuals. For American Hospital Supply, the goal has always been improving service to the customer. For Amazon.com, alliances with suppliers and competitors do not detract from the fact that at its base, Amazon is a retailer, with an overriding emphasis upon the customer relationship. Finally, Cisco, who began the strategic initiative discussed here with automation of its supply chain, ultimately developed its system to encompass the customer as a strategic target as well. Thus, it appears that while strategic systems may target suppliers or competitors, the most likely target, particularly over time, is customers.

In terms of *strategic mode*, organizations with the strongest market positions are most likely to develop offensive strategic systems, while those operating from weaker positions are most likely to develop defensive systems. Thus, we see that American Airlines' SABRE system was originally a defensive weapon against a biased reservation system controlled by a competitor. As SABRE terminals were installed in travel agencies, SABRE evolved into an offensive weapon. Amazon's systems began and remain offensive. When Amazon had the first mover advantage, its systems were primarily offensive. Over time as the technology became commonplace in the bookselling industry, Amazon expanded to include other products, and formed alliances, providing back-end operations for both competitors and purveyors of complementary products. Cisco's approximately 80 percent market share in routers and switches (Reinhardt, 1999) allows it to operate offensively in these marketplaces, but it is in a defensive position in the service provider market where it holds a much smaller share.

A consideration of *strategic orientation* demonstrates the impact of the Internet. When American Airlines, AHSC, and Cisco began the strategic initiatives discussed here, they were focused internally, on gaining control over inventory, order processing, and the like. Over time, the external focus in these systems increased. Amazon, on the other hand, began with both an internal and external focus. Not weighted down by the burden of their legacy systems, Amazon was able to create a unique infrastructure, which undoubtedly contributed to its ability to focus its strategic systems both internally and externally. This bi-directional focus also may be a result of the fact that the e-commerce marketspace, with its accelerated time-to-market for strategic systems, is cruel to single-dimensional organizations, and rewards those like Amazon, whose strategic initiatives are multi-dimensional and "morphing." Unlike the other cases studied here, Amazon strategic initiatives target multiple categories within the five dimensions of the framework. Amazon exploits both technology and information. It applies differentiation, innovation, and growth through alliances. It focuses on customers, suppliers, and competitors. And, it emphasizes building sales volume externally while minimizing costs internally. By competing in so many ways, Amazon has built an organization that is more difficult for competitors to attack. To the extent that Amazon is successful, it is likely to become a model for others in the future. The literature is full of accounts of organizations copying technology, and of organizations copying strategy from competitors in the same industry. However, relatively little notice has been given to the extent that organizations copy IT strategy from other organizations in unrelated industries. If Amazon is successful in evading aggressive competitors by constantly "morphing" across many facets of each of the five dimensions, then its strategy is likely to be copied, just as AHSC did with American Airlines.

CONCLUSION

Strategic systems face inevitable changes in their external environment. They are affected by both changes in their competitive marketplace and advances in technology. To maintain their competitive advantage, strategic systems must evolve, significantly changing in at least one of their five dimensions. The classic systems analyzed here demonstrate that organizations maintain strategic advantage over extended time periods by moving across boundaries within the framework of the Five Dimensions of IT Strategy. Thus, the five dimensional framework proposed here can help organizations identify opportunities to develop existing strategic systems in new directions, allowing them to better address changes in the competitive marketplace and/or technology and extend the period of strategic benefit.

Perhaps most importantly, the classic cases analyzed here support the hypothesis that the five-dimensional framework could be used by organizations to balance risk in their strategic IT portfolios. Such a balanced portfolio would have a broad spread of strategic systems. Some of an organization's strategic systems would leverage technology, while others would leverage information. Some would be aimed at relationships with customers, while others would be aimed at relationships with suppliers or competitors. Some would be aimed at achieving competitive advantage, while others would be aimed at reducing competitors' real or potential strategic advantages. Some would be aimed at the external marketplace, while others would be aimed at improving internal

Copyright © 2003, Idea Group Inc. Copying or distributing in print or electronic forms without written permission of Idea Group Inc. is prohibited.

processing efficiency. Finally, some might rely on differentiation, and others on cost, innovation, growth, or alliances. When an organization's total strategic portfolio is balanced with respect to these five dimensions, its marketplace position is less vulnerable to strategic competitive risk. The framework presented here enables organizations to identify areas where they are most open to an aggressive competitor's move. Further, it reveals the vulnerabilities that come from clustering strategic initiatives, emphasizing one or two approaches, while ignoring others. When an organization's strategic systems have the same or similar profiles on the five dimensions of the framework presented here, then that organization's strategic IT portfolio is particularly susceptible to competitors' moves. An organization can use the five dimensional framework to diversify its portfolio of strategic IT systems, thus minimizing risk.

The practical applications of this research are three-fold. First, this research integrates prior research on strategic initiatives into a single comprehensive framework for use in identifying strategic opportunities. Second, this research proposes that this framework can be used to extend systems' strategic potency. Third, and most significantly, this research suggests that balancing risk in the total IT project portfolio (McFarlan, 1981), while important, is insufficient, and that organizations should also balance the risk in their strategic IT systems portfolios. In addition to identifying opportunities to extend the strategic lifespan of IT systems, the framework specified by this research can also be used to identify and control exposure to strategic IT risk.

REFERENCES

Anonymous (2002). Virgin Entertainment Group and Amazon.com Announce Strategic Alliance, published June 24, 2002. Retrieved on June 28, 2002 from:http://hoovnews.hoovers.com/fp.asp?layout=displaynews&doc_id=NR20020624290.2_725c0050aa9d36d6&ticker=AMZN&l=ticker_news&sym=AMZN&s=21.

Ansley, M. (2000). Virtual Manufacturing. *CMA Management* 74(1), 31-35.

Bakos, J. Y., & Treacy, M. E. (1986). Information Technology and Corporate Strategy: A Research Perspective. *MIS Quarterly* 10(2), 107-119.

Benjamin, R. I., Rockart, J. R., Scott Morton, M. S. & Wyman, J. (1984). Information Technology: A Strategic Opportunity. *Sloan Management Review* 25(5), 3-10.

BusinessWeek (1999). Q&A: Jeff Bezos: Amazon.com (the pioneer of online selling) says that eBay doesn't have to lose for Amazon to win. *Business Week* 3631, 137-141.

Clemons, E. K. (1999). Risk Watch. CIO Magazine 12(21), 38-43. Retrieved on October 5, 2001 from: http://www.cio.com/archive/081599/expert_content.html.

Fryxell, D. A. (1996). eaasySABRE. *Link-Up* 13(3), 10-11.

Grant, D. (2002). A wider view of business process reengineering: technology alone does not enable organizational change. *Communications of the ACM,* 45(2), 85-91.

Hayes, F. (1999). Amazoned! *Computerworld* 33(20), 116.

Hopper, M. D. (1990). Rattling SABRE - New Ways to Compete on Information. *Harvard Business Review* 68(3), 118-125.

King, W. R., Grover, V., & Hufnagel, E. H. (1989). Using Information and Information Technology for Sustainable Competitive Advantage: Some Empirical Evidence. *Information & Management* 17(2), 87-93.

Knight, L.V., White, J.D., & Steinbach, T.A. (2002). Five Dimensions of IT Strategy: A Framework for Minimizing Risk and Extending Strategic Impact. *Issues and Trends of Information Technology Management in Contemporary Organizations: Information Resources Management Association International Conference,* pp. 1018-1020.

Konicki, S. (2000). Amazon taps Excelon to redo supply-chain system. *Informationweek* 26(810), 26.

Leininger, K. E. (1992). Open Systems Slam the Door on the Days of Competitive Advantage by IT Alone. *Chief Information Officer Journal* 5(1), 47-50.

Mata, F. J., Fuerst, W. L., & Barney, J. B. (1995). Information Technology and Sustained Competitive Advantage: A Resource-based Analysis. *MIS Quarterly* 19(4), 487-504.

McFarlan, F. W. (1981). Portfolio Approach to Information Systems. *Harvard Business Review* 59(5), 142-150.

Mellahi, K. & Johnson, M. (2000). Does it pay to be a first mover in e.commerce? The case of Amazon.com. *Management Decision* 38(7), 445-452.

Miller, W. H. (1999). Airlines Take to the Internet, published August 16, 1999. Retrieved on June 28, 2002 from: http://www.industryweek.com/CurrentArticles/asp/articles.asp?ArticleID=598.

Neo, B. S. (1988). Factors Facilitating the Use of Information Technology for Competitive Advantage: An Exploratory Study. *Information & Management* 15, 191-201.

Nolan, R. L. (2001a). Cisco Systems Architecture: ERP and Web-enabled IT. Harvard Business School 9-301-099.

Nolan, R. L. (2001b). Cisco Systems: Building Leading Internet Capabilities. Harvard Business School 9-301-133.

NUA. (2002). Internet Surveys: Record Traffic for Travel Sites, published February 12, 2002. Retrieved on July 18, 2002 from: http://nua.ie/surveys/index.cgi?f=VS&art_id=905357653&rel=true.

Porter, M. E. (1980). *Competitive Strategy.* New York: Free Press.

Porter, M. E., & Millar, V. E. (1985). How Information Gives You Competitive Advantage. *Harvard Business Review* 63(4), 149-160.

Prior, M. (2002). Amazon alliance could put Web sales on the map. *DSN Retailing Today* 41(7), 50, 76.

Rackoff, N., Wiseman, C., & Ullrich, W. A. (1985). Information Systems for Competitive Advantage: Implementation of a Planning Process. *MIS Quarterly* 9(4), 285-294.

Reinhardt, A. (1999, September 13). Mr. Internet. *BusinessWeek* 3646, 128-140.

Short, J. E. & Venkatraman, N. (1992). Beyond business process redesign: Redefining Baxter's business network. *Sloan Management Review* (Fall): 7-21.

White, J. D. (2000). Dissertation proposal: Why bad things happen to good systems; Proposal for research into key elements responsible for accidents during the maintenance and operation phases of strategic information systems. DePaul University School of Computer Science, Telecommunications and Information Systems.

Wingfield, N. (2002, March 15). Amazon finds partners Toys 'R' Us, Expedia, Hotwire are growing restless. *Wall Street Journal*.

Wiseman, C. (1988). Attack & counterattack: The new game in information technology. *Planning Review* (September/October): 6-12

Wiseman, C., & MacMillan, I. C. (1984). Creating Competitive Weapons from Information Systems. *Journal of Business Strategy* 5(2), 42-49.

Chapter VIII

Partnering for Success in Application Service Provision

D. E. Sofiane Tebboune
Brunel University, UK

Philip Seltsikas
University of Surrey, UK

ABSTRACT

Application Service Provision (ASP), which consists of deploying, managing and remotely hosting software applications through centrally located servers, is emerging as a new form of application outsourcing that is attractive to many sectors. This chapter shows that the concept of strategic alliances is highly relevant to the ASP model. The chapter illustrates this with two cases, one of which was a failure because of inappropriate partnership management. The authors highlight the importance of focusing on the management of alliances instead of how to form them, by presenting a life cycle approach to alliances. The chapter also relates the immaturity of the ASP market to the difficulty in measuring the success of strategic alliances formed in this context. This chapter concludes by presenting predictions about the future of ASP.

INTRODUCTION

In recent years, more and more companies have entered into relationships through alliances. Corporations have often adopted structures that were large and centralised and based on hierarchical modes of communication. Such corporations used various methods for eliminating competitors, such as, mergers, price wars, and the weight of large advertising budgets (Alter & Hage, 1993). For several reasons, such as the pressure for the globalisation of business, organizations began focusing more on cooperating with others. In this context, Alter & Hage (1993, p. 2) argued that *"...many companies are developing structures that are smaller, decentralized, and based on strategies of cooperation and horizontal relationships."* Moreover, such relationships developed between organizations in the same product market niche, which led previously competing companies to collaborate, thus marking an important institutional change (Alter & Hage, 1993).

Developing alliances, *as a strategy*, has been adopted by organizations in different sectors, which have aimed to differentiate their products or enter markets more quickly. Application Service Provision, which is still in a developing stage, is a field in which strategies of partnering and forming alliances are commonplace. As the new wave of delivering software as a service began to take off, many companies tried to exploit the opportunity of entering this embryonic market, which led to an excessive number of competitors. As a result, these companies found difficulties in making profits, and therefore adding value to their offering became indispensable. Many entered into strategic alliances as *leverage* for their business.

This chapter aims to investigate strategic alliances in the context of the Application Service Provision (ASP) model. It investigates the ASP market and its development, and the role of alliances in the context of the ASP model using illustrative cases. The chapter provides a background drawn from the literature on strategic alliances and discusses the formation and management of alliances. Issues relevant to the development of the ASP market through strategic alliances are presented.

BACKGROUND

The Application Service Provision Model

Application Service Providers (ASPs) have created a new form of outsourcing that can be seen as 'application outsourcing' (Cherry Tree & Co., 1999). In its simplest form the model consists of deploying, managing and remotely hosting software applications through centrally located servers (Cherry Tree & Co., 1999). Customers use the hosted applications through a 'rental' arrangement (see Figure 1). This model represents a very new approach to software distribution and effectively results in the delivery of software as a *service*.

Figure 1: The basic ASP model (Source: Cherry Tree & Co., 1999, p. 3)

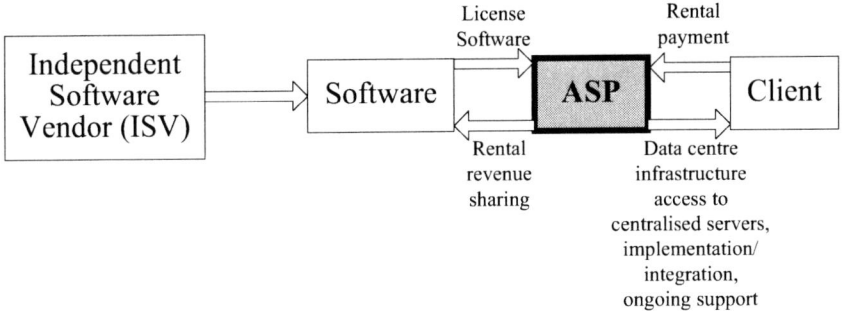

According to the ASP Industry Consortium (ASPIC), an ASP *"manages and delivers application capabilities to multiple entities from a data centre across a wide area network"* (cited in Cherry Tree & Co., 1999). As a result, the ASP model gives organizations the opportunity to focus on their core functions, without being distracted by issues such as systems management (Columbus, 2000).

There have been many stimuli to the emergence of the ASP model. Most notably, the small and medium sized enterprise (SME) segment of the market was virtually excluded from the enterprise applications market, largely due to their inability to afford them.

The ASP model offers SMEs the possibility of leveraging these costs because of the economies of scale that ASP vendors can enjoy. In fact, based on the principle of *one-to-many*, the ASP model is believed to create enormous cost savings of the order of 20% to 50% (Miley, 2000). Furthermore, Miley (ibid.) argued that the *ubiquity* of the Internet, its integral and open standards, and the devaluation of computers led this media – the Internet – to revolutionise business practices, and delivering applications through the Internet is only a *"natural"*.

Other *drivers* of the ASP model are as follows (Cherry Tree & Co., 1999):
- The shortage of IT experts, where some companies, especially the smaller, cannot afford to pay for IT experts on a long-term basis. ASPs offer access to skilled personnel at minimum cost;
- Improvement in application deployment time, reducing it from months to days or weeks;
- Access to latest technology and software;
- Minimising the total cost of ownership (TCO) of applications, as fixed costs shift from application users to the ASPs;
- More focus on core competencies, by eliminating non-core functions.

The size of the ASP market, as forecast by many analysts, is also an important sign of the importance of this business model. IDC, for instance, expected the market to grow from US$ 300 million in 1999, to US$ 25 billion in 2004 (cited in Miley, 2000). Furthermore, IDC expect US enterprise ASP spending alone to grow to US$ 2.5 billion by 2004. Even if the ASP market is in continuous expansion, many issues still form a strong barrier to its development. Such issues are as follows:

- Security is a main concern for prospective customers causing ASP uptake to suffer. In fact the uncertainty of whether ASPs are capable of ensuring the security of proprietary information is emerging as a major factor inhibiting the deployment of the ASP business model. This issue is intensified when *mission critical* applications are to be supplied.
- Performance concerns, where many analysts argue that deploying existing applications, based on client/server architecture, on an ASP delivery presents significant degradation in performance, as these applications were not designed to be 'hosted'. Instead, Web-enabled applications of suitable architecture can ensure optimal performance.

The original ASP model (see Figure 1) presented many weaknesses. The model suffered lack of *product differentiation* (Porter, 1985), as different ASP

Figure 2: Competitive forces for the ASP market initially (Adapted from Porter, 1985)

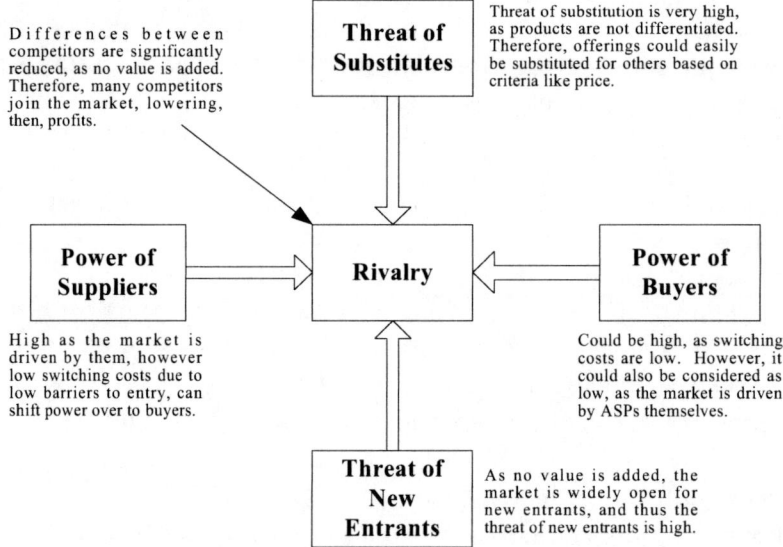

vendors focused mainly on hosting applications. In fact, the similarity of offerings in the marketplace was fuelled by low entry barriers (Cherry Tree & Co., 2000) and caused an explosion of similar services. According to the competitive forces model, illustrated in Figure 2, it should be noticed that the ASP market is highly accessible, as entry barriers are low. This left the market wide-open to new entrants. The high number of competitors made *profit* a difficult target to achieve. Consequently, many players in the ASP market felt the need for *differentiating* their product(s): *"...in order to build a sustainable company, additional value-added components need to be offered in order to build long-term, strategic relationships with customers"* (Cherry Tree & Co., 2000, p. 7). Thus, for ASPs, simply hosting and managing applications did, in general, not provide sustainable strategies. Instead, *"companies that ultimately build sustainable ASP related businesses will also offer a value-added component(s) to their service that is simultaneously difficult for competitors to replicate and customers to replace"* (Cherry Tree & Co., 2000, p. 8).

Moreover, the ASP market witnessed major changes with the emergence of different variations of the initial concept, classified as (Cherry Tree & Co., 2000; Currie & Seltsikas, 2000; Lehman Brothers, 2000): ***Enterprise ASPs*** where ISVs deployed their own ASP strategy, choosing to offer their services directly to their customers, accessing thus a wider segment; ***ASP Enablers*** who support the infrastructure through which ASPs deliver their offerings; ***Pure Play ASPs*** characterised by owning their delivered resources, and acting as a single point taking responsibility of all the requirements for delivering their resources; ***Vertical ASPs***, targeting industry-specific applications and processes; ***Horizontal ASPs*** offering, mainly, collaborative applications such as email; and ***Full Service Providers (FSP)*** providing an end-to-end solution.

The variations cited above are significantly supported by the focus on leveraging partnerships to create differentiation, and thus raising barriers to entry (Columbus, 2000). Alliances are developed for the benefit of two partners or more. These benefits consist of acquiring skills and resources that are unlikely to be developed by a single organization. Thus, the formation of a strategic alliance can be an important enabler for creating a differentiated product or service.

In general, we argue that the poor take-up of the ASP model has been aggravated by the lack of differentiated product offerings. To overcome this lacuna, many ASPs have entered into a set of partnerships and alliances that allow them to acquire additional skills and resources for differentiating themselves. Columbus (2000, p. 171) argued: *"In the business plans of many application service providers today there is a strong focus on leveraging partnerships to create differentiation."* However, as different ASPs have different backgrounds, and thus different skills, they need to partner with companies with different skills in order to bring additional resources, where according to Columbus (2000, p. 171): *"Many ASPs today are partnering for access to technology, while many others with strong technical expertise are partnering to get access to distribution channels."*

Partnerships are also becoming an important part of an ASP's strategy as the ASP market grows, where, according to Columbus (2000), customers' expectations concerning an ASPs performance will grow, and therefore partnerships will be increasingly adopted in order to ensure the highest level of *performance*. However, such achievements cannot be guaranteed, as partnering has to be successful in order to bring advantages. Gartner Group (2001) forecast that 60% of ASPs created before 2001 will fail due to poorly developed business models, the **wrong choice of partners**, an inability to execute high levels of service, and consolidation in the ASP market. This is indicative of recent progress in the ASP industry. What is emerging is an understanding (that is demonstrated in successful ASPs) that partnering issues are among the most important to the success of ASP.

Consequently, issues such as *choice* of partners and the *management* of alliances will play a major role in the on-going success of an ASP. As organizations from different sectors have deployed strategic alliances for many decades, the literature in this area could be a valuable source of information regarding the success and failure factors for alliance formation and management. Frameworks such as the *alliances life cycle*, discussed in the next section (see Figure 3), could be of major use for alliance management.

Currently, the ASP market is full of both successful and unsuccessful alliances. We believe that the cases of Cable & Wireless a-Services and Pandesic are good illustrations of, respectively, successful and unsuccessful ASP partnering arrangements. Both cases implemented a full service provider strategy and although both have now failed and cease to operate in the market, the Cable & Wireless a-Services case demonstrates a number of successful characteristics.

Case Study: Cable & Wireless a-Services

Cable & Wireless, a telecommunication company, started in the late 1990s to expand its offering to exploit the Internet. It offered Internet access as an ISP and Web hosting provider. A further enlargement of its strategy led the company to enter the world of Application Service Provision. Cable & Wireless set up a wholly owned subsidiary, *"a-Services"*, to manage its ASP offerings. In November 1999, Cable & Wireless announced a plan to form a global relationship with the Compaq Computer Corporation, and planned to commit a total of US$500 million for the relationship during a period of five years, with Compaq sharing revenues and providing a traditional supplier contract. According to Cable & Wireless (Cable & Wireless Press Release: http://www.cw.com), this relationship would position them as a leading application service provider, targeting small and medium sized enterprises (SMEs), to provide them with complete end-to-end e-business solutions.

Starting from the relationship with Compaq, the objectives of Cable & Wireless a-Services were to offer a complete end-to-end integrated solution including application hosting, network connectivity, and e-Business consulting (Cable & Wireless Press Release: http://www.cw.com). The next major step that Cable & Wireless a-Services achieved was its strategic alliance with Microsoft in June 2000. Within this relationship, Microsoft provides *"marketing, product and support professionals as well as making available the facilities and staff of the Microsoft Partner Solutions Center (MPSC) labs for development of future services, products and testing"* (ibid). By doing so, Cable & Wireless a-Services based a range of new services on the Windows platform, featuring initially Microsoft Windows 2000, Microsoft Office 2000, and Microsoft Exchange with integrated messaging and collaboration tools.

In May 2001, following the implementation of the first phases of its ASP strategy, Cable & Wireless acquired Digital Island, a leading provider of managed Internet services for business customers. Digital Island supplies integrated managed hosting, content delivery and intelligent network services. This enhanced Cable & Wireless' capabilities. Digital Island planned to add new services to those offered by Cable & Wireless a-Services such as 'content delivery'. Through this partnership, Cable & Wireless' hosting capabilities were increased with an additional nine hosting centres worldwide (previously managed by Digital Island). The Digital Island deal also gave Cable & Wireless access to a very strong customer base (including Microsoft, Cisco, and Sony).

The general aim of Cable & Wireless a-Services was to evolve to being a Full Service Provider (FSP). Unfortunately, a-Services faced many problems in attracting customers, and as a result a-Services was closed in November 2001 (Crn, 19/11/2001). Although a-Services cannot now be considered among successful ASPs, the formation of a strategic alliance through the aggregation of resources from best of breed suppliers is of interest. The case provides a good example of how ASPs can complement their skills through partnering and acquisition. These are skills that are not found internally but are critical to the development of the business. However, the case also highlights that being backed by strong partners does not necessarily lead to success.

Case Study: Pandesic

Pandesic was an ASP that specialised in Business-to-Consumer e-Commerce. The company was launched in 1997 as a joint venture between Intel and SAP. Pandesic was launched during the golden era of the dot.com explosion, when there were tremendous expectations about profits that could be realised. As its main strategy, Pandesic focused on enabling the emerging e-tailers and retailers that wanted to have fast access to the dot-com market. The investment community had high expectations of Pandesic, however it has been an important illustration of a failure in the ASP industry. When it announced its closure, it had recorded estimated losses of around US$ 20 million per year. The causes of such a failure were not clear, and many analysts (such as IDC) remained confused. It was clear however that its founders – Intel and SAP – were deeply involved.

Pandesic specialised in Business-to-Consumer e-Commerce but started by targeting SAP's existing customers. These were mainly large corporations that were not interested in the consumer-oriented services that Pandesic offered. According to IDC, Pandesic did make attempts to shift its strategy toward Business-to-Business opportunities. With hindsight, Pandesic's failure appears to be strongly linked to its 'inappropriate' strategy, but most notable is that Intel and SAP occupied all six board seats at Pandesic (IDC). As a result (ibid.), blame for Pandesic's failure was directed to both parents – Intel and SAP. The parents were accused of playing a *"laissez-faire"* role, and doing very little to help Pandesic to develop and update its strategy. What was needed was a shift to more profitable Business-to-Business e-Commerce. Whilst Pandesic did not enter into a typical strategic alliance, the case illustrates that significant failures can result from poor partnership management.

Strategic Alliances

Mockler (1999, p. 1) defines strategic alliances as *"associations important to alliance partners and formed to further their common interests."* This is a situation where two companies or more forge an agreement to leverage combined resources, knowledge, and capabilities in order to achieve, enhance, or maintain competitive advantage for each participant (Clarke-Hill, Robinson, & Bailey, 1998; Spekman, Forbes, Isabella, & MacAvoy, 1998). Strategic alliances can be found in different forms (Mockler, 1999): franchising and licensing agreements, partnership contracts, equity investments in new or existing joint ventures and consortia.

The reasons why strategic alliances are formed are several; a common view is that *"firms need to concentrate on core competencies, to outsource more activities and use outside partners as sources of complementary knowledge and competence"* (Nooteboom, 1999, p. 43). Furthermore, strategic alliances are a way of establishing a set of enablers that help companies penetrate or expand in new or existing markets (Mockler, 1999). Child & Faulkner (1998) also identified two rationales for cooperative strategies, being: learning, where each partner having a weakness in a certain area cooperate in order to learn from the other partner; and skill substitution, where the area in which a partner is weak, is taken over by the other partner. Moreover, Nooteboom (1999) identified a variety of additional purposes served by alliances including the spread of fixed costs, circumvention of entry barriers, and speed to market.

As a general classification, Lorange and Roos (1993) suggested two types of alliances: offensive alliances and defensive alliances. The former category has as objectives, creating or penetrating new markets, or defining or setting new standards. In this case, companies form alliances in order to strengthen themselves for an offensive action. The second category – defensive alliances – has as objectives strengthening and protecting existing positions of partners.

The development of strategic alliances, and the increasing interest in them, has been enormous in recent years, due to many drivers such as globalisation, the increase in competition, and shortening product life cycles (Büchel, 2000; Hwang & Burgers, 1997; Sulej, 1998). Globalisation is one of the major drivers; as organizations aim to globalise their businesses, the scopes of their projects increase, and therefore the development of strategic alliances becomes very important in order to spread the risks involved (Sulej, 1998), or to use them as a source of learning (Child & Faulkner, 1998; Inkpen, 2000). The rapid development of technology is also an important driver for the adoption of strategic alliances (Sulej, 1998). As technology is developing at a rapid pace, organizations are unable to provide all the resources and skills necessary for their business. Therefore strategic alliances have gained high importance as a solution for gaining access to skills and knowledge (Büchel, 2000; Child & Faulkner, 1998).

Partnerships and strategic alliances are very important for the development of today's businesses in creating value for all partners. Spekman et al. (1998, p. 758) argued: *"Value is created through synergy as the partners achieve mutually beneficial gains that neither would have been able to achieve individually."*

However, even if the concept of strategic alliances seems to bring many benefits, it is still argued that *cooperation* between organizations could be difficult to manage. On this, Mockler (1999, p. 6) argued: *"The essential concept of sharing control and management on a continuing basis is what makes managing strategic alliances such a critical, difficult and demanding task."* As a result, many failures of alliances in different industries were recorded, which led research interest to shift to focus alliances *management*. In fact, as the rate of failures climbed significantly, it became clear that the success of a given alliance is not only limited to the choice of the right partners, but also to the right management that is practiced after the formation phase. In this context, some research attempted to investigate the whole lifecycle of alliances, as a means of analysing the development and management of an alliance. Spekman et al. (1998), for instance, described the life cycle of an alliance as containing seven stages, as illustrated in Figure 3. It is however difficult to separate these stages because of the difficulty in establishing when each stage begins or ends (Spekman et al., 1998). The diagram illustrated in Figure 3 describes the key activities involved in the lifecycle of an alliance.

Figure 3: Alliances life cycle (Adapted from Spekman et al., 1998)

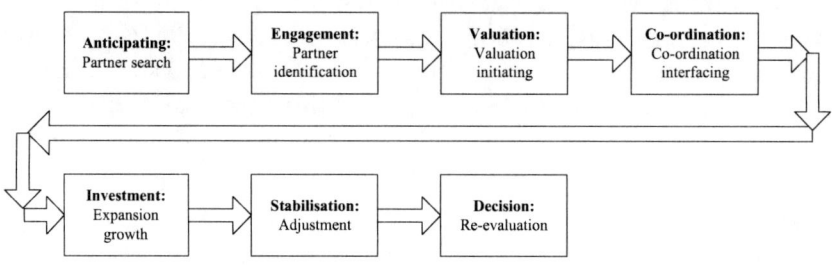

- *Anticipating:* at this stage, the organization starts considering the need for an alliance;
- *Engagement:* in the next stage, having identified the partner, the different partners start building their mutual expectations from the alliance;
- *Valuation:* at this stage, each partner in the alliance starts valuing the different assets and resources offered by the other. During this stage, terms and conditions are defined, contribution of each partner is evaluated, and the benefits are identified;
- *Co-ordinating:* at this stage, the partners involved in the alliance start collaborating. According to Spekman et al. (1998, p. 762), the focus during this stage is on *"the integration/co-ordination of complementary business activities so that the alliance can leverage the anticipated gains derived from the alliance."*
- *Investment:* during this stage, investment from partners is achieved for the future development of the alliance. It is at this stage that *"assets are formally committed and resources are dedicated to the alliance's mission"* (Spekman et al., 1998, p. 762)
- *Stabilisation:* this is the maturing stage of the alliance. At this step, the alliance is already put to work, and therefore measurement and comparison of the objectives initially stated against the performance currently delivered, are possible;
- *Decision:* finally, this stage concerns the re-evaluation of the alliance, and thus the decision of whether to keep the current situation with the current partners, or to plan future changes.

MAIN THRUST OF THE CHAPTER

As mentioned above, Gartner Group (2001) predicted that a poor choice of partners is one of the main causes of failure (and imminent failure) for many

ASPs. According to the alliances life cycle diagram in Figure 3, this problem fits in the very early stage of the life cycle – *'anticipating'* stage – which concerns the formation stage of the alliance. However, for many ASPs the substantive issues are more about *managing* alliances than about forming them. The objective should be the achievement of a successful partnership that can be effectively managed. According to Figure 3, in order for an alliance to be successful it should progress successfully through all the seven stages described. Moreover, the success is further enhanced if the *'decision'* stage closes the loop and goes back to the *'anticipating'* stage. In this case, the partnering firms decide that the alliance is still needed, and is still seen as successful.

However, it is very unlikely that partners' objectives stay static during the life of the alliance, where Spekman et al. (1998, p. 766) argue that *"partners' strategic intent is likely to change over time and the objectives and expectations that guide early stage alliances are very much likely to differ in later stage alliances."* As a result, the assessment and measurement of the success of any given alliance becomes a hard task to achieve. This is especially true in the context of the ASP model. The *highly dynamic* character of the ASP model makes the strategic intent of partners difficult to predict. Pandesic suffered precisely this problem, as the strategic intent of the joint venture changed over time, and what the company was offering became inappropriate for the target market. Thus the joint venture had to shift its strategy. Being unable to do so, Pandesic failed as a result of inappropriate partnership management of its the parents – Intel and SAP.

Such dynamics of the ASP model could be due to its immaturity. Neither service providers nor customers are certain about the appropriate (successful) elements and drivers of the model. Thus, at a more mature stage, the model may become more stable, with better-predicted strategic intents. Such stabilisation would certainly lead to a better base for assessing partnership success.

At present, cases of alliances in the ASP market that are considered successful do exist such as in the case of Cable & Wireless' a-Services cited earlier, even if their business model, as a whole, was not successful. In such cases, the life cycle approach, as described in Figure 3, is appropriate. By examining each stage of how the alliance is managed and how it is considered by the partnering firms, or why it is considered to be successful, a good mix of success criteria is demonstrated.

FUTURE TRENDS

Strategic alliances in the ASP model are a key part of the strategy. With current developments in the industry, it is inconceivable that a single company could perform well in all of the activities required by this new business model. A major prediction that researchers and practitioners in the ASP field increasingly share is that the ASP market will go through major consolidation. Jaruzelski, Ribeiro, & Lake (2000) predicted that, because ASPs will find difficulties in making profit and differentiating their offerings, the ASP market will see two major trends: **Consolidation**, taking place mainly between ISVs and ASPs with infrastructure. According to Jaruzelski et al. (2000), ASPs with infrastructure are the best positioned to gain success in the market, as they can offer customers one-stop-shopping from multiple vendors, and as they have the required technical skills. Furthermore, it will be difficult for such ASPs to develop the appropriate economy of scale needed for covering their infrastructure, a major consolidation will take place in this fragmented market; and *Verticalisation*, where as seen above in the description of the different variations of ASPs, vertical ASPs have a strong focus on offering differentiation, by developing appropriate skills for a precise vertical market. This could become a major differentiator between different players, helping them, thus, to raise barriers to entry.

The validity of these predictions is still uncertain. The market is still maturing and is highly dynamic. However, it is becoming clear that strategic alliances are critical, as large-scale aggregation of skills and resources is necessary for the successful functioning of an ASP business.

CONCLUSION

The ASP market is still in an embryonic stage. This could be less attractive from a customer's perspective. However, we argued that the future of the ASP market is likely to be positive, where the delivery of applications *as a service* will form a major means of software distribution (Jaruzelski et al., 2000).

This chapter has attempted to forge a link between strategic alliances and the ASP business model. It has shown how important strategic alliances are for the development and sustainability of such a model. Two case studies were included in order to illustrate the importance of partnering for the success of the ASP model.

This chapter has also investigated the life cycle of alliances, and has developed understanding of the different phases through which an alliance evolves. When applied to the ASP model, this view showed how difficult it is to assess and measure the success of a given alliance, due to the dynamics of this model.

This has essentially been a discussion chapter about partnering issues in ASP. Further research could develop a more critical approach in order to produce frameworks and guidelines for the effective development and management of alliances that ASPs could employ.

REFERENCES

Alter, C., & Hage, J. (1993). *Organizations Working Together* (191). London: Sage.

Büchel, B. (2000). Framework of Joint Venture Development: Theory-Building through Qualitative Research. *Journal of Management Studies, 37*(5), 637-661.

Cherry Tree & Co. (1999). *Application Service Providers*. Cherry Tree & Co. Retrieved October, 2000, from the World Wide Web: http://www.cherrytreeco.com/current/res_rep.htm.

Cherry Tree & Co. (2000). *2nd Generation ASPs*. Retrieved October, 2000, from the World Wide Web: http://www.cherrytreeco.com/current/res_rep.htm.

Child, J., & Faulkner, D. (1998). *Strategies of Co-operation: Managing Alliances, Networks, and Joint Ventures*. New York: Oxford University Press.

Clarke-Hill, C. M., Robinson, T. M., & Bailey, J. (1998). Skills and Competence Transfers in European Retail Alliances: A Comparison between Alliances and Joint Ventures. *European Business Review, 98*(6), 300-310.

Columbus, L. (2000). *Realizing e-Business with Application Service Provision*: Sams.

Currie, W. L., & Seltsikas, P. (2000). Evaluating the Application Service (ASP) Provider Business Model. *Executive Publication Series (Brunel University), CSIS2000/004*.

Gartner Group. (2001). *Sanity Check on the ASP Opportunity*. Retrieved November 2001, from the World Wide Web: http://www.gartner.com.

Hwang, P., & Burgers, W. P. (1997). The Many Faces of Multi-Firm Alliances. *California Management Review, 39*(3), 101-117.

Inkpen, A. C. (2000). Learning through Joint Ventures: A Framework of Knowledge Acquisition. *Journal of Management Studies, 37*(7), 1019-1043.

Jaruzelski, B., Ribeiro, F., & Lake, R. (2000). *ASP 101: Understanding the Application Service Provider Model*. Booz.Allen & Hamilton. Retrieved, from the World Wide Web: http://www.bah.com.

Lehman Brothers. (2000). *Servers in the Sky: The Application Service Provider*. Retrieved April, 2001, from the World Wide Web: http://www.lehman.com.

Lorange, P., & Roos, J. (1993). *Strategic Alliances: Formation, Implementation and Evolution*. Oxford: Blackwell Publishers.

Miley, M. (2000). Reinventing Business: Application Service Providers. *Oracle Magazine*, November/December, 48-52.

Mockler, R. J. (1999). *Multinational Strategic Alliances*. Chichester: Wiley.

Nooteboom, B. (1999). *Inter-Firm Alliances: Analysis and Design*. London: Routledge.

Porter, M. E. (1985). *Competitive Advantage: Creating and Sustaining Superior Performance*. London: Macmillan.

Spekman, R. E., Forbes, T. M., Isabella, L. A., & MacAvoy, T. C. (1998). Alliance Management: A View from the Past and a Look to the Future. *Journal of Management Studies, 35*(6), 747-772.

Sulej, J. C. (1998). UK International Equity Joint Ventures in Technology and Innovation: an Analysis of Patterns of Activity and Distribution. *European Business Review, 98*(1), 56-66.

Chapter IX

The Resource-Based Theory of the Firm: The New Paradigm for Information Resources Management?

Kalle Kangas
Turku School of Economics and Business Administration, Finland

ABSTRACT

This chapter explores the theoretical foundations of the digital economy. In doing that, it first discusses micro-economics – actually the eight main theories of the 20th century firm. A reasoning, through a literary review, is presented, which shows that no other theory of firm explored provides a suitable background for the digital economy, except the resource-based view of the firm. Starting from this finding, the paper further explores the strategic formulations based on the resource-based view of the firm, as well as its implications to organizational learning and competitive advantage created by information resources management. The conclusions suggest that the resource-based view of the firm, and its implications to strategic management and information resources management, form a solid base for further studies on the foundations of the digital economy. Therefore, the paper suggests that studies of the digital economy could be more fruitful, when studied under the premises of the resource-based theory, than any other modern theory of the firm.

Copyright © 2003, Idea Group Inc. Copying or distributing in print or electronic forms without written permission of Idea Group Inc. is prohibited.

INTRODUCTION

The overall change in the world business environment is a very radical one, arising from three phenomena: networking of organizations and their information systems, increasing utilization of market mechanisms in mutual transactions, and a global emphasis on business operations. The organizational structures of enterprises have become flatter, and the barriers among them lower. Companies have started to resemble chasms of interrelated corporate functions that involve, however, deformed structures. In those structures, each new function is introduced in the form of a patch, and added to the structure – brikolage, as Ciborra (1998) calls it. Business organizations have to decide where to collaborate and where to compete, as well as which parts of their business are fundamental – or *core*.

Turning now to the organization context, businesses – particularly in competitive, more market-driven environments – need to manage their resources efficiently and effectively. This is particularly true for information resources. 'Information Resources Management' (IRM), i.e., the design, implementation, management and control of information resources (Reponen et al., 1995; Kangas, 1997), becomes a vital means for business transactions in companies where products and communication become "informated" (Zuboff, 1988). Operators in the international market often perform occasional, one-time transactions through electronic devices with their business partners. In today's digital economy, extensions of the traditional intra-firm value chain (Porter, 1985) concept are emerging. These value chains could be described as customer-centered "wheels of fortune" chains that happen more by coincidence than by plan or design. This means that there is a need to build a one-time value chain for almost every transaction. This chain is ephemeral, and dissolves after the transaction has been conducted.

The traditional value chain and industry cluster analysis (Porter, 1985), as well as most other recent firm theory approaches, appears to be obsolete in the new information economy. Also, the discussion about centralization and decentralization seems to be purely academic, and has no practical value in the new economy.

At the beginning of the 1990s, the convention was to align information systems to the corporation's overall business strategy. However, in a networked organizational structure, a streamlined alignment would seem a difficult task. Moreover, too much streamlining and standardizing tended to lead to the loss of innovation, and to predictable management concepts. Predictability is seldom a good source of competitive advantage, because predictable – even though successful – firm behavior can be imitated easily, allowing other firms to obtain the same competitive edge.

It is, nonetheless, important to understand how firms create and sustain competitive advantage in today's digital economy. New methods of competitive analysis and competence-building must be found. Promising approaches in this regard include:
1) The resource-based theory of the firm and its implications for strategic management;
2) The relationship between organizational learning and competitive advantage; and
3) The role of information technology in these endeavors.

This study explores whether these approaches also can be applied to areas of mobile business and e-commerce and, more commonly, to the digital economy.

SOME NOTIONS FROM THE MICRO-ECONOMIC THEORY

It can be claimed that any theoretical discussion concerning strategy is based on some theory of the firm. There are several economic theories of the firm guiding strategy research. All the theories try to address two basic questions: why firms exist and what determines their scale and scope (Holmstrom and Tirole, 1989)? A third question, though less-relevant economic theory also is posed: What is the function of the firm and its managers (Seth and Thomas, 1994)? It is, therefore, essential to review some basic assumptions behind the economic theories of the firm.

Two broad outlines of strategic theory development have proved to be useful. The first is strategy formulation research, stemming from economics. The second is strategy implementation research, which has its roots more in organization theory, sociology and psychology (Seth and Thomas, 1994). Of course, strict economic theory and management theory have different research traditions, but it is sometimes worthwhile to combine them. Barney (1996) says, "Many books and articles seem to adopt the fiction that it is possible to study strategy formulation and strategy implementation independently. This is obviously incorrect. It would be clearly be a mistake for firms to formulate their strategies without considering how they were going to implement those strategies" (p. x).

The classic Ricardian economics assume land to be the most important factor of value. However, in the digital economy, land has no significant value, nor do most other forms of tangible capital. Dynamic knowledge has replaced them as the most valuable factor.

THE MAIN THEORIES OF THE FIRM OF THE 20TH CENTURY

The Neoclassical Theory

The Neoclassical Theory, which is part of the wider theory of value, sees the firm basically as an input/output process. The firm exists to produce end products through combining resources, i.e., putting together two inputs: labor and capital. The scope and scale are determined by the extent to which the firm owns the rights to the productive services of the inputs (Alchian and Demsetz, 1972).

The Neoclassical Theory is based on the perfect competition model, which Shepherd (1990) describes as having the following attributes: perfect knowledge by all participants; perfect mobility of resources and participants; rational behavior by all participants; stability of the underlying preferences, technology, and surroundings; no non-market interdependencies among consumers or producers; and pure competition on both sides on every market.

The attributes above lead to a situation where firms are identical: each firm is equally able to obtain exactly the right input, and an input's price equals the input's marginal productive value to the firm. Thus, the individual firm's ambition to maximize its profits yields a market equilibrium of zero economic returns to each firm (Conner, 1991). This, in turn, leads to a zero-sum game in the market, and a static view of competition.

The Bain Type Competition Model

The Bain Type Competition Model involves restraining other firms' outputs. This can happen through exercising monopoly power or through collusion. It says that a large firm can exercise monopolistic behavior, because it is most likely to control substantial proportions of industry output. The firm's conduct is determined by its industry's structure, as well as by the firm's size and its industry's concentration. Seth and Thomas (1994), therefore, call the model the traditional Bain-Mason structure-conduct-performance paradigm of early industrial organization economics. The main difference of the Bain Model from the Neoclassical Theory is that its focus is on the theory of market structure, not the theory of price.

Both theories treat the firm as a "black box," and do not discuss firm heterogeneity within an industry, except concerning scale (Seth and Thomas 1994). In addition, both theories treat the "outside world" very much as given. However, the ontological stances of most contemporary strategy research approaches start from the idea that the firm is surrounded by a variety of environmental variables. Of these, some the firm can control, some it cannot. As Seth and Thomas (1994) put it, "An organization is a purposive and entrepreneurial entity with specialized unique resources which interacts with its environment to maintain long-term viability." They say, further, that "a theory of the firm must be consistent with these elements to serve as a useful backdrop for strategy research" (ibid.). Put together, the above leads to an idea that Neoclassical Theory and the Bain Type Competition Model have limited relevance for strategy research.

New Industrial Economics

As already seen above, the traditional industrial economic theories of the firm do not fit very well into strategy research. That is because of their static nature, and their view of environment, which they treat as a given. Therefore, other theories must be explored. Seth and Thomas (1994) suggest that the focus should be turned to the structure and behavior of firms. This, they say, also blurs the boundaries between strict economic theory and the more management-oriented strategic discussion. By that, they mean a systematic and rigorous way to analyze the structure and behavior of the firm.

Such a theory is game theory. It offers a mathematical way to analyze competition among competitors, all of whose decisions immediately affect the behavior of other players. During the game, all players have symmetry and completeness of information concerning outcomes. The goal of the game is to maximize individual payoffs. The basic concept of a game is that that all players try to maximize their payoffs by taking advantage of their best strategies. This kind of strategy combination is called Nash equilibrium – "where each player has an optimal strategy such that a unilateral change by any single player cannot possibly improve his/her profit" (Seth and Thomas, 1994).

The game-theoretic models emphasize managerial rationality and motivation. "The profit maximization assumption of these models implies that decision-makers are assumed to be rational and are subject to no uncertainty, i.e., that the environment can be predicted with perfect foresight and managers have unlimited information-processing ability" (Seth and Thomas, 1994). However, Nash equilibrium, and managerial rationality through perfect certainty of the environment, lead to a zero-sum game, where there is no place for the market to grow or to change through, for example, managerial entrepreneurship. Thus, they treat the world as a given, and cannot envisage a situation in which all firms in an industry could create competitive advantage simultaneously.

The Behavioral Theory of the Firm

The next theory is the behavioral theory of the firm. It argues that organizations should be viewed as collections of individuals with multiple goals who operate in a defined structure of authority (Simon, 1957). Simon claimed that managers have bounded rationality when facing uncertainty, and that behavioral rules replace profit maximizing. One of the rules is called "satisficing," which means that the firm tries to achieve a satisfactory level of profit instead of maximizing profit.

An extension of the behavioral theory of the firm is the evolutionary theory of economic change (Nelson and Winter, 1982). This theory seeks to explain disequilibrium, not the behavior of the firm. The decision-making rules are characterized by certain routines acquired by adaptive memory that is, however, incomplete. These routines involve standard operating procedures, search behavior and investment behavior. Those firms that select the best combination of routines survive and prosper. The rule-following and routine-based nature of behavioral theories of the firm suggests their contribution is more on the operational side, and thus, add little to the strategic discussion.

Agency Theory

Agency theory of the firm arose from the critique against Neoclassical Theory, and its failure to consider risks. Such risks involve factors preventing costless diffusion of specialized resources. Those factors involve impediments to information transfer, regulatory constraints, managers' competence, and problems in labor, production factors, or output.

The basic idea behind agency theory is that, in corporations, stockholders (principals) delegate decision-making authority to managers (agents). However, the utility function curves of agents and principals diverge. This is because the agents are motivated by their self-interest, while principals aim to maximize their prosperity. This divergence of interests usually is called "agency problem."

Several tools are used to lessen the agency problem. Such tools involve monitoring, bonding, and the design of incentive programs. Agency problems cause agency cost, such as monitoring and bonding cost. However, as managers contribute their human capital to the firm, their stake might be even greater than the shareholders. Therefore, in their own interest, managers are likely to reduce agency costs as well. This leads to an idea that there is no real conflict and thus, that agency costs can be treated as operational issues only. As such, agency theory does not seem to offer any contribution to the strategic discussion.

The Industrial Organization Approach – Positioning

Seth and Thomas (1994) say that the industrial organization (IO) approach advocated mainly by Michael Porter originates from game theory. The industrial organization strategy approach has its roots in positioning in academe and, in the work by Boston Consulting Group, in consulting. These both, in turn, have long histories in applying military strategy in their frameworks. "In this view, strategy reduces to generic positions selected through formalized analyses of industry situations" (Mintzberg and Lampel, 1999).

As already described above, emphasis is placed on the structure of the industry in which the firm is located. The strategy-structure-system triad was a revolutionary discovery in the 1920s. Barney (1986) says the strategy concept in the IO approach has been fundamentally unchanged since it was originally developed by Mason in the late 1930s, and further, by Bain, in the 1950s. It was a wonderful way to describe big companies, and provided a good mental toolkit to govern and coordinate immense conglomerates. But times changed, and companies that had a clear strategy and structure became more systematic, and their actions, predictable. For example, Ghoshal et al. (1999) say that machine-like systems of control are not helpful.

Ghoshal et al. (1999) also note that, over and above predictability, another issue also causes problems. Companies are wrapped in the grip of theories, which is part of their problem. Theories have dominated managerial discourse for the entire 20th century, starting from F. W. Taylor's (1912) scientific management, through today. In short, the theory of positioning means grabbing everything oneself, and preventing anyone else from doing the same. In order to do this, managers must prevent free competition by all means, and that happens at the cost of social welfare.

Another point in Porter's theory is that it emphasizes competition among industry clusters (Porter, 1985, 1998, 2001). As long as any cluster has competitive advantage, so do all the firms within that cluster. This, however, leads to predictable, systematic strategic solutions. On the other hand, if all firms enjoy competitive advantage, over whom do they enjoy it?

Transaction Cost Theory

Transaction cost theory, which sees "firms as avoiders of the cost of markets exchange" (Conner, 1991) is said to provide "the market failures framework" (Seth and Thomas, 1994). It originally arose from the early work of 1991 Nobel Laureate Ronald H. Coase's (1937) critique of Neoclassical Theory and, more generally, the price mechanism and value-based economic thought. In his paper, Coase emphasized market behavior and the firm's governance structure, in contrast to the traditional theories' input/processes of land and capital approach. Coase's general idea was that firms and market are alternative methods for coordinating production (Conner, 1991), with the firm seen as a chasm (nexus) of contracts.

The production coordination is made by some authority (entrepreneur) that is allowed to direct resources so that costs for operating the market and marketing are minimized. "The firm exists to avoid (economize on) the cost of conducting the same exchange between autonomous contractors" (Conner, 1991). The authority's responsibility is to negotiate contracts so that this becomes possible.

Williamson (1975, 1989, 1993) extends Coase's (1937) idea of the existence of the firm for avoiding cost of using market price mechanism (customary in economics) (Williamson, 1993). He claims that particular attention has to be given to situations with opportunistic behavior. Such situations involve simultaneous occurrence of the following conditions: asset specificity, small number of transactors and imperfect information (Conner, 1991; Barney, 1996). "Opportunistic behavior is any action engaged in by an exchange partner, enjoying an informational (or some other) advantage, to exploit that advantage to the economic detriment of others" (Barney and Ouchi, 1986). According to Williamson (1975, 1989), firms exist when all the above conditions are filled, i.e., opportunistic potential is significant.

Ghoshal et al. (1999) have also strongly criticized transaction cost economics. They say that the answer – given by the proponents of transaction cost economics to the question "why do firms exist" – is that companies exist because the market fails. Ghoshal et al. (1999) say that accepting this is dangerous, and leads to an assumption that markets represent some sort of ideal way to organize economic activities.

The transaction cost theory emphasizes static, rather than dynamic, efficiencies. Static efficiency tries to exploit existing resources as effectively as possible. Innovations creating new options and resources create dynamic efficiencies. In insisting that companies are actually second-rate postures of market mechanisms, the transaction cost view locks companies into the market logic of static efficiency (Ghoshal et al., 1999).

There is a further problem in applying the transaction cost theory. It does not fit well with strategic management. It is too normative for that. It applies well for designing or examining, for example, state-of-the-art processes. But, when it is applied to creating new organizational knowledge, it seems to fail.

The Resource-Based View of the Firm

The theory of the growth of the firm (Penrose, 1955, 1959, 1985, 1995), or resource-based theory (Conner, 1991), was developed by Edith Penrose in the 1950s. Seth and Thomas (1994) see it as part of the theory of value, and a descendant of Neoclassical Theory. It also has been called the resource-based approach (Mahoney and Pandian, 1992; Robins and Wiersema, 1995); resource-based model (Barney, 1991); and resource-based perspective (Foss, 1998). Penrose (1995) claims that, although the analysis in the theory concentrates on industrial firms, it may well apply to other firms.

Penrose's (1959) original theory notes that, in order for a firm to exist, it has to grow continuously. She claims that a business firm is both an administrative organization and a collection of productive resources. "The administrative structure of the firm is the creation of the men who run it; the structure may have developed rather haphazardly in response to immediate needs as they rose in the past or it may have been shaped largely by conscious attempts to achieve a 'rational' organization" (Penrose, 1959).

A firm is, thus, "a collection of human and physical resources bound together in an administrative framework, the boundaries of which are determined by the area of 'administrative coordination' and 'authoritative communication'" (Penrose

1995). She also notes that, "Strictly speaking, it is never resources themselves that are 'inputs' in the production process, but only the services that the resources can render" (Penrose, 1959). The distinction between resources and services is not their relative duration. Resources consist of a bundle of potential services and can, for the most part, be defined independently of their use, while the word "service" implies a function or an activity. This means that the services yielded by resources are a function of the way in which they are used.

Bartlett and Ghoshal (1993) describe a large firm's management's reduction from a hierarchical multi-layered structure to an organization of business units with front line managers (manager entrepreneurs). This includes small teams, in touch with customers, and backed by a layer of middle management in a supportive role. This type of management is based on strongly manipulative, but supportive guidance, and advice from higher line management (Penrose, 1995). However, "the very nature of the firm requires that the existing responsible officials of the firm at least know and approve, even if they do not in detail control all aspects of, the plans and operations of the firm" (Penrose, 1959).

External inducements include: growing demand of particular products, changes in technology, discoveries and inventions, special opportunities in market positions and changes that might affect the firm's existing operations. External obstacles include keen competition in markets for particular products, existence of patent rights and other restrictions on the use of knowledge and technology, and entry costs, as well as shortage of resources.

Internal inducements arise from the existence of a pool of unused resources and special knowledge. Internal obstacles arise when some specialized types of services are not available in sufficient amounts internally, e.g., managerial capacity or technical skills.

Conclusions from the Discussion on Theories of the Firm

In summarizing (see Table 1) the review of the modern economic theories of the firm, the following conclusion can be drawn: all of the theories, except one, are rather static. They treat the economic world as rather static, and as a zero-sum game where all the cards have been dealt already.

Competition in that kind of environment is somewhat superficial. Most firms are striving to gain competitive advantage over others. However, there seems to be a dilemma in the static theories. If all firms enjoy competitive advantage over others, then how can any firm enjoy it?

The only exception is the resource-based theory, which is dynamic, and thus allows firms to grow forever. By implication, the economy can carry on growing, as well. As Ghoshal et al. (1999) put it, It is time to expose the old, disabling assumptions and replace them with a different, more realistic set that calls on managers to act out a positive role that can release the vast potential still trapped in the old model. The new role for management breaks from the narrow economic

Table 1: Summary of the theories explored

The Theory	Theoretical origins	Reason for existence	Scope & Scale	Basic view of the market	Basic vocabulary	Feasibility to management strategy research
RECENT APPROACHES TO THE THEORY OF THE FIRM						
The Neoclassical Theory	Theories of value and price	Production by putting together labor and capital	Owning rights to inputs and productive services	Static, non-market interdependencies, perfect competition	Profit maximization, Equilibrium, Perfect information	Only minimal
The Bain Type Competition Model	Theories of value and market structure	To restrain other firms' output	Control through monopoly power	Given static view of the "outside world"	Structure, Size, Industry concentration, Perfect information	Only minimal
New Industrial Economics						
- Game Theory	Mathematics	Profit making	Maximize individual payoffs	Zero-Sum, Static	Managerial rationality and motivation, Best strategy	Only minimal
- Nash Equilibrium					Unilateral change by any single player	
The Behavioral Theory of the Firm	Mathematics, Behaviorism	Collections of individuals with multiple goals	Defined structure of authority, behavioral rules replace profit maximizing	standard operating procedures when facing uncertainty, Static	"satisficing", bounded rationality	Only minimal
Agency Theory	Critique against neoclassical theory	Principals aim to maximize their prosperity	Principals delegate decision-making authority to managers	Operational static uncertainty	Contracts, Utility Functions, Agency Problems	Only minimal, operative research
The Industrial Organization Approach – Positioning	Game Theory Warfare	To prevent free competition of others	Generic positioning by formalized analyses of industry situations	Zero-Sum, Static machine-like system of control	Positions, Generic Strategies, Clusters, Competitive Forces	Only minimal, Suitable for operative industry positions comparisons
Transaction Cost Economics	Critique of neoclassical theory, and value-based economic thought.	To avoid the cost of markets exchange, firms exist, because market fails	Firms and market are alternative methods for coordinating production, firm seen as a chasm (nexus) of contracts	Insisting that companies are second-rate postures of market mechanisms, the view locks companies into the market logic of static efficiency	asset specificity, small number of transactors, Contracts, imperfect information, opportunism	Only minimal, very feasible for operative research
The Resource-Based View of the Firm	partly theory of value, traces of neoclassical theory	In order for a firm to exist it has to grow continuously	a firm is both an administrative organization and a collection of productive resources	Organizational learning, enabled through a dynamic view of the firm and entrepreneurship	Resources, assets, dominant logic, competencies, capabilities	The only dynamic theory assuming constant growth of the market, thus feasible for strategy research

assumptions of the past to recognize that. Modern societies are not market economies, they are organizational economies, in which companies are the chief actors in creating value and advancing economic progress. The growth of firms and, therefore economics, is primarily dependent on the quality of their management. The foundation of a firm's activity is a new "moral contract" with employees and society, replacing paternalistic exploitation and value appropriation with employability and value creation.

The strategy-structure-system trilogy was a revolutionary discovery in the 1920s. It was a wonderful way to describe big companies and provided a good mental toolkit to govern and coordinate immense conglomerates. However, times changed and companies that had a clear strategy and structure became more systematic and their actions, predictable; and machine-like systems of control are not helpful, of course (Ghoshal et al., 1999).

The shift to a new paradigm in the digital economy can happen only through organizational learning, which is enabled only through a dynamic view of the firm and entrepreneurship. From the ones described above, the only theory of the firm to make this possible is the resource-based theory. Therefore, the resource-based management and its concomitants, competence- and capabilities-based management, should be studied more thoroughly in connection with strategy formulations.

RESOURCES AND COMPETITIVE ADVANTAGE

Barney (1991a) claims that, whenever identical firms populate an industry, any one firm cannot enjoy sustained competitive advantage. This is true even if a firm is a 'first mover' (Lieberman and Montgomery, 1988). It cannot have sustained competitive advantage, unless the firms in its industry are heterogeneous in terms of the resources they control. On the other hand, even when the firms in an industry are perfectly homogenous, such firms collectively may be able to obtain sustained competitive advantage over firms in other industries, as long as there are strong entry or mobility barriers. Where such barriers do exist, this sustained advantage will be reflected in above normal economic performance for these firms (Porter, 1980). Barney (1991a) assumes that barriers to entry and mobility only exist when competing firms are heterogeneous in terms of the strategically relevant resources they control. The resource-based view, therefore, takes the value chain logic (Porter, 1985) a step further, by examining the attributes that resources identified by value chain analysis must posses in order to be sources of sustained competitive advantage.

Barney (1991a) discusses four indicators of a firm's resources that generate sustained competitive advantage:

Value: Can the firm's resources respond to environmental opportunities and/or threats? Firm's resources can be a source of sustained competitive advantage only when they are valuable, meaning that they enable a firm to conceive of or implement strategies that improve its efficiency and effectiveness.

Rareness: How many competing firms already possess these valuable resources? Some strategies require a particular mix of physical capital, human capital, and organizational capital (immaterial) resources in order to be implemented.

Imitability: Are these resources costly to imitate? Imitation can be done through duplication or substitution (e.g., through strategic alliances). Costliness depends on any or a combination of the following issues: (i) whether there is a complex history as to the creation of a given resource; (ii) whether a resource involves numerous 'small decisions' in its creation; and (iii) whether the resources are very complex socially, e.g., involving many stakeholders.

Supportive Organizational Arrangements: Do organizational arrangements support and exploit resources? Within this context, the emphasis is on managerial and organizational resources. Organizational resources include close interpersonal relationships among managers, which, in turn, enhance mutual trust, reduce monitoring cost and enhance the search for new opportunities.

Figure 1: The VRIO framework for evaluating the competitive positioning of a firm's resources and capabilities (Adapted from Barney, 1994)

Valuable?	Rare?	Costly to Imitate?	Efficiently Organized?	Competitive Implications
No	--	--	No	Competitive Disadvantage
Yes	No	--		Competitive Parity
Yes	Yes	No		Temporary Competitive
Yes	Yes	Yes	Yes	Sustained Competitive Advantage

Barney, in analyzing sources of competitive advantage (1991a), makes two further assumptions that contradict traditional accounts (Porter, 1985) as to how a firm's resource homogeneity and mobility create such advantage:

(i) Firms within an industry (or group) may be heterogeneous with respect to the strategic resources they control;
(ii) These resources may not be totally mobile across firms, and thus heterogeneity can be long-lasting.

The implications of these two assumptions are examined in the context of Barney's VRIO framework – Value, Rareness, Imitability, and Organization – as depicted in Figure 1.

The next section articulates the role of information technology in support of organizational competencies and capabilities.

COMPETENCIES, CAPABILITIES AND INFORMATION TECHNOLOGY

Organizational *competencies* refer to the unique knowledge owned by the firm. Firms are presumed to focus on a few key or core competencies, which they can exploit effectively to their competitive advantage. For Rumelt (1994), the concept of core competencies relates directly to the resource-based framework. As such, the competitive advantage of a firm is determined, not only by the industry or environment, but also by its possession of unique skills, knowledge and resources (competencies). This can be seen as complementary to market structure analysis, as captured by the seminal competitive forces model by Porter (1990).

In the work of Rumelt (1994), 'corporate core competence' – the concept developed by Prahalad and Hamel (1990) – includes:

1. **Corporate span.** Core competencies span [several] business [functions] and products within a corporation. Put differently, powerful core competencies [can] support several products and businesses.
2. **Temporal dominance.** Products are but momentary expressions of a corporation's core competencies. Competencies are more stable, and evolve more slowly than do products.
3. **Learning-by-doing.** Competencies are gained and enhanced by work. Prahalad and Hamel (1990) say 'core competencies are the collective learning in the organization, especially how to coordinate diverse production skills and integrate multiple streams of technologies. ... Core competence does not diminish with use ... competencies are enhanced as they are applied and shared.'
4. **Competitive locus.** Product-market competition is merely a superficial expression of a deeper competition over competencies (Rumelt, 1994).

Organizational *capabilities* refer to the firm's ability to *use* its competencies. They represent the collective tacit knowledge of the firm in responding to its environment. Capabilities are developed by combining and using resources with the aid of organizational routines, i.e., those specific ways of doing what the organization has developed and learned. Capability development, therefore, involves organizational learning. This learning takes place within the context of the firm and is path-dependent and firm- specific; as a consequence, it is impossible to imitate and may, therefore, create competitive advantage. Core capabilities differentiate a company strategically in terms of beneficial behaviors that will not be observed in its competitors. Such capabilities evolve from the competitive environment and business mission of the firm through a 'capability learning loop' (Andreu and Ciborra, 1996). As these authors put it, "Core capabilities clarify their role and scope through acquiring a sense of why they are important" (Andreu and Ciborra, 1996). From the above reasoning, one can conclude that core capabilities are important or, in Barney's terms, 'valuable.' They are firm-specific, thus, heterogeneously distributed across competing firms, and are path-dependent and, thus, imperfectly mobile. The consequence of this is that core capabilities are sources of sustained competitive advantage (Andreu and Ciborra, 1996).

Sanchez, Heene and Thomas (1996) posit that, as the combining of "internal" and "external" environments is of a systemic nature, it is hard to identify strict borders between the "in" and "out" in the analysis of a specific case. In a similar analysis, Sanchez, Heene and Thomas (1996) say that firms can be distinguished by (i) distinctive strategic goals, (ii) strategic logic, (iii) resources available, and (iv) the coordination of resources' deployment. A firm's management processes provide the mechanisms for coordinating and directing its resources under the governance of strategic logic. A firm achieves competence when it is able to sustain coordinated deployment of resources in ways that help it to pursue its goals. This pursuit takes place through the following dual activities, although these do not have to be complementary in all cases.

Competence leveraging: coordinated deployment of resources that do not require qualitative changes in the resources, or in the mode of their coordination.

Competence building: acquisition or use of qualitatively different resources or modes of coordination.

It follows that competence-based competition is based on:
(i) Dynamic single loop learning (Argyris and Schön, 1978) processes of coordinating and leveraging organizational processes (e.g., current or new market opportunities) into competencies, without qualitative changes in existing stock of assets and capabilities (changing only the way of acting, not the underlying assumptions).

(ii) Dynamic double-loop learning (Argyris and Schön, 1978) processes of coordinating and building competencies, with qualitative changes in existing stocks of assets and capabilities (changing the way of acting, as well as the underlying assumptions). In this framework, "strategic change within a firm is motivated by managers' perceptions of strategic gaps between their firm's current stocks and flows of assets and capabilities ... and the stocks and flows they believe will be needed to achieve the firms goal's in its competitive environment" (Sanchez, Heene and Thomas, 1996).

The link just set out among competencies, capabilities and single and double loop learning highlights the important role that information technology (IT) and telecommunications (TC) could play in the coordination and learning support (automation) of organizational processes and, by implication, competitive advantage.

The issues involved here are by no means straightforward. Barney (1991), for instance, questions the claim that information systems are a source of sustained competitive advantage. For him, this very much depends on the type of system involved. He contends that machines – be they computers or otherwise – are part of the physical technology of a firm, and usually can be bought across markets. As such, any strategy that exploits just the machines (computers) in themselves is likely to be imitable and, thus, not a source of sustained competitive advantage.

Mata et al. (1995), in their resource-based analysis, found that, out of four attributes of IT – capital requirements, proprietary technology, technical IT skills, and managerial IT skills – managerial IT skills is the only resource that can bring sustained competitive advantage. Keen (1991) comes to similar conclusions, stating that, while IT may be a commodity, IT management is not—it is the value-added element that *leads to* competitive advantage. Mata et al. (1995) point out, of course, that we cannot consider the other three attributes unimportant, because they may still produce, admittedly temporary, competitive advantage. Mata et al.'s analysis suggests that IT managers should work closely with other managers within the firm to support their information needs. It must be recognized that the information needs of various stakeholders vary in different types of firms, depending on the firm's industry, resources and structure.

Mata et al.'s findings suggest two factors that can contribute effectively to gaining sustained competitive advantage:
1. Developing methods for strategy generation involving information resources management that emphasize and enforce the learning of these skills across the whole organization.
2. Developing shared goals within the whole organization.

Andreu and Ciborra (1996) have come to similar conclusions in their resource-based discussion, combining IT, organizational learning and core capabilities development. These authors view IT as a central support for routinization and capability learning loops. Moreover, IT is seen also as instrumental in making capabilities become core. Andreu and Ciborra (1996) also suggest four guidelines, if IT is to play a key role in making core competencies and capabilities really count for a firm.

- *Look for IT applications that help to make capabilities rare.* An example of this could be the American Airlines computerized reservation system (Copeland and McKenney, 1988), which, at least at the beginning, was unique and thus rare.
- *Concentrate on IT applications that make capabilities valuable.* Rosenbluth Travel Agency could be an example of this (Clemons and Row, 1991).
- *Identify capabilities that are difficult to imitate.* This also points to the American Airlines case (Copeland and McKenney, 1988) where systems were complex and thus difficult to imitate.
- *Concentrate on IT applications with no clear strategically equivalent substitutes.* Sometimes, certain functionality can be achieved only by means of particular IT applications. Thus, IT contributes to the lack of substitution. An example of this could be World Wide Web pages where the producer has included certain features that can be viewed only on specific browser versions.

Andreu and Ciborra (1996) provide a list of issues where IT-based support for capability creation is feasible that includes the following.

- Supporting the firm's capabilities learning process (capability learning loop).
- Supporting the sharing of capabilities.
- Facilitating reflection, experimentation and training on routines and capabilities.
- Supporting and enabling capability diffusion.
- Using IT applications that provide information about the competitive environment.
- Using IT applications that disseminate the business mission.

CONCLUSIONS

As a summary of this review of the modern economic theories of the firm, the following conclusion can be drawn: all of the theories, except one, are rather static. They treat the economic world as rather static, and as a zero-sum game, where all the cards have been dealt already.

Competition in that kind of environment is somewhat superficial. Most firms are striving to gain competitive advantage over others. However, there seems to be a dilemma in the static theories. If all firms enjoy competitive advantage over others, then how can any firm enjoy it?

The only exception is the resource-based theory, which is dynamic and, thus, allows firms to grow forever. By implication, the economy can continue to grow as well. As Ghoshal et al. (1999) put it, It is time to expose the old, disabling assumptions and replace them with a different, a more realistic set that calls on managers to act out a positive role that can release the vast potential still trapped in the old model. The new role for management breaks from the narrow economic assumptions of the past to recognize that. Modern societies are not market economies; they are organizational economies in which companies are the chief actors in creating value and advancing economic progress. The growth of firms and, therefore economics, is primarily dependent on the quality of their management. The foundation of a firm's activity is a new "moral contract" with employees and society, replacing paternalistic exploitation and value appropriation with employability and value creation.

The shift to a new paradigm in the digital economy can happen only through organizational learning, which is enabled only through a dynamic view of the firm and entrepreneurship. From the ones described above, the only theory of the firm to make this possible is the resource-based theory. Therefore, the resource-based management and its concomitants, competence- and capabilities-based management, should be studied more thoroughly in connection with strategy formulations information resources management.

REFERENCES

Alchian, A., & Demsetz, H. (1972). Production, Information Cost, and Economic Organization. In M. Casson (Ed.) (1996). *The Theory of the Firm*. Cheltenham: Elgar, 92-110.

Andreu, R. & Ciborra, C. (1996). Organizational learning and core capabilities development: the role of IT. *Journal of Strategic Information Systems*, 5, 111-127.

Argyris, C. & Schön, D. A. (1978). *Organizational learning: A theory of action perspective*. Reading, MA: Addison-Wesley.

Barney, J. B. (1986). Types of competition and the theory of strategy: Toward an integrative framework. *Academy of Management Review*, 11(4), 791-800.

Barney, J. B. (1991). Firm resources and sustained competitive advantage. *Journal of Management*, 17(1), 99-120.

Barney, J. B. (1994). Bringing managers back in: a resource-based analysis of the role of managers in creating and sustaining competitive advantage. In

J.B. Barney, J.C. Spender & T. Reve (Eds.), *Does management matter? On competencies and competitive advantage*. Lund: Institute of Economic Research.

Barney, J. B. (1996). *Gaining and sustaining competitive advantage*. New York: Addison-Wesley.

Barney, J. B. & Ouchi, W. G. (1986). Basic concepts: Information, opportunism, and economic exchange. In J. B. Barney & W. G. Ouchi, (Eds.), *Organizational economics: Toward a new paradigm for understanding and studying organizations*. San Francisco: Jossey Bass Publishers.

Bartlett, C.A. & Ghoshal, S. (1993). Beyond the m-form: Towards a managerial theory of the firm. *Strategic Management Journal,* 14, (Winter, Special Issue: Organization, Decision Making and Strategy).

Ciborra, C. (1998). Design of computer-based systems for the 21st century. (Lecture at the 4th Summer School of Design and Management of Information Technology, May 3-8, 1998, Magleås, Denmark.

Clemons, E. K. & Row, M. K. (1991). Information technology at Rosenbluth Travel: Competitive advantage in a rapidly growing service company. *Journal of Management Information Systems.* 8(2), Fall, 53-79.

Coase, R. H. (1937). The nature of the firm. In O. E. Williamson & S. G. Winter (Eds.) (1993). *The Nature of the Firm; Origins, Evolution, and Development*. New York: Oxford University Press, 18-74. (Originally in *4 Economica N.S.*)

Conner, K. R. (1991). A historical comparison of resource-based theory and five schools of thought within industrial organization economics: Do we have a new theory of the firm? *Journal of Management.* 17(1), 121-154.

Copeland, D. G. & McKenney, J. L. (1988). Airline reservations systems: Lessons from the history. *MIS Quarterly*, September, 353-370.

Foss, N. J. (1998). The resource-based perspective: an assessment and diagnosis of problems. *Scandinavian Journal of Management,* 14(3), 133-149.

Ghoshal, S., Bartlett C. A. & Moran, P. (1999). A new manifesto for management. *Sloan Management Review,* Spring, 40(3), 9-20.

Holmstrom, B. R. & Tirole, J. (1989). The theory of the firm. In R. Schmalensee and R. D. Willig (Eds.), *Handbook of Industrial Organization* (Vol. I). New York: North Holland, 61-126.

Kangas, K. (1997). Case of a Finnish multinational; coordination mode and a resource-based view to core capabilities. Proceedings of the 1997 Information Resources Management Association Conference, May 20-22, Vancouver, BC, Canada.

Keen, P. W. G. (1991). *Shaping the Future*. Boston, MA: Harvard Business School Press.

Lieberman, M. B. & Montgomery, D. B. (1988). First-mover advantages. *Strategic Management Journal*, 9 (Special Issue), 41-58.

Mahoney, J. T. & Pandian, R. (1992). The resource-based view within the conversation of strategic management. *Strategic Management Journal*, 13, 363-380.

Mata, F., Fuerst, W. L. & Barney, J. B. (1995). Information technology and sustained competitive advantage: a resource-based analysis. *MIS-Quarterly*, 19(4), December.

Mintzberg, H. & Lampel, J. (1999). Reflecting on the strategy process. *Sloan Management Review*, Spring, 21-30.

Nelson, R. R. & Winter, S. G. (1982). An evolutionary theory of economic change. Cambridge: The Belknap Press.

Penrose, E. (1955). Research on the business firm: limits to the growth and size of firms. *American Economic Review*, XLV (2), 531-43.

Penrose, E. T. (1959). *The Theory of the growth of the firm*. Oxford: Basil Blackwell.

Penrose, E. T. (1985). *The Theory of the growth of the firm twenty-five years after*. Acta Universitatis Upsaliensis, Studia Oeconomiae Negotiorum, 20, Uppsala.

Penrose, E. T. (1995). Preface. In *The Theory of the growth of the firm*, Third Edition. Oxford: Oxford University Press.

Porter, M. E. (1980). Competitive strategy; techniques for analyzing industries and competitors. New York: Free Press.

Porter, M. E. (1985). Competitive advantage: Creating and sustaining superior performance. New York: Free Press.

Porter, M. E. (1998). Clusters and the new economics of competition. *Harvard Business Review*, November-December, 77-90.

Porter, M.1 E. (2001). Strategy and the Internet. *Harvard Business Review*, March, 62-78.

Prahalad, C. K. & Hamel, G. (1990). The core competence of the corporation. *Harvard Business Review*, May-June, 79-91.

Reponen, T., Auer, T., Pärnistö, J. & Viitanen, J. (1995). Tietoresurssien johtamisstrategia kilpailukyvyn välineenä. Turku: Publications of the Turku School of Economics and Business Administration, Series C-8: 1995.

Robins, J. & Wiersema, M. F. (1995). A resource-based approach to the multibusiness firm: empirical analysis of portfolio interrelationship and corporate financial performance. *Strategic Management Journal*, 16, 277-299.

Rumelt R. P. (1994). Foreword. In G. Hamel & A. Heene (Eds.), *Competence-Based Competition*. Chichester: Wiley.

Sanchez, R., Heene, A. & Thomas, H. (1996). Introduction: towards the theory and practice of compctence-based competition. In R. Sanchez, A., Heene & H. Thomas (Eds.), *Dynamics of competence-based competition; theory and practice in the new strategic management*. Exeter: Pergamon, 1-35.

Seth, A. & Thomas, H. (1994). Theories of the firm: implications for strategy research. *Journal of Management Studies*, 31:2, March, 165-191.

Shepherd, W. G. (1990). *The economics of industrial organization* (3rd ed.), Englewood Cliffs: Prentice Hall.

Simon, H. (1957). *Administrative behavior*. New York: Macmillan.

Taylor, F. (1971). Scientific management. In D.S. Pugh (Eds.), *Organization theory*. Penguin Books: London. Originally in Taylor, F. (1947). *Scientific management*. New York: Harper & Row, 39-73. Testimony to the House of Representatives Committee, 1912.

Williamson, O. E. (1975). *Markets and hierarchies: Analysis and antitrust implications*. New York: Free Press

Williamson, O. E. (1989). Transaction cost economics. In R. Schmalensee & R.D. Willig (Eds.), *Handbook of Industrial Organization*, Vol. I. New York: North Holland, 137-182.

Williamson, O. E. (1993). Introduction. In O. E. Williamson & S. G. Winter (Eds.), *The nature of the firm; origins, evolution, and development*. New York: Oxford University Press, 3-17.

Zuboff, S. (1988). In *The age of the smart machine: The future of work and power*. New York: Basic Books.

Chapter X

A Theoretical Framework for Measuring the Success of Customer Relationship Management Outsourcing

Babita Gupta
California State University Monterey Bay, USA

Lakshmi S. Iyer
The University of North Carolina at Greensboro, USA

ABSTRACT

Dramatic growth of e-commerce has increased the bargaining power of customers requiring changes in strategies for Customer Relationship Management (CRM) development and implementation on the part of firms. Success of CRM implementations is thus critical for firms to survive in the 21st century. Because of the complex technologies involved in CRM, companies are choosing to outsource to vendors that specialize in CRM. In this study, we propose a theoretical framework that examines the CRM outsourcing success. Based on prior literature, we propose that CRM outsourcing success is influenced by degree of CRM outsourcing, partnership quality between the outsourcing firm and the vendor, organizational factors of the outsourcing firm, and the service quality of the vendor.

Copyright © 2003, Idea Group Inc. Copying or distributing in print or electronic forms without written permission of Idea Group Inc. is prohibited.

INTRODUCTION

Explosive growth of e-commerce is changing the nature of competition among companies and customer service is emerging as a key differentiator among competitors. With firms increasing their Web operations, customers now have the ability to contact the organizations they do business with through various interactive and non-interactive means (such as email, fax, call centers, FAQs, online chats, newsletters, "snail mail," retail stores and Web-based forms). This has changed the customer-related business requirements for all types of companies, and has led companies to consider Customer Relationship Management (CRM) as an important part of their competitive strategy. As the focus is shifting to retention of the most valuable customers, rather than acquisition (Winer, 2001), companies are looking for ways to engage customers. To build a long-term, sustained relationship with customers, and create long-term value for the firm, CRM tactics are used to deliver customized information in an interactive and responsive manner to each valuable customer.

CRM generally is stated as a strategy that companies use to identify, manage, and improve relationships with their customers. Thompson (2001) defines CRM as a company's activities related to developing and retaining customers through increased satisfaction and loyalty. eCRM is a term generally used when a company's customer service operations are on the Web. According to Cahners In-Stat Group (2001), worldwide revenues from CRM software application will increase from $9.4 billion in 2001 to approximately $30.6 billion in 2005. According to Tom Kaneshige of *CIO Enterprise Magazine*, CRM investments are expected to exceed $90 billion by 2003 (Kos, 2001).

CRM initiatives have high costs of implementation, (typically $1 million), as well as high failure rates, estimated to be between 55 percent to 75 percent (Ericson, 2001). For large-scale CRM implementations at very large businesses, reported spending on CRM software, hardware, services, internal labor, and training have been as high as $30-90 million (Young, 2001).

For effective CRM, companies generally must adopt a customer-centric philosophy to achieve goals, such as increase in sales, customer loyalty, customer service and support, and better and effective distribution of products. CRM can produce additional profits for firms through cross-selling, up-selling, reduced product marginal costs and lower customer acquisition costs (Winer, 2001). CRM applications must be designed to integrate all the customer communication points across various functional areas of a company.

CRM products generally are classified into three categories (Karimi, Somers and Gupta, 2001). These are:

1. *Operational* – for improving sales, marketing and customer service efficiency through marketing campaign management, service request management and automation that integrate with existing processes and infrastructure.

2. *Analytical* – for collecting better customer data containing customer buying history and demographics data; mining this data to generate customer profiles and anticipate their needs; and, thus, formulating more effective customer-centric strategies.
3. *Collaborative* – for integrating communications, across various channels, to improve information sharing across the organization and build an integrated view of the customer, ensuring the consistency of the message to the customer; for eCRM, one-to-one personalized Web marketing, customized product and services offering for individual customers, etc.

Despite the rise in popularity of CRM outsourcing, there is little literature in IS outsourcing that is specific to CRM functions. This study hopes to contribute to the IS field, by studying CRM outsourcing partnerships through an integrated framework of resource dependence, transaction cost economics and social exchange theory. This study focuses on the CRM vendor-company relationship by extending the work of Grover, Cheon and Teng (1996) and Lee and Kim (1999). We develop a framework to evaluate how these companies select a CRM vendor, how they adopt and integrate CRM technologies into their existing infrastructure and what factors affect CRM outsourcing success.

The following section provides a background on IS outsourcing literature. We follow that with our proposed framework to measure the success of CRM outsourcing, underlying theories and constructs, hypotheses and research methodology. We conclude with summary and future plans.

GENERAL BACKGROUND ON OUTSOURCING

Outsourcing is more and more a reflection of the strategic partnerships in the digital economy. While there are many definitions of IS outsourcing found in literature, there are three common components to these definitions: "first an external provider takes over part or all of an organization IS functions; second, external provider should take the responsibility; and third, customers transfer IS functions to external provider as well as employee and part of computer facilities" (Yang and Huang, 2000, p. 227).

The nature and extent of IS outsourcing has evolved throughout the past few decades, and information systems functions—of increasingly high-asset specificity, involving responsibilities not only for the technology, but also the business processes—and targeted business results are being outsourced (Grover, Cheon and Teng, 1994; Grover *et al.*, 1996; Gurbaxani, 1996; Nam, Rajagopalan, Rao and Chaudhury, 1996; Lee, Huynh, Chi-wai and Pi, 2000). More and more, the nature of this relationship has shifted, from a contractual relationship to a tightly integrated partnership relationship, for mutual benefit of the vendor and outsourcing firm, as firms consider outsourcing a key strategic choice (Grover et al., 1996; Lee and Kim, 1999; Lee et al., 2000).

Although high in asset specificity, companies are outsourcing CRM functions. CRM implementations require far more coordination among functionally disparate organizational units, including IT and senior management involvement in IT planning, organization, control and integration (Karimi et al., 2001). CRM initiatives are not confined to a particular function, but rather cut across various functions of an organization, therefore, they complicate the nature of CRM implementation through outsourcing. While there are many off-the-shelf CRM software packages, it generally is very difficult to integrate these into company-wide CRM initiatives and, also, into other existing applications, like Enterprise Resource Planning (ERP). Because of the complex technologies involved in CRM, companies are choosing to outsource to vendors that specialize in CRM. IDC research shows that the worldwide CRM services market will increase from $19.4 billion in 2001 to $45.5 billion in 2006 (Morphy, 2002).

Outsourcing offers various strategic, technological and economic advantages to a firm (Grover et al., 1996; Smith, Mitra and Narsimhan, 1998; Lankford and Parsa, 1999; Ngwenyama and Bryson, 1999; King and Malhotra, 2000; Lee et al., 2000; Yang and Huang, 2000). These are:

- *strategic benefits,* by allowing a firm to focus on its core competencies by outsourcing routine IT functions and, therefore, acquiring state-of-the-art knowledge beyond the firm's resources, and, as a result, improving IS service quality;
- *technological benefits,* through the acquisition of complex technologies from an external vendor that otherwise would have high internal acquisition and coordination costs, high obsolescence risks and longer time-to-market; and
- *economic benefits,* through reduced costs and improved efficiencies (long-term) by utilizing external vendors' expertise and economies of scale, and favorable allocation of fixed costs.

Cost reductions through outsourcing to external vendors result through two primary approaches. One approach is adversarial involving bidding among competing vendors to drive down prices. The other approach is through collaboration between the vendor and firm to lower transactional costs (Canon and Homburg, 2001). Outsourcing strategies involve contracting with either a single vendor or multiple vendors, although developing a relationship with a single vendor is more cost effective, and leads to better outsourcing performance throughout the long term (Ngwenyama and Bryson, 1999).

Notwithstanding the advantages, outsourcing IS functions may fail, due to complexities involved in managing long-term relationships with its vendor, and result in loss of control of organizational assets; loss of firms' internal IS expertise and capacity to learn new skills and technologies; threat of opportunism from vendors; uncertainties and lack of decision models in choosing the outsourcing vendor; and loss of morale and performance among the firm's employees (Rao, Nam and Chaudhury, 1996; Ngwenyama and Bryson, 1999; King and Malhotra, 2000). High asset specific IS outsourcing may also result in competitive threats from the vendors, and in addition, a firm may lose out on future business opportunities if the skills and competencies being outsourced appreciate in value (King and Malhotra, 2000).

CRM OUTSOURCING FRAMEWORK

While there are a number of studies for evaluating outsourcing of IS functions (Grover *et al.*, 1996; Lee and Kim, 1999; Maltz and Ellram, 1999; King and Malhotra, 2000; Kini, 2000; Lee *et al.*, 2000; Yang and Huang, 2000), there is very little literature specific to outsourcing of CRM functions. This study hopes to contribute to the IS field by studying CRM outsourcing partnerships through an integrated framework of resource dependence, transaction cost economics and social exchange theories.

Resource-dependency theory refers to outsourcing to external vendors to fill resource gaps within the firm for the purpose of providing the firm with strategic competitive advantage (Lee *et al.*, 2000).

Transaction cost theory provides an economic viewpoint to outsourcing, via a set of principles for analyzing buyer-supplier (outsourcer-vendor) transactions, and determining the most efficient mode of structuring and managing them (Nam *et al.*, 1996; Ngwenyama and Bryson, 1999; Lee *et al.*, 2000). Yang and Huang (2000) consider five factors—management, strategy, technology, economics and quality—in considering the outsourcing benefits to the firm.

Social exchange theory is used to explain the close partnership-style outsourcing relationship between the firm and vendor, by taking into account prior relationships, trust and culture, and their effect on ongoing outsourcing relationship (Lee and Kim, 1999; Lee *et al.*, 2000; Yang and Huang, 2000). Trust is perceived as the firm's belief that the vendor has the best interests of the firm and will perform accordingly to achieve desired goals for the firm (Lee and Kim, 1999).

This study focuses on the CRM vendor-company relationship by extending the works of Grover *et al.* (1996) and Lee and Kim (1999). We develop a framework to evaluate how these companies select a CRM vendor, how they adopt and integrate CRM technologies into their existing infrastructures and what factors affect CRM outsourcing success, based on resource-dependency, transaction cost and social exchange theories. We hope this framework will help answer questions, such as:

1. How do the tangible characteristics of a CRM vendor (such as, the length of operation, market reputation, geographic proximity, product features, and other tangible components) influence CRM outsourcing success?
2. How do the CRM product features provided by the CRM vendor, such as reliability, security, compatibility, database quality and centralization, data warehousing capabilities, accuracy, and maintenance requirements influence CRM outsourcing success?
3. Is there any relationship between partnership quality (between the company and CRM vendor) and CRM outsourcing success?

Proposed Model to Measure CRM Outsourcing Success

In our proposed model, we study the success of outsourcing CRM functions to an external vendor. This could take place at various levels, depending on the distinct level of technological and management complexity. We consider CRM outsourcing at three CRM categorization levels—*operational*, *analytical* and *collaborative* (Karimi et al., 2001).

The model (Figure 1) proposes to study the relationship between the level of CRM outsourcing and its success, how the CRM outsourcing success is

Figure 1: Research model to measure the success of CRM outsourcing

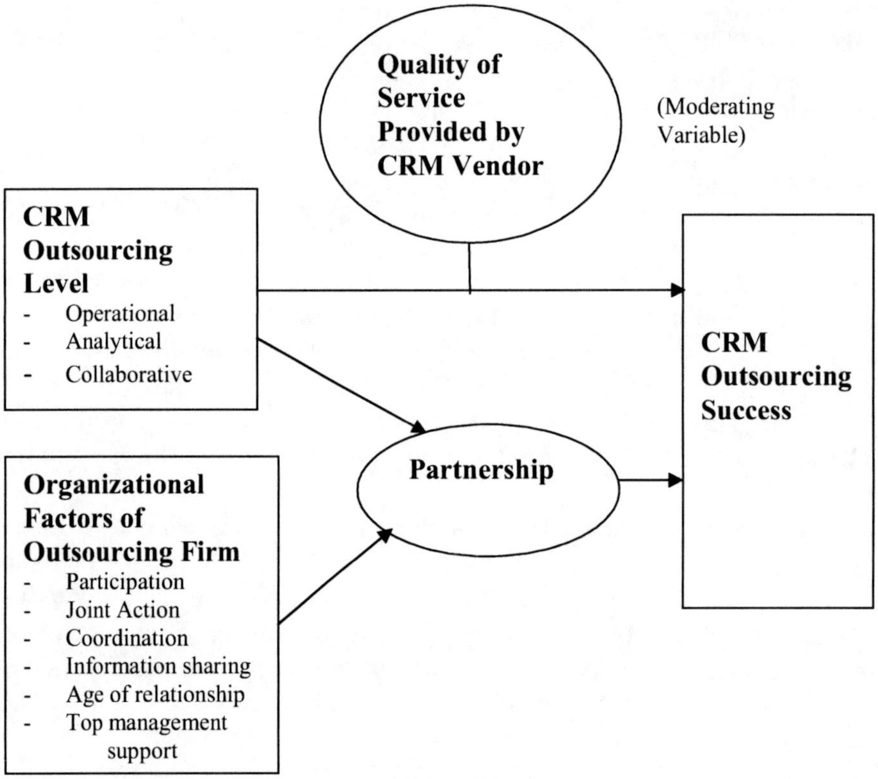

influenced by the quality of service provided by the CRM vendor, and the partnership quality between the outsourcing company and the external vendor.

Partnership relationship between vendor and firm is considered an important factor in predicting the success of outsourcing (Lee and Kim, 1999; Lee *et al.*, 2000). Generally, relationships between organizations are categorized as being either transactional- or partnership-style. A transactional style relationship is well specified in its contractual obligations. In contrast, the partnership-style relationships include sharing risk and benefit with a view to establish long-term commitment (Henderson, 1990; Lee and Kim 1999; Lee *et al.*, 2000).

The model also considers the effect of internal management issues and other organizational factors of the outsourcing company on the partnership quality and the success of CRM outsourcing. We consider prior outsourcing experiences of an outsourcing firm, as this may affect outsourcing decisions (Nam *et al.*, 1996; Lee and Kim, 1999; Lee *et al.*, 2000).

Model Constructs

CRM Outsourcing Level

As stated earlier, we adopt the classification of CRM products into three levels (operational, analytical, and collaborative) by Karimi *et al.* (2001). First, we would like to explore the relationship between the level of CRM outsourcing and outsourcing success. Based on transaction cost, as well as resource dependence theory, and examples of outsourcing success in literature, if strategic, technological or economic considerations influence organizations to outsource, then the relationship between outsourcing and its success should be positive and significant (Grover *et al.*, 1996). Hence, our first hypothesis is in the CRM context.

Hypothesis 1: The degree of CRM outsourcing will be positively related to outsourcing success.

Quality of Service Provided by CRM Vendor

Quality of service provided by the CRM vendor is an important factor that will influence the success of CRM outsourcing. The relationship between the CRM outsourcing level and CRM outsourcing success will be stronger if service quality is higher. Thus, our next hypothesis is:

Hypothesis 2: The relationship between CRM outsourcing level and CRM outsourcing success is moderated by service quality level.

This study adopts and adapts the two dimensions of SERVQUAL instrument construct used in the Grover *et al.* (1996) study, tangibles and reliability, and adds a new one, CRM technology:

- Tangibles (e.g., physical space, geographic proximity, number of employees, number of other customers, etc.);
- Reliability of the vendor; and
- CRM Technology (product features, i.e., does one vendor provide a better fit with the outsourcing company's existing technology than others, etc.)

Partnership

Konsynski and McFarlan (1990) and Lasher *et al.* (1991) state that partnership between the outsourcing firm and the vendor plays an important role in the success of outsourcing strategy. Grover *et al.* (1996) considered partnership as a mediating variable. However, Lee and Kim (1999) view partnership quality as an antecedent to outsourcing success. They also show that partnership quality is influenced by other factors (which we discuss next). Hence, in this study we treat partnership as an intermediate variable. To evaluate the company-CRM vendor-partnership relation, we use four dimensions: communication, trust, cooperation and satisfaction (Grover *et al.*, 1996; Lee and Kim, 1999).

Organizational Factors of Outsourcing Firm

Organizational factors of outsourcing firms that also include internal management issues influence partnership quality, which, in turn, affects the outsourcing success (Lee and Kim, 1999). We consider the following factors from literature that are relevant to CRM outsourcing:

- degree of participation between firm and vendor;
- joint actions taken by firm and vendor to negotiate and agree on mutual benefits and common goal;
- coordination among employees of firm and vendor to effect intended objectives, provide support and maintain balance;
- information sharing between firm and vendor;
- age of relationship between vendor and firm; and
- top management support.

Thus, our next hypothesis is:

Hypothesis 3: There is a positive relationship between organizational factors and partnership quality.

CRM Outsourcing Success

High partnership levels between the CRM outsourcing company and the CRM vendor will help achieve the organizational objectives and provide a competitive advantage. The dependent variable, success of CRM outsourcing, is measured by using the widely used concept of satisfaction, due to benefits gained by the CRM outsourcing company, from a business perspective (Grover et al., 1996; Chin and Lee, 2000; Lee et al., 2000). Thus our last hypothesis is:

Hypothesis 4: There is a positive relationship between partnership quality and outsourcing success.

RESEARCH METHODOLOGY

We plan to validate this framework by conducting a survey of companies that have an active CRM implementation and are outsourcing these functions to a single vendor (see Ngwenyama and Bryson, 1999, for discussion on single vendor versus multiple vendor outsourcing strategy).

Data will be collected using a pilot-tested survey based on above constructs. Both mail, as well as, Web-based surveys will be conducted to increase the number of responses. The survey will be aimed at senior level executives in sales/marketing/customer support functions of the CRM and/or e-CRM outsourcing companies. Structural equation modeling will be used to determine the overall effect of the variables on the final determinant, i.e., CRM outsourcing success.

SUMMARY

We present a testable theoretical model that examines the relationship among CRM outsourcing levels, organizational factors of the outsourcing firm, partnership quality and the success of CRM outsourcing from a business perspective. The model also considers how quality of service provided by vendor influences the CRM outsourcing success. This model seeks to answer questions, like how companies select CRM vendors, how they adopt and integrate CRM technologies into their existing infrastructure and what factors affect CRM outsourcing success? To validate the model, we plan to conduct a survey of companies that have an active CRM implementation and are outsourcing these functions.

REFERENCES

Cahners In-Stat Group (July 2001). Retrieved September 29, 2001 from the World Wide Web: http://www.instat.com/pr/2001/ec0105st_pr.htm.

Canon, J. P. & Homburg, C. (2001). Buyers-supplier relationships and customer firm costs. *Journal of Marketing, 65* (1), 29-43.

Chin W. W. & Lee, M.K.O. (December 10-13, 2000). A proposed model and measurement instrument for the formation of IS satisfaction: The case of end-user computing satisfaction. *Proceedings of the Twenty-first International Conference on Information Systems*, Brisbane, Australia.

Ericson, J. (August 2001). The "failure" of CRM. *e-Business Executive Daily, Line 56*. Retrieved July 12, 2002, from the World Wide Web: http://line56.com/print/default.asp?ArticleID=2808.

Grover, V., Cheon, M. J. & Teng, J.T.C. (1994). An evaluation of the impact of corporate strategy and the role of information technology on IS functional outsourcing. *European Journal of Information Systems*, 3 (3), 179-190.

Grover, V., Cheon, M.J. & Teng, J.T.C. (1996). The effect of service quality and partnership on the outsourcing of information systems function. *Journal of Management Information Systems*, 12 (4), 89-116.

Gurbaxani, V. (1996). The new world of information technology outsourcing. *Association for Computing Machinery. Communications of the ACM*, 39 (7), 45-46.

Henderson, J.C. (1990). Plugging into strategic partnerships: the critical IS connection. *Sloan Management Review*, 30, 37-18.

Karimi, J., Somers, T. M. & Gupta, Y.P. (2001). Impact of information technology management practices on customer service. *Journal of Management Information Systems*, 17 (4), 125-158.

King, W. R. & Malhotra, Y. (2000). Developing a framework for analyzing IS sourcing. *Information & Management*, 37 (6), 323-334.

Kini, R. B. (2000). Information systems outsourcing evaluation strategy: A precursor for outsourcing. *International Journal of Management*, 17 (1).

Konsynski, B.R. & McFarlan, F.W. (1990). Information partnerships-shared data, shared scale. *Harvard Business Review*, 68 (5), 114-120.

Kos, A. J., Sockel, H. H. & Falk, L. K. (2001). Customer relationship management opportunities. *Ohio CPA Journal*, 60 (1), 55-57.

Lankford W. M. & Parsa, F. (1999). Outsourcing: a primer. *Management Decision,* 37 (4).

Lasher, D.R., Ives, B. & Jarvenpaa, S.L. (1991). USAA-IBM partnerships in information technology: managing the image projects. *MIS Quarterly*, 15 (4), 551-565.

Lee, J. & Kim, Y. (1999). Effect of partnership quality on IS outsourcing: Conceptual framework and empirical validation. *Journal of Management Information Systems,* 15 (4), 29-61.

Lee, J., Huynh, M. Q., Chi-wai, K. R. & Pi, S. (January 2000). The Evolution of Outsourcing Research: What is the Next Issue? *Proceedings of the 33rd Hawaii International Conference on System Sciences.*

Maltz, A. & Ellram, L. (1999). Outsourcing supply management. *Journal of Supply Chain Management*, 35 (2), 4-17.

Morphy, E. (April 2002). CRM Web services trend building. CRMDaily.com.

Retrieved July 12, 2002 from the World Wide Web: http://www.ecommercetimes.com/perl/story/17437.html#story-start.

Nam, K., Rajagopalan, S., Rao, H. R. & Chaudhury, A. (1996). A two-level investigation of information systems outsourcing. *Association for Computing Machinery. Communications of the ACM*, 39 (7), 36-44.

Ngwenyama, O. K. & Bryson, N. (1999). Making the information systems outsourcing decision: A transaction cost approach to analyzing outsourcing decision, *European Journal of Operational Research*, 115 (2), 351-367.

Rao, H. R., Nam, K. & Chaudhury, A. (1996). Information systems outsourcing. *Association for Computing Machinery. Communications of the ACM*, 39 (7), 27-28.

Smith, M. A., Mitra, S. & Narasimhan, S. (1998). Information systems outsourcing: A study of pre-event firm characteristics. *Journal of Management Information Systems*, 15 (2), 61-93.

Thompson, B. (2001). What is CRM? Retrieved from the World Wide Web January 29, 2001: http://www.CRMguru.com.

Walter, A., Ritter, T. & Gemunden, H.G. (2001). Value creation in buyer-seller relationships: Theoretical considerations and empirical results from a supplier's perspective. *Industrial Marketing Management*, 30 (4), 365-377.

Winer, R. S. (2001). A framework for customer relationship management. *California Management Review*, 43 (4), 89-105.

Yang C. & Huang, J. (2000). A decision model for IS outsourcing. *International Journal of Information Management*, 20 (3), 225-239.

Young, D. (2001). CRM: Miscalculated ROI projections can result in multimillion-dollar IOUs. *Wireless Review*, 18, 10-14.

Yu, L. (2001). Successful customer-relationship management. *MIT Sloan Management Review*, 18-19.

Chapter XI

Implementation of the ASP Organizing Vision: The Role of Participation and Trust

Rajiv Kishore
The State University of New York at Buffalo, USA

ABSTRACT

A new breed of IT service providers, termed Application Service Providers (ASPs), has emerged during the last several years. While the ASP paradigm is opening new options for strategic governance of organizational IT infrastructures, implementation of this model is fraught with several uncertainties. This chapter describes a particular type of uncertainty, termed the "know-what" uncertainty, that firms generally face as they implement any techno-organizational innovation, and discusses some specific know-what uncertainties associated with the client adoption of the ASP paradigm. The chapter then discusses the role that participation and trust (in the ASP organizing vision) play in mitigating the client-side know-what uncertainties during the course of adoption and implementation of this new IT governance model. The chapter also provides some recommendations for clients and vendors for making this new IT services paradigm a successful reality.

BACKGROUND

Fundamental changes in the way Information Technology (IT) and related business applications are owned, operated, and managed are being brought about by a rapidly emerging class of IT service providers, termed "Application Service Providers" (ASPs). ASPs, enabled by Internet technologies, are redefining the notion of "IT outsourcing" by altering the IT assets ownership and control equation. In this IT governance paradigm, business applications are rented/leased from ASPs on a recurring fee basis, and are run by individual and corporate users in a browser window on their desktops. The software application and the client data reside on ASP platforms and are accessed by customers through public and private computer networks (quite often the Internet).

The ASP governance model has been touted as providing several strategic advantages to the IT function and, thereby, to the overall enterprise. Some of the potential advantages of the ASP paradigm that can accrue to the IT function of an enterprise include: an accelerated speed of deployment of IT applications, seamless connectivity and integration among diverse business partners through shared Web-based applications, scalability of IT infrastructure, and a lower and predictable total cost of ownership ("e-Sourcing the corporation: Harnessing the power of web-based application service providers," 2000). These advantages, indeed, have the potential to allow an enterprise to refocus on firm competencies and to provide flexibility in acquiring new business capabilities (*Application Service Providers (ASP)*, 1999).

However, the ASP governance model does not come without its share of challenges and risks. The fact that client data resides on ASP-owned servers poses new threats pertaining to data security and privacy. Software applications are operated and managed by ASP vendors, generally, as "packaged solutions" for multiple clients, because that is precisely what the ASP model provides for a one-to-many relationship. However, in such a scenario, there are risks of getting "locked in" with older versions of "vanilla" applications. Because the "value network" in the ASP model is quite complex, aggregating products and services from a number of vendors—including telecommunications and network providers, hardware vendors, application vendors, software tools vendors, service firms, and distributors and resellers (Gillan et al., 1999)—the overall quality of service to clients may be an important concern that needs to be fully addressed prior to adoption of this governance model. Finally, the financial viability of specific ASP vendors in the current financial climate, especially after the dot.com bust that started last year, is a matter of immense concern to potential adopters.

IMPLEMENTING THE ASP PARADIGM
Know-What Uncertainties

Knowledge about any phenomenon can be broken down into three components: *know-what*, *know-why*, and *know-how* (Garud, 1997). Know-what "represents an appreciation of the kinds of phenomenon worth pursuing," know-why "represents an understanding of the principles underlying phenomenon" and know-how "represents an understanding of the generative processes that constitute phenomenon" (Garud, 1997).

In the context of technological innovations, the three knowledge components can be viewed either from the vendor perspective or from the client perspective. Know-what from a vendor perspective involves knowing about customer needs and wants. This component of knowledge is extremely important for the vendors, because it provides the basis for developing newer products and newer product features that meet customer needs. From a customer/client perspective, however, know-what is the flip side of the coin. Vendors and their partners have developed newer products and services, and/or newer features/functionalities in existing products/services, based on their understanding of customer needs and wants. It is now the clients and the customers who have to know about these newer products/services that are available in the marketplace, and about their features and functionalities, in order to be able to find solutions for organizational problems; and/or to implement these leading-edge innovations within their firms to gain strategic advantage; or, to at least maintain strategic parity with their competitors. The other two knowledge components—know-why and know-how—can be viewed similarly from both the perspective of vendors and that of the clients. However, these components are not discussed in this chapter, as they are not of immediate interest from the perspective of implementation of the ASP paradigm.

In its current nascent state, both the vendor and client know-what about the ASP model is fairly limited. However, it is the client-side know-what about the ASP paradigm that is of interest and concern from the perspective of adoption and implementation of the ASP paradigm by client organizations. In the context of the ASP paradigm, client-side know-what represents an appreciation and understanding about the promises and perils of the ASP paradigm; client-side know-why represents an understanding about why this phenomenon will provide the benefits it promises; and client-side know-how represents specific methods and techniques required to utilize this phenomenon, both in terms of managing the contractual relationship and in terms of using the IT services provided through this model.

A lack of *client-side know-what* about the ASP paradigm constitutes what I have termed *know-what uncertainties* for potential adopter organizations of this IT governance choice. Overcoming these "know-what" uncertainties is essential for potential adopters, so they are not only able to adequately discriminate the substance from the hype about this IT governance model, and make informed choices during the adoption process, but also to negotiate "win-win" contracts and service level agreements with ASP vendors. The following section discusses two mechanisms for overcoming the client know-what uncertainties.

Overcoming Know-What Uncertainties
Participation and Trust in the ASP Organizing Vision

The IS field has developed a considerable body of literature in the area of systems implementation during the last two decades. IS literature also has devoted much attention, during the last decade, to the phenomenon of IS outsourcing, of which the ASP paradigm is a specific incarnation. However, there is a paucity of literature, in both these streams, that focuses on how the know-what uncertainties can be overcome in the context of adoption and implementation of strategic information technologies or IT governance mechanisms. I propose that participation (Huber, 1991; Rai & Patnayakuni, 1996) and trust (Rousseau, Sitkin, Burt, & Camerer, 1998) in the ASP paradigm, which I equate to an *organizing vision* (Swanson & Ramiller, 1997), can help organizations reduce know-what uncertainties as they evaluate the ASP option.

An *organizing vision* has been defined formally by Swanson and Ramiller (1997) as "a focal community idea for the application of information technology in organizations." Organizing visions are created by the larger IS community, comprised of IT vendors, IT consultants, potential adopters, research and advisory firms, etc., to facilitate the development and deployment of IT innovations. Then, organizing visions are iteratively crafted and refined in a community discursive domain, through such means and channels as trade shows, professional meetings, trade magazines, virtual communities, etc. The ASP paradigm is a perfect example of an organizing vision because, as discussed above, it is a specific application of new information technologies to provide IS/IT services to organizations in a novel and unique manner. It started as a concept for the provision of discrete and standalone IT applications such as word processing, scheduling, e-mail, etc., but gradually developed and evolved into a viable mechanism for governance of entire IT infrastructures of organizations throughout the last several years. The gradual evolution of this vision took place in a discursive arena populated by a community of IT vendors, service providers, consultants, professionals, academics, researchers, etc. who have some academic, professional, and/or business interest/stake in this paradigm. The two mechanisms for managing know-what uncertainties are discussed next.

Participation in the Organizing Vision

Participating in the organizing vision discourse provides potential adopters with an opportunity to know, more comprehensively, the context and content of the focal innovation—ASP paradigm in our case—and its advantages and attendant risks, thereby reducing their know-what uncertainty pertaining to the ASP phenomenon. This participation not only provides potential adopters with knowledge about "… the existence and potential gains of a new innovation" (Attewell, 1992), or "signaling" information, it also provides the potential adopter with the opportunity to actually connect with the external IT community and engage in richer two-way interactions with the various players in the ASP arena. Therefore, the ASP organizing vision is a much larger mechanism than signaling for helping to reduce the know-what uncertainties, and it is expected to affect a potential adopter's perceptions about the advantages of and risks inherent to the ASP paradigm.

Therefore, participation in the organizing vision discourse, and connectedness with the external IS community, provides potential adopters of the ASP paradigm with an opportunity to know more comprehensively about the focal innovation—ASP paradigm in our case. Such adopters better understand the context for application of this paradigm through seminars and discussions, where vendors provide information and ideas about the circumstances when the ASP model makes sense for organizations to adopt and utilize. Such connected and participating adopters also stand to gain a better understanding about the advantages and attendant risks of the ASP paradigm from their peers in other organizations. The notions of connectedness and participation are supported by the organizational learning literature (Huber, 1991) and empirical studies in the IT innovation adoption area (Rai & Patnayakuni, 1996).

Trust in the ASP Organizing Vision

"Trust is a psychological state comprising the intention to accept vulnerability based upon positive expectations of the intentions or behavior of another" (Rousseau et al., 1998). A heightened awareness about the relative advantages and risks of the ASP paradigm will result from a higher degree of participation in the organizing vision discourse. However, a potential adopter may still be uncertain about the "truthfulness" of the claims about the ASP vision, and those made by specific ASP vendors, and the likelihood of successful implementation of this paradigm. Trust—both an institutional trust in the ASP paradigm and calculative trust between the vendor and the client organizations—provides yet another mechanism for reducing know-what uncertainties pertaining to the fruition of benefits and the occurrence of risky and undesirable outcomes (Rousseau et al., 1998). Trust is expected to moderate the relationship between the key drivers of adoption—perceived relative advantages and perceived risks of the ASP paradigm—and the adoption/implementation of the ASP model. Trustworthiness characteristics (Sheppard & Sherman, 1998) also act as mitigators for the various kinds of risks that are inherent to the ASP paradigm, and not only alleviate adopter concerns during initial adoption decisions, but also provide mechanisms to manage inherently "incomplete" ASP outsourcing contracts through a judicious combination of control and trust (Das & Teng, 1998).

RECOMMENDATIONS FOR CLIENTS AND VENDORS

Based on the notions discussed above, some concrete recommendations can be provided to client IT managers who are involved in the evaluation and implementation of the ASP model within their organizations. First, client managers will be well-advised to "get connected" with and within the ASP community, so that they not only get to know what is on the anvil, but are also able to shape the evolving ASP vision. They can get connected either in a one-way technology-scanning mode or in a two-way discourse participation mode. Technology scanning is possible through subscription to e-mail services and/or browsing of Web sites and documents provided by technology research and advisory firms (such as IDC at www.idc.com, Gartner Group, at www.gartner.com, Yankee Group at www.yankeegroup.com, etc.), ASP consortia (such as ASP Industry Consortium at www.aspic.com), and ASP portals (such as www.aspindustry.org/index.html, www.aspisland.com, etc.). Several IT magazines, such as *CIO* at www.cio.com also maintain special-interest sections on ASPs and related topics on their Web sites. Two-way discourse participation is possible by subscribing to e-message boards and attending ASP-related conferences, organized by several of the aforementioned organizations, in addition to IT outsourcing-related consulting and advisory firms (such as The Outsourcing Institute at www.outsourcing.com and Outsourcing Center at www.outsourcing-center.com), systems integration firms (such as EDS at www.eds.com, IBM at www.ibm.com, etc.), and IT consulting firms (such as PriceWaterhouseCoopers at www.pwc.com and Cap Gemini Ernst and Young at www.capgemini.com).

Second, it is important for client managers also to assess their trust in the ASP vendors and that they consider such vendor factors as reputation, size of the firm, willingness to customize applications, discretion, reliability, competence/ability, integrity, predictability, and foresight. Some of these factors can be assessed based on "brand" name and publicly available information, while others can be judged only by prior experience. Given that the ASP sector is young, and has had a volatile history since its inception, it is particularly important that client managers assess their trust in the vendors realistically, and do not swap control mechanisms, such as penalty clauses, with trust-based mechanisms in their ASP vendors.

The ASP vendors have an important responsibility to get their clients connected into the discursive arena, preferably in a two-way communication mode. This will help educate their clients about the various services currently offered by ASP vendors, and also will help the vendors understand customer needs—based on which, they can create products and offerings that will have appeal and utility for their customers. Moreover, such two-way communication also will foster closer ties between vendors and clients, providing the vendors with an opportunity to signal their trustworthiness characteristics and their desire to work with their clients to solve their clients' problems.

Finally, ASP vendors also have a great responsibility toward creating and reinforcing institutional trust in the overall ASP paradigm. Toward this end, ASP vendors can adopt "best practices" that will contribute positively toward building of institutional trust in this paradigm. Such industry-accepted best practices can be created by ASP industry consortia, in consultation with their membership base, and may include pledges of full adherence to disclosure policies, standard service levels and standard penalty clauses. Creation of institutional trust in the ASP paradigm is particularly important, because lower institutional trust in this model has the potential to greatly hamper adoption of the this governance choice by client organizations jeopardizing the very existence of this innovative IT governance model.

CONCLUSIONS

This chapter discussed some know-what uncertainties associated with the adoption of the novel ASP paradigm by client organizations. Two broad mechanisms—participation and trust in the ASP organizing vision—were discussed, as a means to facilitate adoption and implementation of the ASP paradigm within organizations. Finally, some practical recommendations for client and vendor organizations were presented to foster successful adoption and implementation of this IT governance model.

ACKNOWLEDGMENTS

An earlier version of this chapter was presented at the 2002 International Conference of the Information Resources Management Association. The author would like to thank the two anonymous reviewers who reviewed the earlier version of this paper, and the several attendees of the session in which the paper was presented, for their insightful comments. The author also would like to gratefully acknowledge the financial support provided by NSF to the author under grant #9907325 which partially supported this research. Any opinions, findings, and conclusions or recommendations expressed in this material are those of the author and do not necessarily reflect the views of the National Science Foundation.

REFERENCES

Application Service Providers (ASP). (1999). (Spotlight Report). Cherry Tree & Co.

Attewell, P. (1992). Technology diffusion and organizational learning: The case of business computing. *Organization Science,* 3, 1-19.

Das, T. K., & Teng, B.-S. (1998). Between trust and control: Developing confidence in partner cooperation in alliances. *Academy of Management Review,* 23(3), 491512.

e-Sourcing the corporation: Harnessing the power of web-based application service providers. (2000). *Fortune,* March 6, S1-S27.

Garud, R. (1997). On the distinction between know-how, know-what and know-why. In A. Huff & J. Walsh (Eds.), *Advances in Strategic Management* (pp. 81-101): JAI Press.

Gillan, C., Graham, S., Levitt, M., McArthur, J., Murray, S., Turner, V., Villars, R., &Whalen, M. M. (1999). *The ASPs' impact on the IT industry: An IDC-wide opinion.* International Data Corporation.

Huber, G. P. (1991). Organizational learning: The contributing processes and the literature. *Organization Science,* 2(1), 88-115.

Keil, M., Tan, B. C. Y., Wei, K.-K., Saarinen, T., Tuunainen, V., & Wassenaar, A.(2000). A cross-cultural study on escalation of commitment behavior in software projects. *MIS Quarterly,* 24(2), 299-325.

Rai, A., & Patnayakuni, R. (1996). A structural model for CASE adoption behavior. *Journal of Management Information Systems,* 13(2), 205-234.

Rogers, E. M. (1995). *Diffusion of Innovations* (Fourth ed.). New York: The Free Press.

Rousseau, D. M., Sitkin, S. B., Burt, R. S., & Camerer, C. (1998). Not so different after all: A cross-discipline view of trust. *Academy of Management Review,* 23(3), 393404.

Sheppard, B. H., & Sherman, D. M. (1998). The grammars of trust: A model and general implications. *Academy of Management Review,* 23(3), 422-437.

Sitkin, S. B., & Pablo, A. L. (1992). Reconceptualizing the determinants of risk behavior. *Academy of Management Review,* 17(1), 9-38.

Sitkin, S. B., & Weingart, L. R. (1995). Determinants of risky decision-making behavior: A test of the mediating role of risk perceptions and propensity. *Academy of Management Journal,* 38(6), 1573-1592.

Swanson, E. B., & Ramiller, N. C. (1997). The organizing vision in information systems innovation. *Organization Science,* 8(5), 458-474.

Chapter XII

Measurement Issues in Decision Support Systems

William K. Holstein
The College of William and Mary, USA

Jakov Crnkovic
State University of New York at Albany, USA

ABSTRACT

After a brief discussion on the history of decision-making, this chapter focuses on metrics for justifying investment in information systems and technology and for measuring business and management performance. The discussion of metrics is linked to current practices in decision support systems and focuses on the needs for future systems. With several examples drawn from contemporary practice, we introduce implementation guidelines for DSS development incorporating new metrics that go beyond ROI and Balanced Scorecard-like measures. Suggested guidelines include simplicity, selectivity, a focus on research and learning, and benchmarking. These guidelines suggest that future metrics to support decision support systems should be grouped into meaningful categories and tied more closely to system architecture.

INTRODUCTION

The past decade has seen tremendous progress in systems for information support including flexible and adaptable systems to support decision makers and to accommodate individual needs and preferences. These model- or data-driven or hybrid systems incorporate diverse data drawn from many different internal and external sources. Increasingly, these sources include sophisticated enterprise resource planning systems, data warehouses and other enterprise-wide systems that contain vast amounts of data and permit relatively easy access to that data by a wide variety of users at many different levels of the organization. Decision support and DSS have entered our lexicon and are now increasingly common topics of discussion and development in large, and even in medium-sized, enterprises.

Recent economic conditions, particularly the downturn in the fortunes of e-commerce, suggest that the road ahead for DSS may be fraught with problems. In our view, many of those problems have to do with inadequate procedures and metrics for measuring business and management performance. As this is written, in mid-2002, daily headlines about overstatement of revenues, and the recording of expenses as capital expenditures at collapsing companies such as Enron and WorldCom indicate that we clearly have problems with aggregate metrics on issues previously thought to be well understood (revenues, expenses, etc.), but the issue is also present at lower levels.

A SHORT DISCOURSE ON THE HISTORY OF DECISION-MAKING

Decision-making as we know it today, supported by computers and vast information systems, is a relatively recent phenomenon. But the concept has been around long enough to permit the methods and theories of decision-making to blossom into "a plethora of paradigms, research schools, and competing theories and methods actively argued by thousands of scientists and decision makers worldwide."[1]

The fundamental considerations of contemporary decision-making were enunciated almost 100 years ago by the French philosopher and statistician Jules Henri Poincaré. Here is a Poincaré quote from the source cited just above: "But of all these paths, which will lead us most promptly to the goal? Who will tell us which to choose? We need a faculty, which will help us perceive the goal from afar. This faculty is intuition ... Logic and intuition both have a necessary part to play. Both are indispensable. Logic alone can convey certainty: it is the instrument of proof. Intuition is the instrument of invention."[2]

Intuition ... perceiving the goal from afar. Today we use different terms, such as judgment, experience, and soft data, but the ideas are the same as Poincaré's – we must find ways to combine logic (and technology) and the soft skills and experience of managers to support decision-making.

Copyright © 2003, Idea Group Inc. Copying or distributing in print or electronic forms without written permission of Idea Group Inc. is prohibited.

Early computer systems focused primarily on accounting and financial data. It is said that information systems are about transforming data. We could say that early systems transformed data into aggregated or summarized data – for example, wage rates, hours worked, benefits and tax data etc. transformed into departmental or corporate payroll reports.

In the mid-1960s, the development of the IBM System 360 and rapidly proliferating competitive systems from other vendors ushered in the era of Management Information Systems (MIS). Applications quickly moved beyond finance and accounting data and into operations. Transaction processing systems began to generate order, usage, and customer data that could be analyzed with (what quickly became quite sophisticated) models. Real transformation of data into information became commonplace. For example, the transformation of data on sales and usage, costs, supplier lead times and associated uncertainties were transformed into re-order points, safety stocks and comprehensive inventory management and production scheduling systems.

Despite the broader reach of MIS, such systems are characterized by highly structured, infrequent reports, often with standard formatting. Frequently, because it was "easier" (for the IT staff), each manager in a given function, e.g., marketing, received the same voluminous report – even though a manager of activities in Japan could not care less about data relating to New Jersey. Despite the tremendous advance of MIS over previous generation systems, most of the data in management information systems was internal, historical (related to already concluded transactions), and financial.

Parallel to the development of computers and information systems that supported the acquisition and processing of useful data, others were working on decision-making per se. A particularly interesting approach was developed by Charles Kepner and Benjamin Tregoe that survives to this day as the Kepner-Tregoe method for problem solving.[3] Their practical methodology for decision-making isolates clearly defined problems, generates alternative solutions, and defines criteria and a weighting scheme to evaluate the alternatives and choose a solution.

Despite its clarity and power, the Kepner-Tregoe method has problems with judgment factors, or what we now call soft data – Poincaré's "intuition." Judgment plays an important role in decision-making, and the consideration of judgments is tricky. Not all judgments, or everybody's judgment, should be considered, or even weighted. The difficult balancing of subjective and objective values is frequently not amenable to straightforward weighting and formal analysis.

By the end of the 1970s, it was clear that model-based decision support had become a practical, useful tool for managers. Decision support systems (DSS) "evolved from the theoretical studies of organizational decision-making done at the Carnegie Institute of Technology during the late 1950s and early 1960s and the technical work on interactive computer systems, mainly carried out at the Massachusetts Institute of Technology in the 1960s."[4]

The dramatic increase in computing power in the 1990s, coupled with rapid development of the Internet, has led us finally to the true era of information support. Contemporary software including database management systems and enterprise resource planning systems, together with the interconnection of businesses through supply chain management and Internet-based communications, offer limitless opportunity for further development of decision support systems and methodology.

IT INVESTMENT METRICS

Many large investments in enterprise systems and e-commerce infrastructure have been made without clear justification from traditional measures such as Return on Investment (ROI) or Payback, or even newer measures such as Total Cost of Ownership or Economic Value Added. Many managers have been content to follow poet Elizabeth Barrett Browning's advice:

Measure not the work
Until the day's out and the labour done
Then bring your gauges.

Two additional, more contemporary, quotes make the same point: "Only three years ago, using return on investment as a guide to technology purchases seemed so ... Old Economy. Technology strategists at many firms used other criteria, such as a product's distinctiveness, its degree of innovation, even the 'eyeballs' it might attract to a Web site."[5] "Most don't know what the ROI is on CRM [and other large IT investments]. They're making big, expensive, politically risky blind faith investments."[6]

But now, as might be expected in economic hard times, managers are calling for more formal justification of new IT investments. Many are finding that adequate metrics do not exist. There is a considerable literature dealing with metrics related to IT investments. We will take a broader view, because we believe the problems with metrics go well beyond IT investment justification, but we begin with some brief data on IT investment metrics.

An *Internet Week* survey reported in October 2001 that 82% of 1,000 managers surveyed said they expect their company's overall e-business operations to be profitable in 2001. Yet only 34% said their company had developed a formal model to measure the success of those operations. A Jupiter Media Metrix survey reported in the same article indicates that most companies use ROI metrics that are inconsistent from one project to another, making it "nearly impossible to correctly choose which projects should be funded and which should be killed."[7]

The times when any investment related to Internet-enabling an enterprise was considered too strategic to require detailed justification are over. But what metrics are valid and useable? The *Internet Week* survey suggests that more than half of IT investment projects related to e-businesses have problems with measurement:[8]

25%	Don't have the time or budget to conduct detailed justification studies
19%	Available metrics are not satisfactory
13%	ROI doesn't apply

We are convinced that the problem goes beyond metrics to justify and support IT investments and extends to broader questions of methods and metrics for measuring business and management performance. Although recent headlines highlight questionable or even fraudulent accounting practices, for most managers the issues relate to more routine decision-making.

Examples of routine decision-making include questions such as:
- Should we outsource our human resources information system?
- Even though we are growing, we lost 10% of our customers last year. What would it cost, and what would be the savings, of reducing that turnover to 5%?
- Should we require our major suppliers to grant us a 5% price reduction?
- What can be done to reduce the turnover of engineers by at least 20%?
- Should we enter the market in Bulgaria?
- Can all of our units use a common data warehouse, or do we need several specialized data marts?
- What is the effect of reducing our sales force by 15% across the board vs. 20% in Europe only?

Answers to questions such as these will not only have an important impact on the success of the business, but provide examples of the frame in which the decision support systems of the future will be defined – relating to external data (e.g., customers, suppliers, foreign markets), involving large issues that approach strategic implications and are difficult to analyze (e.g., outsourcing, turnover, and the impact of IT systems on performance).

Copyright © 2003, Idea Group Inc. Copying or distributing in print or electronic forms without written permission of Idea Group Inc. is prohibited.

METRICS OF BUSINESS AND MANAGEMENT PERFORMANCE

Decision support means supporting managers who are running the business. Increasingly, it refers to supporting middle-level managers who rely on a mix of internal and external data that is steadily tilting towards external data on customers, markets, competitors, and the political, regulatory and economic environment. If we define the process of *control* as tasks undertaken by middle- and lower-level managers to *ensure that plans come true*, we see clearly the role of data and information in decision support: managers use data and convert it into information to *monitor* the implementation of plans to ensure that strategic goals are met. If the monitoring indicates that plans will not be fulfilled, corrective *action* must be taken *in time* to ensure that the plan is, in fact, met. If the information from a decision support system cannot serve as the basis for action (i.e., cannot first help the decision maker to decide to do something, and then help to decide what to do) the information will not be used and the system will therefore be useless.

The key words in the previous paragraph that lead to action are *monitoring* and *time*. Monitoring is the management function that is the primary target for DSS implementation. Timeliness is crucial. Advance warning without enough time to steer around the iceberg, or to make the necessary changes to ensure that strategic plans are successful, is not the kind of decision support that managers seek.

As we think about supporting management decision-making, we must think of how managers work. Their role is easy to describe (despite the fact that it is fiendishly difficult to accomplish): managers abhor irregularities and plans that do not come true, yet they thrive on exceptions. They look for things that don't fit, for things that look funny, for things that are out of line. Then they ask "why?" Much of their time is spent trying to answer that simple question and searching for actions that will make perceived problems disappear and bring things back to normal expectations. Examples of the "whys" that plague managers of large companies include: Why can't Cadillac attract younger buyers? Why did the PC manufacturers who dominated the market in the 1990s lose so much share to Dell Computer? Why do practically none of the profits of the newly merged HP/Compaq come from PCs? Which of the newly merged HP/Compaq's 85,000 products should survive? (Abruptly killing off redundant products might scare customers and deflate revenues, but overlap is costly.)[9]

For each of these questions, one can imagine a manager who is conjuring the question as a response to a perceived exception that needs to be "fixed." What Cadillac sales manager thinks that his/her product is not attractive to young buyers? What HP manager thinks that Dell's share should be where it is? What former Compaq manager thinks his/her product should be dropped?

Copyright © 2003, Idea Group Inc. Copying or distributing in print or electronic forms without written permission of Idea Group Inc. is prohibited.

We cite this process and these questions to focus clearly on metrics of business performance and management performance. Measurement and metrics are the tools for identifying exceptions. Exceptions, in turn, drive management to seek and find actions that will deal with the exceptions and achieve strategic goals. But think for a moment about traditional metrics. The Cadillac manager knows how to measure the average age of Cadillac buyers. But how does s/he measure the potential attractiveness to younger buyers of a proposed new model, of a proposed advertising campaign, or of a proposed discount or rebate program? This is where judgment and intuition come into play – and precisely the area where managers need decision support.

Before we leave the issue of metrics to measure business and management performance, and the important issue of metrics to identify exceptions in the accomplishment of strategic tasks, consider the following annotated quotes from a recent *Business Week* article about management changes at Microsoft.[10]

> Ballmer realized that he couldn't manage Microsoft the way Gates had. There were just too many moving parts, and it was too unwieldy.

(The definition of "success" in the Gates era was certainly different from the definition in Ballmer's era, when the company is several times larger, growing much more slowly, and subject to many more external regulatory influences. Gates' metrics simply could not be Ballmer's metrics.)

> Ballmer realized that Microsoft needed new methods to manage an ever-more-complex company. He first tried to organize around different kinds of customers. The idea was to get product-development groups more connected to users. But the reorganization didn't work. Decisions about such widely used products as Windows, for example, spread across too many of the new divisions.

New non-financial metrics often face a common problem in very large or in small or medium-sized enterprises – problems spread across divisions in large companies, or across people in small enterprises. It is difficult to assign clear responsibilities for performance against metrics such as improved customer service or faster response time.

> Ballmer has stitched together a quilt of management processes that, he says, especially suits Microsoft. (Changing management processes is the essence of management action.) "Ballmer elevated the importance of something he calls the "organizational health index" ... a survey of employees who are asked to rate their bosses on their leadership skills." (The implementation of a metric with clear communications implications.) "Perhaps Ballmer's biggest innovation is

something called the Executive P&L, a balance sheet that divides the company into seven distinct businesses and gives each unit's leader the financial tools to measure its performance. Ballmer hopes the device will empower execs who have long worked in an environment where everything was run by the CEO. In the past, managers would know the costs of developing a product but not the cost of selling it. Now, they can see their costs end-to-end, giving them the information necessary to make decisions about allocating resources without having to run it by Ballmer.

Despite the mixed P&L/balance sheet metaphor, this is an outstanding example of the point that we are trying to make – that decision support involves measurement of strategic tasks, effectively communicated and monitored.

The Microsoft example supports a clear summary: in the current environment, measurement must be related to business matters, business strategies and goals – the stuff that managers deal with in their everyday environment. IT-related metrics related to uptime, downtime, response time and peak capacity mean little to managers under pressure to make plans come true. They are trying to formulate and monitor plans that reflect the strategic mission and goals of the business, (i.e., accomplish strategic tasks). They need IT that can add value to the business in ways that they can clearly understand. IT investment justification and metrics are important, but considered in the larger context of business performance they are only a small part of the story.

DSS AND BUSINESS METRICS

The Balanced Scorecard Collaborative, an organization that promotes the Balanced Scorecard approach to measuring business and management performance, presents discouraging data if the objective for DSS is to support strategic tasks (the table found on page 176).[11]

These data suggest that business metrics, clearly related to strategy, are far more important than metrics related solely to IT investments or even to IT and systems performance.

Pulling together what we have stated thus far, we see a situation that precludes significant progress in the development and implementation of decision support systems unless:
- new metrics that focus more clearly on business and management performance are developed and implemented, and
- more attention is given to metrics that focus on monitoring strategic activities, or activities that will have an important effect on the outcomes of strategic initiatives and high-level company goals.

Only 5%	Of the workforce understands their company strategy
Only 25%	Of managers have incentives linked to strategy
Only 40%	Of organizations link budgets to strategy

The Balanced Scorecard and other initiatives have made it clear that traditional business metrics rely too heavily on financial and accounting measures. Financial measures tend to be hard, historical, and internal, rather than soft (including judgmental data and estimates that, while inaccurate, are vital to future planning), future-oriented (and therefore, by definition, soft) and external (related to the customer, the market and the environment).[12] We see, therefore, that an important question is not just *what* to measure, but *how* to measure, and in which areas of the business to seek meaningful metrics.

Consider a metrics example from the world of professional sports. The Portland Trail Blazers basketball team has implemented an aggressive eCRM strategy to increase fan involvement and change the mix of audience demographics. Changing audience demographics is an excellent example a "strategic task." ROI metrics used to determine the effectiveness of the eCRM strategy indicate it that is paying off handsomely, but that is only part of the story. According to the chief financial officer of the Trail Blazers: "We can measure things like overall revenue, but that wouldn't tell us if we've got more fans because of how we service them or because the team just pulled in two new superstars. We needed to develop other metrics to analyze the impact (of our actions)."[13]

One metric is season ticket sales, which reduces dependency on transitory and more labor-intensive box-office sales. The eCRM system helps the Trailblazers target and service season ticket holders, and the results are clear. Season ticket sales increased by 5.4% in the first year after introduction of the system, and 7.3% the following year.

All of the Trailblazers' measurements are proprietary, but team managers say they indicate conclusively that the eCRM strategy is a keeper. "We ask ourselves continually if we had to do this all over again, would we?" says the Trail Blazer CFO, Jim Kotchik. "The answer is yes – even if it had cost twice as much."

As another example, consider a service company in the current difficult business environment. Following a historic strategy of developing a continuing stream of new and innovative services may not be appropriate at this time. What if management enunciates a strategy of operational excellence – doing things faster, better and cheaper – to support a traditional range of services? How do you measure speed, excellence, and simplicity? Cost per service might be a simple measure, but how do you incorporate complexity of the service provided, the cost of support required, after-sales costs? How would you benchmark your performance against competitors for whom your cost, timeliness and quality data estimates are sketchy at best?

The questions raised by this example are all answerable, individually, one at a time, by individual or small groups of managers. But, in reality, that is not the answer. These questions need to be answered in a *total, systematic manner* that spreads the idea of different measures, and then different business processes and structures to achieve results against the new metrics, throughout the organization. Earlier, we said that information that does not lead to action is useless. Here we paraphrase that comment by observing that new measurements and metrics that do not lead to significant organizational change are useless.

Much of the literature on measurement and metrics focuses on the measurement of IT accomplishments derived from business strategy. This is an important issue, certainly for those of us who promote the application of IT and systems to business problems. However, the terrain is connected to far more than just traditional IT tasks. Managers are trying to enhance customer service, shorten cycle times for existing products and time to market for new products, increase productivity, reduce costs, organize customers into meaningful segments and then develop unique programs to serve them better, etc. These tasks, earlier referred to as strategic tasks, are the stuff of which our systems, and our metrics, should be created. It is also important to note that metrics serve not only to support and measure performance, but also as the basis for communication within the organization – communication that helps to frame discussions in business, not IT, terms. We turn now to implementation issues surrounding these ideas and suggest some guidelines for DSS development incorporating new metrics.

IMPLEMENTATION GUIDELINES
Breadth in Measurement

A first guideline, as we have discussed, is that breadth in measurement (beyond financial and accounting measures) is important. The ideas behind the Balanced Scorecard should be understood and implemented in decision support systems. Breadth, however, does not imply complexity.

Consider the following quote – it may be true since it does not say "only three things" – and it fits the point here: "The ability of companies to boost profits depends on three things: how high they can lift their prices, how much they can increase output per worker, and how fast wages are rising."[14]

The ability to raise prices, often described as "pricing power," is related to many different metrics and measures. Some of these measures are financial, e.g., profitability of other divisions, products and services and capital structure; but many others are not, e.g., customer perception of the company's value proposition, features and benefits of products and services, embedded technology, total quality (not just product quality), competitive position in the marketplace, and relationships with customers, suppliers, and workers. Increasing worker productivity involves similarly complex metrics.

Simplicity

A second guideline is simplicity. Metrics must be easy to understand and communicate. They must relate to relevant activities and tasks, and be drivable, i.e., managers must be able to use the measures to determine (drive) actions that will affect future results.

An example of a simple, but powerful, metric is the pass-through measure offered by Trilogy, an e-business software maker from Austin, Texas. Trilogy prices its products according to the impact they have on their customers' businesses. "If we don't help an automobile manufacturer improve their success rate when they're selling cars, they don't pay," says Trilogy founder Joe Liemandt. "If we and our customers are focused on delivering value for their business, then good things happen for both of us."[15]

Selectivity

Our third suggestion relates to simplicity: DSS designers must avoid the impulse to measure everything. The focus must be only on the most important metrics from the user's (the decision maker's) point of view. Metrics should be built in hierarchies, with more details for lower-level managers, and fewer, more summarized measures for higher-level managers.

Consider the experience of the largest savings bank group in Norway, the Union Bank of Norway. The bank built a data warehouse and uses a CRM solution to create, manage, and analyze programs for building relationships with its customers. A marketing team launched a customer loyalty program targeted at the bank's most profitable customers. Nothing dramatic here – many companies are doing this. But the Union Bank of Norway's dialogue-based program captures information from customers to use as the basis for the *next contact*. The next contact with the customer might be triggered by an event, by elapsed time since the previous contact, or by other developments or circumstances.[16]

Here we see bank management's clear perception that an important element of customer relationship management is planning and executing the next contact with the most profitable customers. The system, models, data and metrics combine to implement that perception with an impressive 70% customer response rate.

Research and Learning

Fourth, DSS design should emphasize data and data collection, not just for reporting, evaluation and auditing, but also for research and learning, for finding exceptions, for learning the causes of exceptions and for exploring alternative courses of remedial action. Research is perhaps a strange term to use in the context of management practice, but research, in the best sense of the term (investigate, study, explore, delve into, examine) is required to find, first, meaningful measures of exceptions and, then, their causes.

Here is an excellent example of a system that facilitates research and enhances learning from the Data Warehousing Institute: "Pep Boys is an automotive after-market enterprise with 629 stores in 36 states and Puerto Rico. Just a few years ago, field sales managers, relying on reports mailed from headquarters, often didn't know whether performance and profitability goals had been met until weeks later. Frustrated, the company embarked on an enterprise-wide business intelligence initiative. The result is a data warehouse with an easy-to-use interface." Roughly 1,000 users now access the system and can conduct their own ad hoc queries and analyses in seconds. Approximately 20 analytical cubes cover areas such as store hierarchy, service, commercial sales, retail sales and human resources. "Where reports are used to generate more questions, the system allows me to find answers – and attain a richer level of detail," says the director of service operations.[17]

Benchmarking

As a fifth guideline, we cannot overemphasize the importance of benchmarking against credible external targets. Indeed, without a firm connection to good external benchmarks (best practice, best-of-class indicators) companies can fall victim to *manumation*, simply automating old, outdated processes. A formula for the process has been around for years:

$$OP + NT = EOP$$
(**Old Processes** plus **New Technology** equals **Expensive Old Processes**)

Benchmark analysis can identify problems and suggest solutions and can serve as an excellent idea bank for new metrics. Benchmarks or comparatives are important because metrics need anchor points for comparison. Without a benchmark for normal or best-in-class, how can you gauge results?

Simple benchmarks might include your own past performance, current goals, customer expectations for things like order-to-delivery time, percentage defects, or on-time delivery. In particular, you should know how you compare to others in your industry and leaders in your functional area. Be sure to think carefully about which comparatives will lead to valid conclusions and sensible action.

In some industries and functions, there are a growing number of highly useful benchmarks from trade associations, consulting companies and other organizations. An example of a widely used set of metrics is the Supply Chain Council's Supply Chain Operations Reference (SCOR) model. SCOR allows companies to objectively measure their supply chain practices and compare them against benchmark standards gathered from the more than 700 manufacturing and related companies that are members of the Supply Chain Council. The SCOR model groups supply chain functions into five process categories: Plan, Source, Make, Deliver, and Return. Metrics at each level of the model are supported by progressively more detailed metrics for processes at lower levels.

The following quote highlights the importance of metrics to support process change when new factors, such as Web-enabled processes, are introduced: "Updating performance metrics for Web-enabled supply chain operations became important the day your company migrated from an information-only Website to one with interactive customer capabilities. Whether you're tracking customer orders or collaborating with partners on products and processes, your new business dynamics likely don't fit the old criteria, and you may need to update your basic supply chain performance measurements to match an advanced level of attainable objectives."[18]

Benchmarking is useful beyond performance measurement. It can help to answer why when exceptions are identified. For example, is a manufacturer's frequent late delivery an inventory-level issue or is it caused by slow order-reaction-time on the part of one or more of the supply chain's participants? Benchmarking can help to target on the exact answer, which can then lead to needed adjustments.

Time

As a sixth and final guideline, we suggest careful consideration of collapsing time. Speeding up of business processes and reaction times has become almost a cliché, but time is the most important element in many new metrics to support decision-making. Consider this example from the previously quoted article: "Take one standard supply chain metric: order fulfillment lead time. Its meaning remains the same as always, but the effective unit of measure applied (time, in this case) has been moving from months down to weeks, from weeks to days, and, in this 'e-' era, to hours."[19]

Another example cited in the same article is a benchmark metric called "*upside production flexibility*," meaning the number of calendar days to achieve an unplanned, sustainable 30% increase in production – perhaps prompted by a sudden change in a supply chain partner's requirements. "If I said today that I need 30% more of something, how fast can my suppliers, and their component suppliers, deliver that? [Only] Part of the answer is in manufacturing lead time, [The other, equally important] part is administrative lead times – getting the information, sharing it, and synchronizing it."

SUMMARY

The previous quote deftly summarizes much of what we have discussed. We see a clear exception – the need to increase output by 30%, quickly – and the immediate following need to organize the required information internally, and then communicate that information externally to suppliers and on to their suppliers.

The key element in the processes that are involved here is time, not cost. So, first, metrics to ensure that these processes are working properly will be drawn largely from non-financial data.

Next, there is a pressing need to focus only on the most important, but not necessarily the most obvious, issues and to collect relevant data to support understanding of how the task will be accomplished. Much of the learning will be based on intensive communication, with suppliers and their suppliers, probably much of it Web-based.

Previous benchmarking outside the organization with suppliers and processes would be highly valuable at this point – indicating who can perform and who cannot.

Summarizing our implementation guidelines for the development of metrics for decision support systems:

- think beyond financial measures,
- focus only on the most important, but not necessarily obvious, issues and collect relevant data to support exploration, analysis and understanding,
- benchmark outside the organization and build relevant knowledge to support change, and
- do it fast, and make it possible for users of the system to work quickly as well.

INDICATIONS FOR FURTHER DISCUSSION

We have only scratched the surface in this chapter. Much more needs to be done to categorize and delineate metrics for decision support and to tie metrics more closely to system architecture and concepts. Metrics for reporting performance, for example, differ significantly from metrics for improving performance. We need a better understanding of how these different types of metrics can be incorporated in decision support systems. It is also important to understand the technical details of measurement and metrics. There is much beyond ROI and payback metrics.[20]

Categories of Metrics

To add just a little more detail to the question of categorization, we present a framework that usefully defines aggregate categories of metrics. The framework is built on the concept of three-part, or perhaps three-force, leverage provided by different categories of metrics.

Managing accountabilities, or performance management, includes the entire process from defining jobs and setting goals to tracking results, reviewing performance and providing rewards.

Leverage first applies when you manage accountability for results. Additional leverage accrues by measuring and managing work processes, since all the future results produced by that process will be improved. Likewise, by measuring and managing organizational capability, all the future processes and results that rely on that capability will be influenced in a positive manner. Leverage over future results increases as you go further and further behind the scenes to manage the factors by which results are produced.[21]

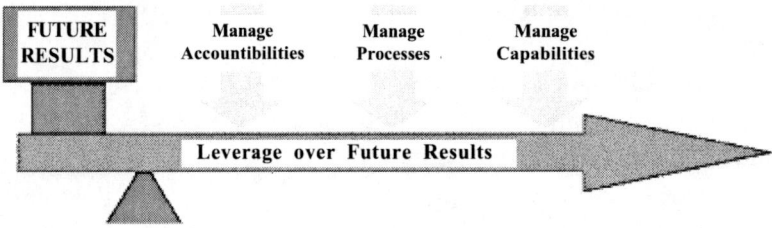

Organization Structure for IS/IT

Organizational approaches to IS have evolved in a cyclic manner over time.[22] At one end of the spectrum, centralized IS organizations bring together all staff, hardware, software, and processing into a single location. Decentralized organizations scatter these components in different locations to address local business needs. Enterprises of all shapes and sizes can be found at any point along the continuum. Over time, however, each enterprise tends to gravitate toward one end of the continuum or the other, and often reorganization is, in reality, a change from one end to the other.

How does a company's approach to its systems and information technology affect its metrics? We offer no answer, but suggest that the question is a lively one that should be considered. The following table[23] summarizes the advantages and disadvantages of the centralized vs. decentralized approach to IT/IS organization. Clearly, given these differences, appropriate metrics might be very different at the two ends of the continuum.

We began with a quote from a turn-of-the-last-century French philosopher, highlighting the importance of "intuition." We all agree that contemporary decision support systems must include more external, soft data and incorporate mechanisms for integrating judgments with facts. But soft data is often dodgy as the British would say – unreliable, inaccurate, and judgmental. While some data might not be usable for reporting and management performance evaluation, it could be invaluable for suggesting avenues for change and for improving performance. What DSS architecture can accommodate these differences in role and data quality and still meet simplicity and transparency requirements?

There are many unknowns, but one thing is sure: rapid progress in DSS will be made, with or without those of us in the academy who are interested in contributing. We must sharpen our understanding and clarify our communication if we hope to influence the future of metrics and DSS.

Approach	Advantages	Disadvantages
Centralized	Global standards, common data	Technology may not meet local needs
	"One voice" when negotiating supplier contracts	Slow support for strategic initiatives
	Economies of scale and a shared cost structure	"Us versus them" mentality when technology problems occur
	Access to large capacity	Lack of business unit control over overhead costs
Decentralized	Technology customized to local business needs	Difficulty maintaining global standards and consistent data
	Closer partnership between IT and business units	Higher infrastructure costs
	Greater flexibility	Loss of control
	Consistency with decentralized enterprise structure	Duplication of staff and data
	Business unit control over overhead costs	

ENDNOTES

1. Robins, E. (2001). A brief history of decision-making. White Paper from the Technology Evaluation Corp. technologyevaluation.com
2. These ideas were first expressed in Poincaré, J.H. (1905). Science and Hypothesis. Translated in The Foundations of Science. (1982) Washington, D.C.: University Press of America.
3. See http://www.kepner-tregoe.com/
4. Keen, P. & Morton, M.S. (1978). *Decision support systems: An organizational perspective*. Reading, MA: Addison-Wesley.
5. Kirsner, S. (2002). How do you spell value? *Newsweek*, June 10, 2002.
6. Zornes, A. (2000). VP Meta Group. *ENT Magazine,* December 13, 2000.
7. InternetWeek.com, October 1, 2001.
8. *ibid*
9. A post-merger checklist sidebar in HP and Compaq: It's showtime, *Business Week*, June 17, 2002.
10. "Ballmer's Microsoft: How CEO Steve Ballmer is remaking the company that Bill Gates built," *Business Week*, June 17, 2002.
11. From an August 20, 2001 advertisement for the Balanced Scorecard Collaborative. See bscol.com
12. The Balanced Scorecard initiative (See bscol.com) has done much to raise awareness of this point, but we believe that much more must be done, particularly to connect Balanced Scorecard-like ideas to DSS.
13. Banham, R. (2001). ROI: Mad to Measure. *eCFO Magazine*, September 17, 2001. See also www.nba.com/blazers
14. Mandel, M.J. (2002). More productivity, more profits? *Business Week,* June 10, 2002.
15. See Endnote 5.
16. Kari Opdal, Head of CRM for Union Bank of Norway, quoted in CRM and event-based marketing initiatives deliver results in *What Works, Best Practices in Data Warehousing and Business Intelligence, Volume 13*, a 101communications Publication in sponsorship with The Data Warehousing Institute.
17. Robert Berckman, Director of MIS, Pep Boys, Pep Boys tunes into its data, driving sharper decision-making, in *What Works, Best Practices in Data Warehousing and Business Intelligence*, 13, a 101 communications Publication in sponsorship with The Data Warehousing Institute. Additional reference: www.ibm.com/bi
18. Schultz, G. (2001). Advanced performance metrics for the e-era. *Technology Edge*, June 2001.
19. George Schultz, see Reference 18. The subtitle of the article is instructive: Your old gauge for measuring and meeting operational and profitability goals may need recalibration.

20   A useful reference on metrics related to IT investments is Theo J.W. Renkema, T.J.W. (2000). *The IT value quest: How to capture business value of IT-based infrastructure*. New York: John Wiley & Sons.
21   Bob Frost, Performance metrics: How to use them and how to get more leverage. Source: http://www.pbviews.com/magazine/articles/performance_metrics.html
22   Pearlson, K.E. *Managing and using information systems: A strategic approach*. New York: John Wiley and Sons.
23   *ibid*

An early version of this chapter was presented at the 2002 Information Resources Management Association International Conference, May 19-22, 2002, in Seattle, Washington, and appeared in the proceedings of the conference.

Chapter XIII

Information Technology Strategic Alignment: Brazilian Cases

Fernando José Barbin Laurindo
University of São Paulo, Brazil

Marly Monteiro de Carvalho
University of São Paulo, Brazil

Tamio Shimizu
University of São Paulo, Brazil

ABSTRACT

This chapter presents a study about the effectiveness of Information Technology (IT) applications in Brazilian companies. IT has been considered a strategic issue for successful companies. On the other hand, the discussion about the results of Information Technology (IT) applications considering the return over the investments and the effectiveness of their management still remains controversial. Effectiveness evaluation allows strategic alignment between IT and company business visions and should be analyzed as a continuous process. In order to discuss these issues, in this chapter, a comparative analysis about IT strategic impacts is performed using different theoretical models. The study is based on multiple cases: financial services, telecommunications, and building materials companies. Interviews with the main actors from different levels of the organization hierarchy have been done.

Copyright © 2003, Idea Group Inc. Copying or distributing in print or electronic forms without written permission of Idea Group Inc. is prohibited.

INTRODUCTION

Information Technology (IT) has assumed an important position in the strategic function of the leading companies in the competitive markets (Porter, 2001). Particularly, e-commerce and e-business have been highlighted among IT applications (Porter, 2001; Evans & Wurster, 1999). Two basic points of view can be used for understanding IT's role: the acquisition of a competitive advantage at the value chain and the creation and enhancement of core competencies (Porter & Millar, 1985; Duhan et al., 2001).

Effectiveness, in the context of this chapter, is the measurement of the capacity of the outputs of an Information System or of an IT application to fulfill the requirements of the company and to achieve its goals, making this company more competitive. In a few words, effectiveness can be understood as the ability to "do the right thing" (Laurindo & Shimizu, 2000; Walrad & Moss, 1993; Maggiolini, 1981; Drucker, 1963).

Several problems have been discussed concerning IT project results in effectiveness of their management. In spite of different approaches about the "productivity paradox," there is a general consensus about the difficulty of finding evidence of returns over the investments in IT (Brynjolfsson, 1998; Willcocks & Lester, 1997; Brynjolfsson, 1993; Strassman, 1990). The evaluation of IT effectiveness allows the strategic alignment of objectives of implemented systems and their results with the company business vision (Laurindo et al., 2002; Laurindo, 2002; Laurindo & Shimizu, 2000; Hirscheim & Smithson, 1998).

The comparison and evaluation of business and IT strategies and between business and IT structures must be a continuous process, since the company situation is constantly changing to meet market realities and dynamics.

In order to understand how IT effectiveness can be managed, a comparative analysis about the role of IT in Brazilian companies is presented. The theoretical models used in effectiveness analysis were based on the Rockart's Critical Success Factors method, McFarlan Strategic Grid (1984), and Henderson & Venkatraman Strategic Alignment Model (1993) approaches. Three case studies are performed in financial, telecommunications and building materials companies.

FINDING STRATEGIC IT APPLICATIONS

Critical Success Factors (CSF) is a widespread method used for linking IT applications to business goals and for planning and prioritizing information systems projects. This method was proposed by Rockart (1979), although King & Cleland (1975 and 1977) had suggested a similar idea (critical decision areas) before.

According to this method, the information systems, especially executive and management information systems, are based on the current needs of the top executives. These information needs should focus on the Critical Success Factors (CSF). Rockart defines CSF as the areas where satisfactory results "ensure successful competitive performance for the organization." This author states that CSF prime sources are the structure of the industry, competitive strategy, industry position, geographic location, environment and temporal factors.

Basically, the CSF method includes the analysis of the structure of the particular industry and the strategy and the goals of the organization and its competitors. This analysis is followed by two or three sessions of interviews with the executives, in order to identify the Critical Success Factors, related to business goals, define respective measures (quantitative or qualitative) for the CSF and define information systems for controlling CSF and their measures.

For Rockart, this process can be useful at each level of the company and should be repeated periodically, since CSF can change through time and can differ from one individual executive to another.

The CSF method had an important impact on managerial and strategic planning practices, even though it was primarily conceived for information systems design, especially management and executive information systems. Besides the utilization in information systems planning and information systems project management, it has been used in strategic planning and strategy implementation, management of change and as a competitive analysis technique (Pollalis & Frieze, 1993). This method leads to a policy-oriented approach, by focusing on the essential issues of companies. Furthermore, the continuous measurement of the CSF allows companies to identify strength and weakness in their core areas, processes and functions (Rockart, 1979; Sullivan, 1985).

More details of the process of implementation of the CSF method can be found in Rockart & Crescenzi, (1984) and Martin (1982).

McFarlan (1984) proposed the *Strategic Grid* that allows the visualization of the relationship between IT strategy and business strategy and operations. This model analyzes the impacts of IT-existent applications (present) and of an applications portfolio (future), defining four boxes, each one representing one possible role for IT in the enterprise: "Support", "Factory", "Turnaround" and "Strategic" (Figure 1).

- "Support": IT has little influence in present and future company strategies.
- "Factory": existent IT applications are important for company's operations success, but there is no new strategic IT application planned for the future.
- "Turnaround": IT is changing from one situation of little importance ("support" box) to a more important situation in business strategy.
- "Strategic": IT is very important in business strategy in the present and new planned applications will maintain this strategic importance of IT in the future.

Figure 1: Strategic grid of impacts of IT applications (McFarlan, 1984)

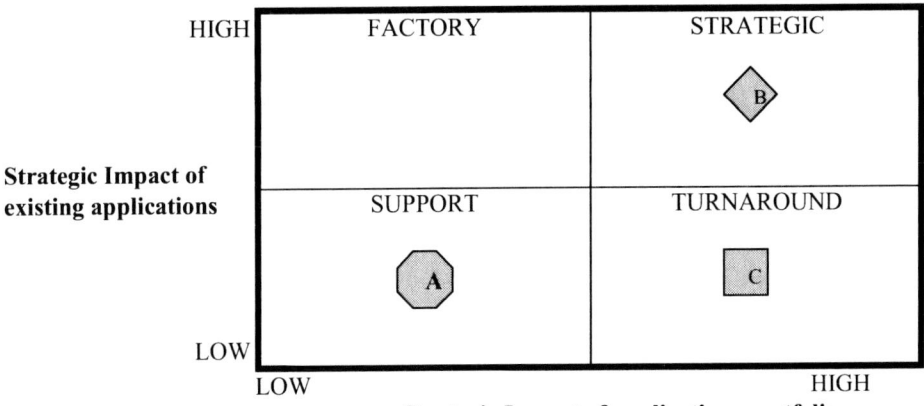

In order to assess the strategic impact of IT, McFarlan proposed the analysis of five basic questions about IT applications, related to the competitive forces (Porter, 1979):
- Can IT applications build barriers to the entry of new competitors in the industry?
- Can IT applications build switching costs for suppliers?
- Can IT applications change the basis of competition?
- Can IT applications change the balance of power in supplier relationships?
- Can IT applications create new products?

These questions should be answered considering both present and planned future situations.

Thus, IT may present a smaller or greater importance, according to the kind of company and industry operations. In a traditional manufacturing company, IT supports the operations, since the enterprise would keep on operating even when it could not count on its IS (Information Systems). However, in a bank, IT is strategic for business operations, since it is a source of competitive advantage and a bank cannot operate without their computerized IS.

Henderson & Venkatraman (1993) proposed the "Strategic Alignment Model" that analyzes and emphasizes the strategic importance of IT in the enterprises. This model is based on both internal (company) and external (market) factors. It is a framework for studying IT impacts on business and understanding how these impacts influence IT organization and strategy, as well as it enables us to analyze the market availabilities of new Information Technologies.

Two fundamental concepts in this model are strategic fit (interrelationships between strategy and infrastructure) and functional integration (integration between business and IT, in the strategic and infrastructure aspects). The authors emphasize that strategy should consider both internal and external domains of the company. Internal domain concerns the administrative structure of the company. External domain concerns the market and the respective decisions of the company. Thus, according to this model, four factors (that the authors called domains) should be considered for planning IT:
(i)   Business strategy;
(ii) IT strategy;
(iii) Organizational infrastructure and processes; and
(iv) IS infrastructure and processes.

Figure 2: Perspectives of strategic alignment (Henderson & Venkatraman, 1993)

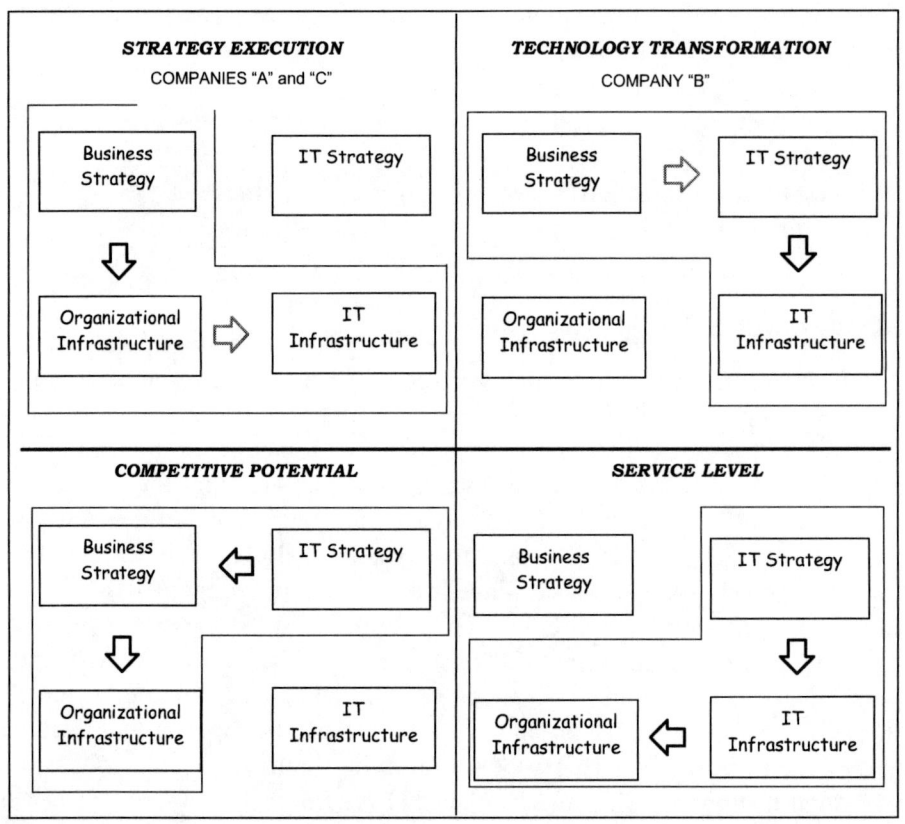

The Strategic Alignment Model brings the premise that the effective management of IT demands a balance among the decisions about the four domains above.

According to Henderson & Venkatraman, there are four main perspectives of strategic alignment, through the combination of the four factors, starting from business strategy or from IT strategy, as shown in Figure 2.

One important innovation of this model is that IT strategy could come first and change business strategy, instead of the usually general belief that business strategy comes before IT planning.

This planning should be a continuous process, since external factors are in a permanently changing situation. If the company does not follow these changes, it will be at a serious disadvantage in the fiercely competitive market. This is particularly true when a new technology is adopted by almost all companies in an industry, passing from a competitive advantage for those that have it to a disadvantage to those that do not use it.

Thus, in this sense, the strategic alignment differs from the classic vision of a strategic plan, which does not present the same dynamic approach.

After the proposal of these four perspectives above, Luftman (1996) described four new perspectives that start in the infrastructure domains, instead of the strategies domains:

- Organizational IT Infrastructure Perspective:
  Organizational infrastructure → IT infrastructure → IT strategy
- IT Infrastructure Perspective:
  IT infrastructure → IT strategy → Business strategy
- IT Organizational Infrastructure Perspective:
  IT infrastructure → Organizational infrastructure → Business strategy
- Organizational Infrastructure Perspective:
  Organizational infrastructure → Business strategy → IT strategy

Luftman (1996) also proposed that in some situations a fusion of two perspectives might occur. In these cases, two perspectives can be simultaneously assessed and impacting the same domain: *IT infrastructure Fusion, Organizational infrastructure Fusion, Business strategy Fusion, IT strategy Fusion.*

Research has been developed in order to find the *enablers* of Strategic Alignment. Luftman (2001) listed five of them: *senior executive support for IT, IT involved in strategy development, IT understands the business, business-IT partnership, well-prioritized IT projects, IT demonstrates leadership.* The absence or poor performance of these same factors are considered *inhibitors* of Strategic Alignment.

Some authors, like Ciborra (1998), state the strategic success of IT applications might be achieved through a tentative approach, rather than structured methods of strategic IT planning. These authors argue that frequently the drivers of strategic IT applications are efficiency issues, instead of a result of a strategic IT plan. Some important and well known successful information systems, with clear strategic impacts, do not present evidences of being previously planned, which seems to be in agreement with this kind of thinking (Eardley et al., 1996).

IT MANAGEMENT IN BRAZILIAN COMPANIES

This chapter intends to verify if companies with significant IT strategic impact tend to develop more elaborate procedures concerned with effectiveness.

In order to investigate the IT role in Brazilian companies, the adopted methodological approach was multiple cases (Yin, 1991; Claver et al., 2000). The selection criteria were the following: local dispersion, different kind of management of IT, different IT strategic impact, and organizational structure and IT application complexity. Based on these criteria, three cases were selected, each one from a different industry: building materials, financial, and telecommunication. Interviews were performed with many players from different hierarchic levels. Table 1 presents the characteristics of the analyzed companies.

It is important to notice that the focus in COMPANY "A" was restricted to a specific business unit, hereafter BU1, which achieved 60% of company total revenue.

Table 1: Characteristics of the studied companies

Characteristic	COMPANY "A"	COMPANY "B"	COMPANY "C" *
INDUSTRY	Manufacturing	Financial	Manufacturing
FOREIGN CAPITAL?	No	No	Yes
BUSINESS AREAS	Agribusiness, Building Materials	Multiple Banks	Electronic, Several Product Lines
REVENUE (M M US$)	400	4.500	2.000 **
NUMBER OF EMPLOYEES	6,000	17,000	2,700
BUSINESS UNITS?	YES	NO	YES
LOCAL DISPERSION?	YES	YES	YES

* Brazilian branch ** Latin American

The theoretical models used in effectiveness analysis were based on Rockart, McFarlan and Henderson & Venkatraman approaches previously described.

UNDERSTANDING IT ROLE IN EFFECTIVENESS

COMPANY "A" belongs to the building materials industry, whose companies in Brazil have been adopting different competitive strategies in order to face the growing market share of lower cost foreign competitors. Two major competitive approaches have been detected: the first one is the cost leadership strategy, and the second one is the differentiation approach (Porter, 2001). Through the years, COMPANY "A" has kept leadership in its market through differentiation strategy (Porter, 1979), since its products are well known by their superior quality and design. Another important differentiation factor is the technical assistance; providing repair services and allowing customers to buy replacing parts easily.

These facts were very important in the search for the CSF for this specific company.

In COMPANY "A", according to its IT and business executives of the corporation and of BU1, Critical Success Factors (CSF) were:
1. final product quality,
2. product design,
3. assistance services,
4. new product time-to-market,
5. costs,
6. flexible and large product mix,
7. product delivery lead-times.

Three of these CSF were closely related with new product development processes. The first four CSF mentioned above are in agreement with the traditional strategic differentiation approach adopted by the firm; the other three represent responses to market changes and pressures. Some IT applications were considered important for some of the CSF, like CAD/CAM, project control system, product development database, an enhanced cost control system, production program and control system, for example.

COMPANY "B" is one of the biggest players of the Brazilian financial market, whose companies are strong IT users and the services provided are world class. Hence, foreign competitors have not seriously threatened them. However, COMPANY "B" has faced fierce competition with other big Brazilian banks in order to maintain its market share, differentiation may be considered as its competitive strategy, although operational efficiency (and consequently, operational costs) is also a very important issue.

In COMPANY "B", the CSF method was not formally adopted as a planning tool; thus it was necessary to identify them through interviews with business and IT professionals and through the analysis of managerial reports. As a result of this process, the following CSF were found:
1. operational costs,
2. potential for developing and implementing new products,
3. focus on the more profitable business.

The reduction of operational expenses present in many IT applications portfolios is due to mainly the use of internet and home banking as an alternative for lowering cost transactions.

COMPANY "C" is a manufacturer of telecommunications equipment, with a strong focus on the final consumer. This industry has been very competitive in recent years and the competitive strategy approach adopted by the company for facing this threatening scenario has been differentiation. Thus, this firm had to be very flexible to meet growing final consumer expectations. Consequently, some important changes occurred both in business and IT management, both locally and globally.

COMPANY "C" uses the CSF method, so their identification was much easier. The CSF list was found in formal documentation and both business and IT executives ratified them during the interviews:
1. commitment with final products quality,
2. outstanding products performance,
3. assistance and consumer services.

One of the most important IT initiatives of this company was the implementation of an ERP (Enterprise Resource Planning) system, aiming an integration of the information among different functional and business areas and also among different plants all over the world. The executive board has strong expectations about this integration that should provide appropriate support for achieving the CSFs.

The effectiveness analysis through the Strategic Grid (McFarlan, 1984) allows classifying the appropriate position of each company, as illustrated in Figure 1.

In COMPANY "A", a traditional manufacturing company, the IT area adopts a support approach and there is no perspective of changing this role in near future. Existent IT applications, and those planned for implementation in the short term, do not present strategic impacts. Hence, it should be classified in the "Support" box of the Strategic Grid. Nevertheless, some IT applications used in new products development may change this situation, since they are having a growing impact on firm performance.

There is no systematic use of formal project management tools for controlling information systems development and implementation.

COMPANY "B" is well known for its aggressive use of IT resources and considers IT as an inherent part of its operations and strategy, since the company cannot work without IT. Besides, all future business strategic plans rely heavily on the implementation and maintenance of IT applications. So, COMPANY "B" is classified in the "Strategic" box.

The importance given to IT can be also noticed by the use of efficiency practices and formal software engineering and project management models (Carvalho et al., 2002).

Although COMPANY "C" is also a manufacturer, IT importance is different from COMPANY "A". There is a concern with efficiency of development, maintenance and implementation of IT applications. Due to a proposal of company organizational restructuring, characterized by the creation of new corporate areas and more centralization, the demand for better integration among business units is increasing. So, IT is moving from a support role towards a new position, with increased strategic impact, making possible the new structure and its operation in the enterprise. This situation justifies the choice of the "Turnaround" box for this company. COMPANY "C" also considers important the use of formal efficiency models in IT activities.

Adopting Henderson & Venkatraman's (1993) point of view, it is possible to verify which strategic alignment perspectives were used in each company, as shown in Figure 2.

In COMPANY "A", corporate and BU1 visions are that IT should provide the necessary IT infrastructure for the organizational structure that enables business strategy. So, the perspective is "Strategy Execution". However, alignment between business and IT is better executed in corporations than in BU1. The corporate IT area, that manages both corporate and business unit resources, negotiates directly with corporate direction, understanding much more its needs than those of the business units. Decisions of what will be implemented and which hardware or software will be bought are almost exclusive of corporate IT. The relationship between IT corporate and BU1 is *ad hoc*.

COMPANY "B" adopted a "Technology Transformation" perspective, due to the search for new IT applications, especially those based on the Internet, to allow a new strategy of closer relations with customers. The company emphasized in the 90's the access of customers through *home banking*, with specific software or by Internet. Both users and IT professionals, in a well-defined process, discuss the choice of IT investments. Then, a steering committee (composed by members of high direction of business and IT) decides which projects will be developed and their priorities.

COMPANY "C" also adopts a "Strategy Execution" perspective, because it searches IT solutions for a new structure that focuses on centralization of some

Copyright © 2003, Idea Group Inc. Copying or distributing in print or electronic forms without written permission of Idea Group Inc. is prohibited.

functions and on interaction among business units. Both business and IT strategies are globally defined, establishing parameters for local strategies. Thus, there is alignment between global and local strategies. This solution provides leveling of technologic possibilities on a worldwide basis. Although IT area is seen as an important agent for reducing costs, it is also considered an important support for business strategy and operations.

Table 2 summarizes the analysis of IT effectiveness in the three cases.

CONCLUSIONS

Effectiveness analysis demonstrates that, only in COMPANY "B" is IT a source of competitive advantage, and clearly emphasizes effectiveness evaluation of IT projects. In the other cases, IT does not present the same strategic relevance, as was shown in the McFarlan strategic Grid (Figure 1). However, COMPANY "C's" status tends to change towards a more strategic position.

Table 2: IT analysis in the studied companies

ITEM OF IT ANALYSIS	COMPANY "A"	COMPANY "B"	COMPANY "C"
IT STRUCTURE	By kind of systems	Client	Product line
IT OPERATION	Decentralized	Centralized	Decentralized
SYSTEM DEVELOPMENT	Centralized; Internal	Centralized; Internal	Centralized; Outsourcing
IT DECISIONS	Centralized; Not systematic	Decentralized; Systematic	Decentralized; Systematic
REASONS FOR IT DECENTRALIZATION	No formal model	Local Dispersion	Local Dispersion; Business Units; Wish for Control
IT PROJECTS CONTROL	Ad hoc	Structured	Partially Structured
STRATEGIC GRID	Support	Strategic	Turnaround
STRATEGIC ALIGNMENT	Strategy Execution	Technology Transformation	Strategy Execution
CRITICAL SUCCESS FACTORS	Final Product Quality, Product Design, Assistance Services, New Products Time-To-Market, Costs, Flexible and Large Product Mix, Products Delivery Lead-Times	Operational costs; Potential for developing and implementing new products; Focus on the more profitable business.	Commitment with final products quality; Outstanding products performance; Assistance and consumer services.

COMPANY "A" presents a poor relationship between corporate IT and business units; also, there is a lack of alignment between IT and business unit strategies. As discussed before, COMPANY "A" should keep IT in the "Support" box, since the search for IT efficiency could be achieved through appropriate IT suppliers. Thus, there is an important possibility of increasing IT outsourcing, which would lead to a "Service Level" perspective of strategic alignment, compatible with IT's role in this business. There is also a possibility of a shift to the "Turnaround" box, if the applications for supporting new products development would have a more decisive impact, as mentioned before.

COMPANY "B" was classified in the "Strategic" box, i.e., effectiveness of IT applications represents the possibility of gains in competitiveness. Besides, this company would benefit from formal efficiency models for the development and maintenance of these applications. In this sense, it confirmed the general idea that companies with IT strategic impact tend to use efficiency and effectiveness in well structured procedures.

COMPANY "C", classified in the "Turnaround" box, tends to drive the adoption of more detailed effectiveness evaluation systems, once this company has already demonstrated initiatives in using IT project efficiency.

Both companies "B" and "C" must keep their strategic alignment perspectives, "Strategy Execution" and "Technology Transformation," respectively.

Further studies would be necessary for a better and deeper understanding of the importance of IT effectiveness for the success of competitive companies. However, this chapter intended to help to find a way for this understanding.

REFERENCES

Brynjolfsson, E. (1993). The productivity paradox of information technology: Review and assessment. *Communications of the ACM, 36*(12), 67-77.

Brynjolfsson, E., & Hitt, L.M. (1998). Beyond the productivity paradox. *Communications of the ACM*, August.

Carvalho, M. M., Laurindo, F. J. B., & Pessôa, M. S. P. (2002). Applying efficiency models in information technology area of Brazilian companies. In *Proceedings of IRMA2002 – Information Resources Management Association International Conference, Issues and Trends of Information Technology Management in Contemporary Organizations, Seattle, WA*, 109-110.

Ciborra, C. U. (1998). Crisis and foundations: An inquiry into the nature and limits of models and methods in the information systems discipline. *Journal of Strategic Information Systems, 7*, 5-16.

Claver, E., Gonzalez, R., & Llopis, J. (2000). An analysis of research in information systems (1981-1997). *Information & Management, 37* (4), 181-195.

Drucker, P. F. (1963). Managing for business effectiveness. *Harvard Business Review,* May/June, 53-60.

Duhan, S., Levy, M., & Powell, P. (2001). Information systems strategies in knowledge-based SME's: The role of core competencies. *European Journal of Information Systems, 10*(1), 25-40.

Eardley A., Lewis, T., Avison, D., & Powell, P. (1996). The linkage between IT and business competitive systems: A reappraisal of some 'classic' cases using a competitive analysis framework. *International Journal of Technology Management, 11*(3/4), 395-411.

Evans, P.B., & Wurster, T.S. (1999). Getting real about virtual commerce. *Harvard Business Review, 77* (6), Nov./Dec., 84-94.

Henderson, J.C., & Venkatraman, N. (1993). Strategic alignment: Leveraging information technology for transforming organizations. *IBM Systems Journal, 32*(1), 4-16.

Hirscheim, R., & Smithson S. (1998). Analysing information systems evaluation: Another look at an old problem. *European Journal of Information Systems, 7*(3), 158-174.

King, W.R, & Cleland, D. (1975). The design of MIS: An information analysis approach. *Management Science, 22*(3).

King, W.R, & Cleland, D. (1977). Information for more effective strategic planning. *Long-Range Planning, 10*, 2.

Laurindo, F.J.B. (2002). Tecnologia da informação: Eficácia nas organizações - São Paulo. *Editora Futura*, 248.

Laurindo, F.J.B., & Shimizu, T. (2000). Evaluating strategies in information technology. In A. Neely (Ed.), *Performance Measurement 2000 Conference - Past, Present And Future. Proceedings.* Cambridge, UK, pp. 323-330.

Laurindo, F.J.B., Carvalho, M.M., & Shimizu, T. (2002). Management of information technology effectiveness in Brazilian companies. In: *IRMA 2002 - Information resources management association international conference: Issues and trends of information technology management in contemporary organizations, Proceedings*, Seattle, WA, pp. 412-414.

Luftman, J.N. (1996). Applying the strategic alignment model. In J.N. Luftman, (Ed.), *Competing in the Information Age - Strategic Alignment in Practice.* New York: Oxford University Press. 43-69.

Luftman, J.N. (2001). Business-IT alignment maturity. In R. Papp, (Ed.), *Strategic Information Technology: Opportunities for Competitive Advantage.* Hershey, PA: Idea Group Publishing, 105-134.

Maggiolini, P. (1981). *Costi E Benefici Di Un Sistema Informativo.* Italy; Etas Libri.

Martin, E.W. (1982). Critical success factors of chief MIS/DP executives, *MIS Quarterly,* June.

McFarlan, W.E. (1984). Information technology changes the way you compete. *Harvard Business Review, 62*(3), May/June, 98-103.

Pollalis, Y.A., & Frieze, I.H. (1993). A new look at critical success factors in IT. *Information Strategy: the Executive's Journal, 10*(1), Fall, 24-34.

Porter, M.E. (1979). How competitive forces shape strategy. *Harvard Business Review, 57*(2),137-145.

Porter, M.E. (2001). Strategy and the internet. *Harvard Business Review*, March, 63-78.

Porter, M.E, & Millar,V. (1985). How information gives you competitive advantage. *Harvard Business Review, 63*(4), Jul./Aug.,149-160.

Rockart, J., & Crescenzi, A.D. (1984). Engaging top management in information technology. *Sloan Management Review, 25*(4), Summer, 3-16.

Rockart, J.F. (1979). Chief executives define their own data needs. *Harvard Business Review, 57*(2), 81-92, Mar./Apr.

Strassman, P. A. (1990). The business value of computers. *The Information Economic Press*. New Canaan.

Sullivan, C.H. (1985). Systems planning in information age. *Sloan Management Review, 26*(2), Winter, 3-12.

Venkatraman, N., & Henderson, J. C. (1998). Real strategies for virtual organizing. *Sloan Management Review*, Fall, 33-48.

Walrad, C., & Moss, E. (1993). Measurement: The key to application development quality. *IBM Systems Journal, 32*(3), 445-460.

Willcocks, L.P., & Lester, S. (1997). In search of information technology productivity: Assessment issues. *Journal of the Operational Research Society, 48,* 1082-1094.

Yin, R.K. (1991). Case study research: Design and methods. Rev. ed. Newbury Park: Sage Publications.

Chapter XIV

Technology Trust in B2B Electronic Commerce: Conceptual Foundations

Paul A. Pavlou
University of Southern California, USA

Pauline Ratnasingam
University of Vermont, USA

ABSTRACT

A comprehensive conceptualization of trust in B2B electronic commerce should include trust in the infrastructure and the underlying control and support mechanisms. We refer to this new target of trust as "technology trust," which is described as the subjective belief by which an organization assesses that the underlying technology infrastructure and support mechanisms are capable of supporting inter-organizational communications, transactions, and collaborations. We describe technology trust as a higher-order construct comprising of transaction (a) confidentiality, (b) integrity, (c) authentication, (d) non-repudiation, (e) access control, (f) availability, and (g) best business practices. We conceptualize technology trust drawing upon the notion of institutional trust, and particularly the dimension of situational normality. We describe how bi-lateral (dyadic) and third-party institutionalized technology-related practices can institute situational normality in B2B electronic commerce. This chapter contributes to the understanding of the conceptual foundations of technology trust by bridging the gap between technological solutions from an institutional trust perspective (technology trust), interorganizational trust, and value creation in B2B electronic commerce. We conclude by discussing the study's theoretical and managerial implications toward instituting and making use of technology trust.

INTRODUCTION

Business to business (B2B) electronic commerce is notably characterized by the extensive use of information technology (IT). The central role of IT in online interorganizational relationships utterly emphasizes the magnitude of the technology aspects of interfirm transactions. Given the abundance of benefits from employing IT, such as reduced transaction and coordination costs and the reduced cost of using the Internet infrastructure (as opposed to private networks), organizations are better off heavily utilizing Internet-based IT to communicate, transact, and collaborate with suppliers and customers. However, Internet-based technologies stress the importance of security, privacy, and proper technology use since online transactions take place over the widely accessible Internet infrastructure. Managers must recognize and appreciate the dangers, uncertainties, and security concerns associated with the reliance on IT for transactions, and find ways to take advantage of IT to improve interorganizational relationships rather than exposing their organizations and trading partners to excessive risk.

The prominence of trust in B2B electronic commerce has been widely touted by practitioners and academicians alike (Heil, Bennis, & Stephens, 2000; Keen, 2000). There is a consensus that trust is a key success factor in interorganizational relationships (Zaheer, McEvily, & Perrone, 1998), and particularly those taking place online (Pavlou, 2003). Trust is a key element of social capital (Mayer, Schoorman, & Davis, 1995), and it has been related to desirable outcomes such as partner performance, satisfaction, and competitive advantage (Barney & Hansen, 1994; Ganesan, 1994). Whereas the concept of trust has predominantly focused on the trading partner (interorganizational trust) or its representatives (interpersonal trust) (see Zaheer et al., 1998 for a review), a comprehensive conceptualization of trust in B2B electronic commerce should include trust in the technology infrastructure and the underlying control and support mechanisms. Given the extensive reliance on IT and the inherent uncertainties from their use, it becomes necessary to consider the technical dimension of trust. We posit that trust in electronic commerce implicitly incorporates the notion of technology trust, which is described as the subjective probability by which an organization assesses that the underlying technology infrastructure and control mechanisms are capable of supporting interorganizational communications, transactions, and collaborations. Drawing

Copyright © 2003, Idea Group Inc. Copying or distributing in print or electronic forms without written permission of Idea Group Inc. is prohibited.

upon the emerging trust literature in B2B electronic commerce (e.g., Lee & Turban, 2001; Tan & Thoen, 1998), we explicitly view trust both from the traditional view (trading partner trust), and also from a technological perspective (technology trust).

Technology trust is conceptualized as a form of institutional trust (Zucker, 1986) that relies on impersonal structures (Shapiro, 1987) to institute trust in a given situation. Drawing upon the two-dimensional conceptualization of institutional trust proposed by McKnight, Cummings, & Chervany (1998), technology trust is theorized as arising from situational normality, the ability to show that technology structures make the technology-driven state (communication, transaction, collaboration) appear regular, standard, and non-risky. Situational normality arising from technology applications may be driven by bi-lateral institutionalized practices, such as common agreements for the proper use of IT in transactions, or through third-party driven general guidelines suggested by intermediaries, such as B2B marketplaces (Pavlou, Tan, & Gefen, 2002). Following McKnight et al. (1998), technology trust does not aim to substitute the traditional view of trading partner trust, but it rather aims to complement it as an important antecedent of trading partner trust.

This chapter's contribution to practicing managers comes from proposing a set of managerial implications for instituting and taking advantage of technology trust in B2B electronic commerce. We believe that given the increasing importance of B2B electronic commerce and the uncertain nature of the Internet environment in the digital economy, understanding the nature and role of technology trust is of fundamental managerial importance.

This chapter examines (1) the nature, conceptual foundations, and role of technology trust in B2B electronic commerce, (2) the nature of third-party institutions and bilateral institutionalized practices on building situational normality, and (3) the impact of technology trust on trading partner trust.

BACKGROUND

Today's digital economy encourages the creation of institutional provisions to support and guarantee transactions among entities that lack the traditional face-to-face context. Most institutional provisions have focused on third-party driven structural assurances (certification and escrows) to certify online transactions with new business partners. For example, Pavlou (2003) proposes a set of specific institutional trust-building assurances in B2B auction marketplaces that promote satisfaction, reduce risk, and encourage transaction continuity. Pavlou & Gefen (2002) examine the role of institutional structures, such as escrows and buyer-driven certification in building trust in business-to-consumer auction marketplaces. Tan & Thoen (2001) propose the term "control trust" to describe trust in electronic commerce built by institutionalized procedures.

McKnight & Chervany (2002) describe institutional trust as a critical part of online transactions. Hence, B2B electronic commerce resembles the environment where institutional trust would be particularly important by necessitating the certification of business partners (Zucker, 1986). In sum, there is a growing literature that aims to understand and develop the role of institutional trust in electronic commerce success.

Institutional Trust

Institutional trust has its origins in the sociological literature suggesting that intentions and behaviors are generated by situations followed by assurances that expectations can be fulfilled. In her seminal study, Zucker (1986) suggests that institution trust is the most important mode by which trust is created in an impersonal economic environment (without familiarity) and similarity (communality), providing evidence that trust was formed not because people knew each other personally (Gefen, 2000), but because of the presence of institutional structures. Zucker describes two dimensions of institutional trust: first, third-party certification, such as licenses, regulations, and laws, which defines a party's trustworthiness and expected behavior and second, escrows, which guarantee the expected outcome of a transaction. Shapiro (1987) describes institution trust as the belief that a party has about the security of a situation because of guarantees, safety nets, and other structures. Institutional trust in the context of B2B electronic commerce resembles a group of organizations that are facilitated by specific structures, agreements, and policies in the form of institutional support, assurances, and guarantees. Institutional trust provides favorable impersonal conditions conducive to transactional success, even if no actual people or organizations are the targets of trust. This suggests that if favorable conditions, such as legal, regulatory, business and technical environment could be perceived to support transactions, it would still be possible to build trust and promote favorable trusting outcomes without familiarity (McKnight & Chervany, 2002).

Situational Normality

McKnight et al. (1998) describe two dimensions of institutional trust – (a) structural assurances and (b) situational normality. *Structural assurances* are beliefs that favorable outcomes are guaranteed because of contextual protective structures, processes, or procedures, such as contracts, regulations, and guarantees. Practical examples of structural assurances are monitoring, legal recourse, third-party certification, and escrows that are conducive to situational success (Shapiro, 1987; Zucker, 1986). Structural assurances thus refer to governance structures (Barney & Hansen, 1994). Following McKnight et al. (1998), structural assurances act as safeguards bounding organizations to behave in a cooperative manner because of cognitive consistency.

On the other hand, *situational normality* is the belief that success is anticipated or expected (though not guaranteed) because the situation seems normal. Situational normality does not involve guarantees, but rather regular patterns that reflect that nothing abnormal or dangerous is present that can jeopardize transactions. The typical normality example in electronic commerce is that the communication infrastructure is protected, in the sense that authorization, integrity, non-repudiation, and confidentiality are insured and proper technology practices are in place. For example, a popular online intermediary, Covisint (www.covisint.com), provides situational normality by insuring that its online communication infrastructure is guaranteed. Situational normality can also be instituted by two transacting companies by setting up their own public key infrastructure for secure communication. Other examples of situational normality are values and norms (Pavlou, 2003), which give the impression that transactions are protected by conducive (non-governance) structures of solidarity and fair play.

CONCEPTUAL DEVELOPMENT

Following Pavlou (2003), interorganizational trust is defined as "the subjective belief with which an organization assesses that another organization will perform a particular transaction according to its confident expectations." The focus on a *particular transaction* suggests that trust in B2B electronic commerce covers *at least* two major targets that need to be trusted for a transaction to occur according to an organization's expectations, namely the specific trading partner and also the respective underlying technological infrastructure (Tan & Thoen, 2001). Therefore, the novel character of trust focuses both on (a) technology trust and (b) trading partner trust.

We propose the term "technology trust" to capture the technical aspect of institutional trust, which is based on technology-driven situational normality. Technology trust is then based on the adherence to technical standards, security procedures, and protection mechanisms that are conducive to supporting (but not guaranteeing) interorganizational transactions.

What is Technology Trust?

Technology trust is based on technical safeguards, protective measures, and control mechanisms that aim to provide reliable transactions from timely, accurate, and complete data transmission derived from institutional technology infrastructures and protocols embedded in IT applications and best business practices. Whereas, trust in the infrastructure focused predominantly on security issues (Cassell & Bickmore, 2000), the proposed construct of technology trust encompasses digital signatures, encryption mechanisms (public key infrastructure), authorization mechanisms (user IDs and passwords), and best business practices. These technology mechanisms create a sense of situational normality through best business practices that include regular audit, top management commitment, standards, and other contingency procedures (Bhimani, 1996; Jamieson, 1996; Marcella et al., 1998; Parker, 1995). This line of reasoning is consistent with institutional trust initially suggested by Zucker (1986) and extended by McKnight et al. (1998) with the situational normality dimension. We define technology trust as "the subjective belief by which an organization believes that the underlying technology infrastructure and control mechanisms are capable of facilitating a particular transaction according to its confident expectations." This definition clearly posits that technology trust is a subjective belief in regards to the uncertain performance of the underlying technology infrastructure and control mechanisms. As with previous conceptualizations of trust, technology trust captures the element of confident expectations toward a favorable outcome (transaction facilitation). Finally, technology trust is defined as a distinct (yet related) construct from trading partner trust or interpersonal trust (Zaheer et al., 1998), which is trust in another organization or organizational member.

Even if the proposed construct of technology trust in B2B electronic commerce may be related to conceptualizations of other researchers, it has a distinct conceptualization on its own right. For example, Tan & Thoen (1998) used the term "control trust" to refer to embedded protocols, policies, and procedures in electronic commerce that help to reduce the risk of seller opportunistic behaviors. However, control trust refers to structural assurances that aim to reduce risk by guaranteeing transactions. Moreover, Lee & Turban (2001) measured trustworthiness of Internet shopping based on consumer evaluations of technical competence and Internet performance levels (such as speed, reliability, and availability). This conceptualization is true for consumer transactions and does not equate with technology trust in B2B electronic commerce.

Technology trust is described as a higher-order construct comprising of transaction (a) confidentiality, (b) integrity, (c) authentication, (d) non-repudia-

Table 1: Description of technology trust dimensions

Source	Confidentiality	Integrity	Authentication	Non-repudiation	Access Controls	Availability	Best Business Practices
Bhimani 1996	Privacy	Accuracy	Genuine	Acknowledgement	Unauthorized access	Allows authorized access	Auditing
Jamieson 1996	Protection from unauthorized reading, copying	Completeness	Originality	Non-denial	Protects transmission media	Protection from hackers	Standards Written policies Procedures
Marcella et al., 1998	Protection against disclosure	Reliability	Authoritative Valid	Acknowledgement	Protects Manipulation	Authorized access	Risk analysis Contingency Procedures
Parker 1995	Privacy	Not being altered	Being true		Authorized access	Right to use	High quality standards

tion, (e) access control, (f) availability, and (g) best business practices. Table 1 presents the characteristics of the proposed seven dimensions of technology trust.

Technology Trust Dimensions

Technology trust dimensions in B2B electronic commerce (Table 1) include transaction (a) confidentiality, (b) integrity, (c) authentication, (d) non-repudiation, (e) access controls, (f) availability, and (g) best business practices. First, confidentiality mechanisms aim to protect electronic commerce transactions and message content against unauthorized reading, copying, or disclosure using encryption mechanisms. Connection confidentiality services protect the data transmitted in a connection versus connection-less confidentiality services that only protect single data units. Second, integrity mechanisms provide transaction accuracy and assurance that electronic commerce transactions have not been altered or deleted. Connection integrity services with recovery provide integrity of data with recovery if lost. Connection integrity services without recovery do the reverse. Third, authentication mechanisms provide transaction quality of being authoritative, valid, true, genuine, worthy of acceptance or belief because of conformity to the fact that reality is present. Peer authentication services aim to provide the ability to verify that a peer entity of an association is the one it claims to be (i.e., it provides assurance that an entity is not attempting to masquerade or perform an unauthorized replay). Alternatively, data authentication services aim to allow the sources of data received to be verified as claimed. Authentication mechanisms are important because they are a prerequisite for proper authorization, access control, and accountability. Fourth, non-repudiation mechanisms protect the originator of online transactions and use acknowledgement procedures applying digital signatures or associated technologies. Non-repudiation services with proof of origin provide the recipient of a message with a source assurance, whereas non-repudiation services with proof of delivery provide the sender a message with proof of delivery (destination assurance). Fifth, availability mechanisms protect transactions against weaknesses in the transmission media and protect the sender against internal fraud or manipulation by using authorization mechanisms. Authorized mechanisms focus both on the technology and also on the 'human' entity. Sixth, access control mechanisms provide authorization mechanisms, thereby assuring that data are sent and received without interruption. Access control mechanisms focus on technology infrastructure by examining the quality and security of network access controls. Finally, best business practices focus on policies, procedures, standards, and top management commitment that enforce regular audit, and ensure the smooth functioning of interorganizational transactions.

Drawing from prior theories, we propose the existence of a multidimensional, higher-order factor of technology trust that spans a set of seven first-order dimensions – transaction confidentiality, integrity, authentication, non-repudiation, access controls, availability, and best business practices. Following Chin (1998), the proposed second-order factor is conceptually related to the seven first-order factors, and it is embedded within a nomological network of related factors, such as interorganizational trust, perceived benefits, and outcomes in electronic commerce performance (Ratnasingam & Pavlou, 2002). Following the complex and multidimensional nature of trading partner trust (e.g., competence, integrity, predictability, benevolence), it is expected that technology trust be also multi-dimensional. In addition, the proposed seven individual dimensions of technology trust should be treated in an interrelated, collective, and mutually reinforcing manner. These seven dimensions should not be treated in isolation since no single dimension can facilitate trust in the infrastructure on an individual basis without the supporting role of all dimensions. We make a modest claim that a trustworthy infrastructure is the result of the collective effort of all seven dimensions; hence, high levels on all dimensions would insure a high degree of technology trust.

Trading Partner Trust and Technology Trust

Following Pavlou (2003), we define trading partner trust as "the subjective belief with which an organization assesses that its trading partner will perform the behavioral aspect of a particular transaction according to its confident expectations." This definition focuses exclusively on the credible and benevolent behavior of the trading partner, excluding performance aspects beyond its control. However, the behavioral aspect of a particular transaction may include influencing the underlying infrastructure and supporting control mechanisms. Hence, a relationship is expected between the two dimensions of interorganizational trust. Following McKnight & Chervany (2002), this study proposes that technology trust (trust in the situation) is a critical antecedent of trading partner trust. McKnight & Chervany (2002, p. 13) argue that in business-to-consumer electronic commerce, beliefs that the Internet has legal or regulatory protection for consumers (institution-based trust) should influence trust in a particular e-vendor (interpersonal trust). Based on these arguments we expect that institutional structures that contribute to technology trust should positively influence buyers' trust in trading partners. However, it is important to note that trust in a trading partner should also influence technology trust by giving perceptions that the trading partner's benevolence would go the extra mile to assure the reliability of the technology infrastructure and prevent abnormal situations (Pavlou, 2002). Hence, a reciprocal relationship between technology and trading partner trust is expected. These two constructs essentially form the two fundamental dimensions of interorganizational trust.

Copyright © 2003, Idea Group Inc. Copying or distributing in print or electronic forms without written permission of Idea Group Inc. is prohibited.

Bilateral and Third-Party Technology Trust

Technology trust can draw both from third-party services (intermediaries or B2B marketplaces), and organizational actors (auditors, security analysts, and top management personnel) who promote best business practices toward instituting situational normality. Following Pavlou et al. (2002), the institutional mechanisms facilitating technology trust can be (a) bilateral (dyadic) institutionalized practices shaped by interorganizational processes, standards, and norms, and (b) third-party institution-based structures, commonly available by online intermediaries, such as B2B marketplaces.

Bilateral Institutionalized Practices

Drawing upon Dyer (2000), bilateral institutionalized practices are stable and predictable dyadic technical routines, processes, and norms to facilitate technology trust. The technical standards of conduct are established technical agreements, or the ground rules, which set the normal context for successful buyer-seller relationships (Dwyer, Schurr, & Oh, 1987). As Dyer (2000) describes, Japanese automakers do not rely on specific people that happen to be there, but on bilateral institutionalized practices that entail current processes and norms of interaction, instituting situational normality. Hence, bilateral institutionalized practices have their basis of trust on technical processes and routines, facilitating technology trust.

Third-Party Institutions

Technology trust can also be facilitated by situational normality driven by technical processes and agreements set by third parties. Common examples of third parties or intermediaries are online B2B marketplaces, which are virtual networked organizational forms (Pavlou & El Sawy, 2002) that provide infrastructure technologies and services to enable online buyer-seller relationships (Hempel & Kwong, 2001). Participation in B2B marketplaces, such as Covisint or Bolero (www.bolero.net) entails adherence to specific technical processes, which provide a normal situation for smooth communications and transactions. Therefore, technology trust in B2B electronic commerce can be driven either by third-party institutions or bilateral institutionalized practices. Pavlou et al. (2002) provide a prescriptive framework as to when organizations should rely on third parties to institute situational normality or depend on their own bilateral agreements with their trading partners.

The Value Potential of Technology Trust in B2B Electronic Commerce

Technology trust draws from electronic commerce technologies, third-party services, and organizational actors (auditors, security analysts, and top management personnel) who are committed to enforcing best business practices. It is important to suggest the value potential of technology trust, other than its proposed antecedent role in building trading partner trust. Following Ratnasingam & Pavlou (2002), we expect that technology trust to have both a direct and an indirect (through trading partner trust) on transaction performance and perceived benefits. Such direct and indirect effects of institutional trust on valued outcomes are also proposed by McKnight & Chervany (2002). The relationship also draws from the literature on security services in electronic commerce (Jamieson, 1996; Lee & Turban, 2001; Marcella et al., 1998). For example, most electronic commerce technologies are embedded with automated security protocols that enable firms to ensure security services.

Ratnasingam (2001) conducted a study of inter-organizational trust in dyadic relationships in B2B electronic commerce. The findings of her study revealed that electronic commerce applications are embedded with intelligence systems that contribute to savings in time and costs, as these systems were able to detect and correct errors in a timely manner. For example, Cisco's B2B electronic commerce extranet application, Cisco Connections Online (CCO) has built-in functions and business transactions such as purchase orders for equipment, delivery, and product information from web sites. Secondary elements included ordering for equipment, delivery, and ability to check lead track time. Cisco's registered trading partners can now download product, equipment, and pricing information from CCO. In addition, the automated online tools are embedded within the system.

Implementing encryption mechanisms protect online transactions from being intercepted, manipulated, and deleted, thus contributing to transaction integrity (Marcella et al., 1998; Riggins & Rhee, 1998; Senn, 2000). Transaction integrity leads to economic benefits from savings in time and costs as transactions are received in a complete, accurate, timely, and reliable manner. For example, Mukhopadhyay, Kekre & Kalathur (1995), conducted a study of nine Chrysler assembly centers and found that EDI improved the quality of information sharing and reduced inventory, transportation, and administrative costs. Thus, efficiency benefits from technology trust concentrate on reducing transaction costs, derived from speed and automation of electronic commerce technologies. As described before, authorized login procedures, e-mail acknowledgments, and confirmations provide confidentiality, authentication, and non-repudiation security services. Such functional acknowledgments provide accurate, reliable, and timely feedback mechanisms. In sum, efficiency economic benefits from technology trust concentrate on reducing transaction costs, derived from speed and automation of electronic commerce technologies.

Electronic commerce applications also provide real-time tracking information technologies allowing firms to log into their trading partners' extranet web sites, track shipment details, and estimate arrival dates of the goods they ordered (Riggins & Rhee, 1998). Trading partners are able to inform their end-customers on the arrival dates of the goods, thus contributing to satisfaction, information sharing, open communications and commitment. Relationship-related benefits focus on long-term investments that in turn contribute to strategic benefits that include improved reputations, business continuity, increased organizational performance and potential for competitive advantage. Organizations who demonstrate skills in producing high-quality goods, products, and services can thus achieve high levels of trustworthiness. B2B e-commerce applications thus enable product and service differentiation, tighter links with trading partners, and overall business value. Subsequently, trustworthy firms are able to satisfy their end customers' needs by delivering the goods on time, thus contributing to increased customer satisfaction and relationship-related business value. Increased satisfaction from technology trust, in turn, leads to perceived strategic benefits and actual economic benefits, increasing the volume, diversity, and dollar value of e-commerce transactions (Doney & Cannon, 1997; Smith & Barclay, 1997). Effective management practices can arguably have an important role in the process of IT strategic intent towards achieving business value and competitive advantage, suggesting that best business practices can increase technology trust and ultimately influence B2B electronic commerce performance.

DISCUSSION

This research attempts to make a theoretical and managerial contribution to the area of trust in B2B electronic commerce by integrating the trust literature with institutional theory to propose a new theoretical construct, technology trust, which describes the importance of trust in the underlying technology infrastructure and control and support mechanisms. This chapter provides several new insights on technology trust in B2B electronic commerce. First, it describes the conceptual foundations of the construct, which originate from the concept of institutional trust (Zucker, 1986), and specifically from the dimension of situational normality (McKnight et al., 1998). Grounding the construct of technology trust in the extant institutional trust literature makes it amenable to integration with the rich trust literature. Second, technology trust is conceptualized as a complex, higher-order construct, comprising of seven underlying dimensions. The proposed first-order effects are proposed to have a mutually reinforcing effect, which collectively comprise the multi-dimensional construct of technology trust. Third, technology trust is theorized as a distinct, self-contained dimension of the two-dimensional construct of interorganizational trust, and mutually related to trading partner trust. Finally, an important argument is the value-added role of technology trust that has the potential to improve online transactions and create business value. The value-added component of technology trust also comes from the fact that it enables geographically disperse organizations to communicate and coordinate business activities, allowing organizations across the globe to effectively utilize it without geographical restrictions. In sum, this research makes a theoretical contribution by extending the work of Zucker (1986) and McKnight & Chervany (2002) and applying it to the emerging literature on trust in B2B electronic commerce, highlighting the importance of technology trust in B2B electronic commerce.

Managerial Implications

Many reflective managers have recognized the importance of trust in developing value for a sustainable competitive advantage in exchange relationships. This research proposes a novel trust dimension for B2B electronic commerce, which may help managers and electronic commerce practitioners to develop trustworthy exchange relationships by ensuring a technology-driven situational normality in their interorganizational dealings. By properly utilizing technology trust, this study paves the way for managers to improve the adoption of B2B electronic commerce that could positively affect their exchange relationships and their own trustworthiness toward creating business value. This study provides a guide particularly for early adopters of electronic commerce technologies by improving their levels of awareness for the role and impact of electronic commerce technologies on building technology trust, and subsequently collaborative exchange relationships. In sum, executives must be aware of the importance of technology trust in the competitive global environment of B2B electronic commerce, and its role in cultivating and sustaining interorganizational relationships.

Although governance mechanisms may provide assurances that help mitigate many risks associated with opportunistic behavior in B2B electronic commerce, this chapter argues that technology trust may be equally fundamental to trading partner trust toward building successful B2B electronic commerce relationships. The presence of technology trust helps managers to undertake strategic initiatives more confidently as their online technical systems are implemented with security mechanisms that are embedded with intelligence checking systems. Competence in operating electronic commerce applications contributes to situational normality through timely, correct, and accurate information for organizations to act upon. This contributes to faster trading time, accurate timely flow of information, which in turn leads to the development of trading partner trust. In general, interorganizational trust leads to strategic decision-making, satisfaction, commitment, and business continuity leading to multiple performance outcomes (Pavlou, 2003). This study informs managers of how the new character of trust can be strategically used to realize business value beyond transaction efficiencies and cost reduction. Hence, managers are able to effectively compete and survive in today's electronic commerce world without fears of putting their organizations in situations of excessive risk.

Copyright © 2003, Idea Group Inc. Copying or distributing in print or electronic forms without written permission of Idea Group Inc. is prohibited.

As described in this chapter, situational normality can be instituted through bilateral (dyadic) institutionalized practices. While technology-oriented organizations may have superior practices that can build technology trust with virtually all trading partners, it is important to mention that technology trust is primarily a relative term related to specific technological infrastructures with a given trading partner. Hence, it may become prohibitively costly to institute technology trust with numerous partners, especially for one-time transactions. Hence, organizations can employ third party services as Covisint or Bolero to build the requisite situational normality. Third parties may be superior to comparable bilateral institutionalized provisions, especially if these provisions employ traditional dyadic practices, such as EDI via VANs. Following Pavlou et al. (2002), third parties may be more applicable to initial relationship states or one-time transactions, while bilateral practices become more cost-effective over time.

This study extends the theory on how online B2B marketplaces can be strategically used beyond mere cost reduction and bargaining power (Bailey & Bakos, 1997). Online B2B marketplaces can also be viewed as virtual network of organizations that depend on third-party institution-based mechanisms to inaugurate technology trust. B2B marketplaces could then diversify their portfolio of value-added services through a sophisticated design of IT-enabled services around the transaction process (El Sawy & Pavlou, 2002), specifically instituting technology-related situational normality. Therefore, online B2B marketplaces should utilize the findings of this study to improve the design of their trust-building structural mechanisms to institute a cost-effective trustworthy trading environment. Perhaps the most important challenge for B2B marketplaces would be to provide customized institutional provisions to complement, or even substitute bilateral provisions, even for long-term interfirm relationships.

CONCLUDING REMARKS

In this study, we proposed a new dimension of interorganizational trust that may help managers develop trustworthy exchange relationships. By understanding and properly utilizing technology trust, this study aims to help managers to understand how technology-driven situational normality could positively affect their exchange relationships in B2B electronic commerce, and their very own trustworthiness. By proposing how technology trust can create business value and enhance effective online collaborative relationships, this chapter opens new avenues for research on facilitating B2B electronic commerce success. This study will hopefully entice researchers and practitioners to further examine how the new character of trust can be employed in B2B electronic commerce to realize value for competitive advantage. Finally, this chapter aspires to entice future research on engineering new third party and bilateral mechanisms that are specifically designed to facilitate situational normality and technology trust.

Copyright © 2003, Idea Group Inc. Copying or distributing in print or electronic forms without written permission of Idea Group Inc. is prohibited.

REFERENCES

Bailey, J. & Bakos, J.Y. (1997). Reducing buyer search costs: Implications for electronic marketplaces. *Management Science, 43*(12), 1676-1692.

Barney, J.B., & Hansen, M.H. (1994). Trustworthiness as a source of competitive advantage. *Strategic Management Journal, 15*(2), 175-216.

Bhimani, A. (1996). Securing the commercial Internet. *Communications of the ACM, 39*(6), 29-35.

Cassell, J. & Bickmore, T. (2000). External manifestations of trustworthiness of the interface. *Communications of the ACM, 43*(12), 50-59.

Chin, W.W. (1998). Issues and opinions on structural equation modeling. *MIS Quarterly, 22*(1), 7-16.

Doney, P.M. & Cannon, J.P. (1997). An examination of the nature of trust in buyer-seller relationships. *Journal of Marketing, 61*(1), 35-51.

Dwyer, R.F., Schurr, P, H., & Oh, S. (1987). Developing buyer-seller relationships. *Journal of Marketing, 51*(1), 11-27.

Dyer, J.H. (2000). *Collaborative advantage: Winning through extended enterprise supplier networks.* Oxford, New York: Oxford University Press.

El Sawy, O. A. & Pavlou, P.A. (2002). Using a process-services perspective to the strategic design of B2B exchanges. Working Paper, Marshall School of Business, University of Southern California.

Ganesan, S. (1994). Determinants of long-term orientation in buyer-seller relationships. *Journal of Marketing, 58*(1), 1-19.

Gefen, D. (2000). Electronic commerce: The role of familiarity and trust. *Omega, 28*(5), 725-737.

Heil, G., Bennis, W., & Stephens, D. (2000). *Douglas McGregor, revisited: Managing the human side of the enterprise.* John Wiley and Sons.

Hempel, P.S. & Kwong, Y.K. (2001). B2B electronic commerce in emerging economics: i-metal.com's non-ferrous metals exchange in China. *Journal of Strategic Information Systems, 10*(1), 335-355.

Jamieson, R. (1996). *Auditing and electronic commerce.* Perth, Western Australia: *EDI Forum.*

Keen, P.G.W. (2000). Ensuring e-trust. *Computerworld.* March 13.

Lee, M.K.O., & Turban, E. (2001). A trust model for consumer Internet shopping. *International Journal of Electronic Commerce, 6*(1), 75-92

Marcella, A.J., Stone, L., & Sampias, W.J. (1998). Electronic commerce: Control issues for securing virtual enterprises. *The Institute of Internal Auditors.*

Mayer, R.C., Davis, J.H., & Schoorman, F.D. (1995). An integrative model of organizational trust. *Academy of Management Review, 20*, 709-734.

McKnight, H.D., & Chervany, N.L. (2002). What trust means in electronic commerce customer relationships: An interdisciplinary conceptual typology. *International Journal of Electronic Commerce, 6*(2), 35-53.

McKnight, H.D., Cummings, L.L., & Chervany, N.L. (1998). Initial trust formation in new organizational relationships. *Academy of Management Review, 23*, 513-530.

Mukhopadyay, T., Kekre, S., & Kalathur, S. (1995). Business value of information technology: A study of electronic data interchange. *MIS Quarterly, 19*(2), 137-156.

Palmer, J.W., Bailey, J.P., & Faraj, S. (2000). The role of intermediaries in the development of trust on the www: The use and prominence of trusted third parties and privacy statements. *Journal of Computer Mediated Communication, 5*(3), Online.

Parker, D.B. (1995). A new framework for information security to avoid information anarchy. *IFIP*, 155-164.

Pavlou, P. A. (2002), What drives electronic commerce? A theory of planned behavior perspective. *Best Paper Proceedings of the Academy of Management Conference,* Denver, CO, August 9-14.

Pavlou, P.A. (2003). Institutional trust in interorganizational exchange relationships: The role of electronic B2B marketplaces. *Journal of Strategic Information Systems.* (forthcoming).

Pavlou, P. A. & El Sawy, O.A. (2002). A classification scheme for B2B electronic intermediaries. In M. Warkentin (Ed.), *Business to Business Electronic Commerce: Challenges and Solutions.* Hershey, PA: Idea Group Publishing.

Pavlou, P. A. & Gefen, D. (2002). Building effective online marketplaces with institution-based trust. Working Paper, Marshall School of Business, University of Southern California.

Pavlou, P. A., Tan, Y. & Gefen, D. (2002). The transitional role of institutional trust in online interorganizational relationships. Working Paper, Marshall School of Business, University of Southern California.

Ratnasingam, P. (2001). Inter-organizational trust in business-to-business electronic commerce. Doctoral Dissertation, Erasmus University, The Netherlands.

Ratnasingam, P., & Pavlou, P (2002). Technology trust: The next value creator in B2B electronic commerce. *International Resource Management Association Conference*: Seattle, Washington, May 21-23.

Riggins, F.J., & Rhee, H.S. (1998). Toward a unified view of electronic commerce. *Communications of the ACM, 41*(10), 88-95.

Senn, J.A. (2000). Business to business electronic commerce. *Information Systems Management.* Spring, 23-32.

Shapiro, S.P. (1987). The social control of impersonal trust. *American Journal of Sociology, 93*, 623-658.

Smith, J.B. & Barclay, D.W (1997). The effects of organizational differences and trust on the effectiveness of selling partner relationships. *Journal of Marketing, 51*(1), 3-21.

Tan, Y., & Thoen, W. (1998). Towards a generic model of trust for electronic commerce. *International Journal of Electronic Commerce, 3*(1), 65-81.

Zaheer, A., Mc Evily, B., & Perrone, V. 1998). Does trust matter? exploring the effects of interorganizational and interpersonal trust on performance. *Organization Science, 9*(2), 141-159.

Zucker, L. (1986). Production of trust: Institutional sources of economic structure, 1840-1920. *Research in Organization Behavior, 8*(1), 53-111.

Chapter XV

The South African Online Consumer

Kevin Johnston
University of Cape Town, South Africa

ABSTRACT

This chapter attempts to develop a profile of online consumers in South Africa. Firstly, a profile of the South African online consumer is developed based on various research sources. The chapter then focuses on what the web consumers in South Africa want, and the challenges facing web developers and organizations developing web sites in South Africa.

INTRODUCTION

Many organizations, particularly financial organizations, are building web sites for South African consumers. Few have investigated the profile or needs of the people they are building these web sites for. This chapter examines the composition of the people of South Africa; it then attempts to develop a profile of what the web consumers in South Africa look like.

The chapter highlights some challenges facing web designers in South Africa. Surveys of web consumers were used to gather the information, as well as to determine the needs of the South African online consumers.

BACKGROUND

Who are the people of South Africa and what is known about them? The last official documented census in South Africa found 41.2 million people in South Africa in 1995. Over one million (1,169,000) newspapers are sold daily in South Africa. Two and a half million (6.2%) of the people of South Africa had any tertiary qualification, and 16.4% (6.8m) had completed high school. Over half the population (50.5%) are female and 53.7% of the South African population live in urban areas.

Thirty-one and a half million (76.4%) of the people of South Africa are Black, 10.9% (4.5m) are White, 8.9% (3.7m) are Colored, and 2.6% are Asians. When asked about home language, most of the people spoke one of the languages native to South Africa. Over nine million people (22.9% or 9.4m) listed Zulu as their home language, 17.9% (7.4m) listed Xhosa as their home language, 14.4% (5.9m) Afrikaans, 9.2% (3.8m) Sepidi, and 8.6% (3.5m) listed English as their home language.

The South African currency, the Rand, has been very volatile over the past few years. An exchange rate of 1 US$ = R12 was used to convert South African salaries into dollars. The picture when looking at monthly incomes is as follows: 3.5% of the employed population earns more than US$667 per month. Twenty percent of employed South Africans earn between US$208 and US$667 per month, the remaining 76.5% earn less than US$208 per month. In fact 26% earned less than US$42 per month. Forty-eight percent of employed African women earn less than US$42 per month, while 65% of white men earn more than US$250 per month. The percentage of South Africans who are unemployed is estimated by various sources to be between 40% to 45% of the population. Less than 7% (2.8 million) of the total population are registered income tax payers.

The information above was gathered from the South African Department of Statistics web site (www.statssa.gov.za).

WHO ARE THE WEB USERS IN SOUTH AFRICA?

No one knows exactly how many web users exist in South Africa. There are various estimates of the continually moving total. There are a number of problematic issues in terms of how these figures are determined. What is meant by terms such as "web users" – arc these e-mail users only, surfers, people who do online transactions, or all of these? Many dial-up subscribers share accounts, and many people have multiple e-mail addresses.

Webchek is a strategic Internet research and insights company primarily focusing on business to consumer research in South Africa (www.webchek.co.za).

Sandra Boer (Boer, 2001) is the managing director of the company, and she provided data and survey results, which have been used throughout this chapter.

Webchek's telephone research study indicated that only 29% of Internet home users in South Africa have exclusive use of the Web at home, while 32% said their spouses also had access, 31% said another adult also had access and 28% said their children (18 years and younger) had access. The number of Web users connected via ISDN or leased lines is unknown. Furthermore, double counting can dramatically increase the number of Web users. A Webchek project in 2000 measured an overlap of 27%, that is, 27% of the sample had access to the web at both home and work.

Webchek (www.webchek.co.za) estimated there were about 1.2 million web users in South Africa in 2000. SAOnline (www.saonline.co.za) estimated that there were about one million web users in South Africa in 2000.

Webchek estimated that 89% of South African web users are less than 45 years old, while SAOnline estimate that 10% of South African web users are over 50 years of age. Webchek estimate that 67% of web uses are English speakers, while SAOnline puts the number at 73%. Both Webchek and SAOnline estimate that 50% are female, and thus 50% are male.

Webchek estimate that 60% of South African web users earn more than US$833 per month, while SAOnline estimates that the average web user in South Africa earns US$916 per month. Webchek estimates that 56% of web users have a tertiary educational qualification.

Jessica Knight, the CEO of a South African online shopping site www.inthebag.co.za, was reported as saying the site has 13,500 registered customers, although only 3,000 are active, with an average basket size of US$33 (Computing SA, 2001). In the same issue of Computing SA, another South African online shopping site www.megashopper.co.za reported having a database of 20,000 users, with 1,000 regular shoppers with an average basket size of US$48.

Kris Jarzebowski (2001), the managing director of www.careerjunction.co.za, an online recruiting site in South Africa whose figures are audited by Deloitte and Touche, showed that they had 64,862 unique visitors in February 2001.

Webchek surveys reveal that 38% of South African web users say they access the web every day from home, while 63% said they access the web every day from work. They mainly use the web for e-mail (93% indicated they use e-mail), searching 91%, and job search 32%. Fifty-nine percent of South African web users have more than one e-mail address.

RATIOS

If we test a few of the statistics we arrive at the following interesting ratios:

Fewer than 9% (8.6%) of the people in South Africa speak English (3,543,200). Webchek estimate that 67% of web users are English speakers. If every South African English speaker is a web user, we get a figure of 2,373,944 English-speaking web users. If this represents 67% of web users, South Africa has a maximum of 3,543,200 web users.

If 53.7% of the people in South Africa live in urban areas (22,124,400) and we estimate that 10.5% of urban people over the age of 18 have web access, we arrive at a figure of 2,323,062, less the people under the age of 18.

If 6.2% of South Africans have tertiary qualifications (2,554,400) and 56% of web users have tertiary qualifications, we get 1,430,464 web users with tertiary qualifications. This means there are a maximum of 2,554,400 web users in South Africa.

If 3.5% (1,442,000) of the people in South Africa earn more than US$667 per month, and 60% (865,000) of the web users earn over US$833 per month, South Africa has a maximum of 1,442,000 web users.

SO HOW MANY WEB CONSUMERS ARE THERE, AND WHO ARE THEY?

In a population of 41.2 million people, we conclude that there are not that many web users, with estimates between 3.5% (1,442,000) and 8.6% (3,543,200) If we split the difference and say 6% are web consumers we arrive at a number of 2,472,000. Remember that this is only an estimate.

What do these 2.4 million web users in South Africa look like? They are at the top of the spectrum in terms of qualifications (56% have tertiary qualification) and earnings (60% earn more than US$833 per month). Most of them speak English (67%) and live in urban areas.

One could safely guess that most of them are white, as whites earn 81% of salaries over US$667 per month. Thirty-nine percent of white South Africans have English as their home language, compared to 0.4% of Blacks. Furthermore, whites hold 58% of the tertiary educational qualifications in South Africa, while blacks hold 3%, coloreds 10%, and Asians hold 24% of South African web users are under 45 years old.

One can, therefore, conclude that the majority of the web users in South Africa today are young (under the age of 45), educated (tertiary educational qualification), English speaking whites living in urban areas.

MEETING THE CHANGING NEEDS OF THE ONLINE FINANCIAL SERVICE CONSUMER

The author did a survey on University Honors students in March 2001. The students were e-mailed a set of seven open-ended questions. One of the questions put to the students was, "What do you need as an online financial consumer?" There were a total of almost 40 responses.

Customizable statements were requested by 38% of students who responded, some requested reporting tools, such as graphs, provided on the sites. Perhaps because they were students, cheaper fees and a cash incentive to use web services were requested by 31%.

Twenty-five percent requested integration of all their accounts, including those in other institutions. The other institutions mentioned included clothing stores, other financial institutes, mobile phone companies, etc.

Quick feedback to e-mail or phone calls were requested by 19%. Students felt that they were often given "rubbish answers," or put into queues, or e-mailed to say, "the company will get back to you" within a certain time. In all cases, the feedback was regarded as too slow.

Nineteen percent felt that the financial institutions insist on obtaining information about the client, but make no use of it. Institutions record name, age, occupation, address, details of income and expenditure on one's accounts. Students asked why institutions never use this information to inform clients on what services they are eligible for at the institution. The students asked why the institutions could not deliver tailor-made services based on the information they have about each individual. Almost every student who responded mentioned speed; everything must be faster. Students said they never wanted to wait more than two minutes to do anything online.

The following figures are from a research study conducted by Webchek in May 2000 amongst a sample of 407 individuals over the age of 18 years, living in the urban areas of Johannesburg, Cape Town and Durban, who accessed the Internet (not e-mail only) at least once a month, either at home or at work and who were responsible or jointly responsible for the financial services decision-making in their households. This study was part of a syndicated financial survey for clients to buy into the survey.

Nine in 10 people connected to the Internet in South Africa were aware of at least one bank that offered online banking. Four in 10 people connected to the Internet had never visited any of the online banks in South Africa. Online banks are not necessarily enticing customers and, therefore, do not have the opportunity to retain them. One in three people had used the Internet before to conduct their banking, while 28% banked online at the time (May 2000). This indicates a retention of 81% of customers who have ever banked online, which shows us that the Internet is not completely satisfactory as a channel in South Africa.

Copyright © 2003, Idea Group Inc. Copying or distributing in print or electronic forms without written permission of Idea Group Inc. is prohibited.

Although all people interviewed had conducted banking transactions on a face-to-face basis, most people had used at least two other channels, as well (ATM, Internet or telephone).

Financial products and services are complex, and the web can provide clarity and reassurance to consumers. The web can allow confidentiality, speed and convenience to financial consumers.

HOW WILL YOUNG CONSUMERS ACCELERATE THE PACE OF CHANGE?

We are in the age of the individual and the young want to be seen and treated as individuals. They want to influence the design, layout, and content of a web site, as well. The young want dynamic and customizable content; they want to see what they want to see, when they want to see it, and how they want to see it.

Young South African consumers want access to decision makers, direct access to the correct people with decision-making power, rather than a switchboard or call center operator who, in many cases, is simply another layer between the consumer and the decision maker.

As mentioned previously, young South African consumers want quick feedback to e-mail or telephone calls. They are not happy with auto-replies if these replies not followed up quickly. One South Africa Bank sends out auto-replies thanking you for your e-mail, and promising to respond within one working day. They then either never respond or, if you are extremely fortunate, come back after a week and say they cannot resolve the problem.

Price is very important to the young South African consumers; a service should have a nominal charge and possibly a micro-fee for registration or membership. Price often gives the impression of quality, but this needs to be backed up with incredible service. The consumer should be able to pay for registration or membership or cost with an online account, rather than with a credit card. The young want full control of their money.

Many young feel that distribution takes too long, and that there is no certainty as to when items will be delivered. There is also no certainty that the consumer will be there to collect it when it arrives. An example given was the delivery of debit cards, which can take weeks, although the promise is delivery within 24 hours. However, what this means is that someone will pitch up somewhere within a 24-hour window, but you may not be there to accept delivery.

Young South Africans have very limited loyalty to web sites or to institutions. Several young people requested no switching costs between institutions so that they could change whenever faster, cheaper or better service was offered.

The young want good web sites. A Giga information group survey on web sites (www.gigaweb.com) found:
- 60% of web sites surveyed failed to provide a link to a privacy policy from the home page,
- 60% failed to provide action links such as "buy online," "learn about a product," or manage your account.
- On 43%, the basic navigation aids were missing or hard to find.
- 39% of sites failed to include a link to a site search tool.
- 35% did not provide a link to company profile – a company profile creates trust.

Young South Africans want to be known by the bank; they want to be treated with no prejudice. They want to be made to "feel good" by the bank, they want the bank to be involved in their communities, they want to feel good that they bank with XYZ because XYZ treats them well, treats their staff well and treats the community well.

Nicholas Negroponte summed it up when he said, "Computing is not about computers any more. It is about living." To the young, IT is an integral part of their lives.

WHAT DO WEB USERS WANT, AND WHAT ARE THE CHALLENGES?

Forty-one percent of web users surveyed by Webchek indicated that web service must be simple, easy to understand and easy to use. Twenty-nine percent mentioned security as an issue. They expressed concern that confidential information may be shared or sent to the wrong e-mail address. Twelve percent of web users mentioned web availability; they become annoyed when bank sites are unavailable. They expect bank sites to be available 24 hours a day, seven days a week.

The main dislike about the web in South Africa is slowness – Webchek found that 55% complained about speed, and in the survey of University students 65% mentioned speed as an issue. Most South Africans surveyed said that transactions take too long Obviously, this is a difficult issue as different people have different line speeds, modems etc., so it is not always the site's fault.

Twenty-seven percent of the South African web users surveyed by Webchek indicated that they are wary of using the web other than for surfing.

South Africa poses several challenges to local web designers and to local organizations developing web sites.

Challenge #1. If 27% of South African web users are wary of the web, how will we ever get the vast majority to use the web, not to mention the estimated 660,000 who have it, but are too scared to use it?

Webchek found that 46% of people surveyed bank on line. This would mean a maximum of 1,137,120 people who bank online. Webchek also found that 22% of those not banking online simply "haven't gotten around to it yet." Convenience was the main reason people stated for using online banking. Eighty percent did their banking from home, while 70% bank while at work.

Of the people Webchek surveyed, 37% of the home users and 33% of the work users have made online purchases. Of these who have purchased, 94% indicated that they would continue to make online purchases. Books were the first online purchase of most South Africans.

Twenty-nine percent of people surveyed had been connected to the web for more than three years.

Challenge #2. If 23% of the people in South Africa speak English or Afrikaans as a home language, and almost 100% of South Africa web sites are in English or Afrikaans (even the Government sites are in English or Afrikaans), how will we ever get the vast majority of people to use the web in South Africa?

Challenge #3. How do we get people to use local sites?

It would be foolish for South African web sites to forget the global challenge. According to www.onlinebankingreport.com, only 18 of USA's top 100 banks did not offer web access to customers as of March 2000. By March 2000, there were 26 true web banks in the USA – the oldest, Security First Network Bank, stated in 1995. Over 800 Banks in the USA offer web accounts.

Challenge #4. How do we change culture and strategy to be customer focused?

A major problem facing South Africa's financial institutions is to change their cultural and strategic approach from being product driven to customer driven. A question debated in many organizations throughout South Africa is: "Who owns the customer?" Departments within organizations continue to squabble over which department found the customer first and which department is entitled to change the customer's details. The issue is to get the most benefit for the organization from the customer, but it needs to be changed to benefit the customer.

Challenge #5. To manage channels and channel integration, giving customers the choice of using the most convenient channel at any time.

Challenge #6. To integrate the back office with the web site.

Challenges 1,2 and 3 are about how one gets people to use the site, while the remaining challenges revolve around changing culture and strategy.

WHAT DO YOUNG CONSUMERS WANT FROM FINANCIAL INSTITUTIONS?

The one word mentioned most often was speed. Faster services comes up in every survey. Speed is no longer important, it is essential. Young South African web consumers want cheaper rates, better interest rates, cheaper or zero switching rates.

They also want a single sign-on and a single password for all channels, phone, ATM, web, WAP.

Young South Africans want one global service for all institutions, that is fast and secure. They expect 24-hours-a-day, seven-days-a-week up-time AND prompt resolution of all support calls or e-mails.

An "all-media," "always-available" customer management interaction center, not a call center, but a single center, which can handle anything and everything, is something the young want from financial institutions. Financial Institutions must listen to customers and manage customer expectations, but they need to listen to the right customers, the 20% who make up 80% of the revenue, and these may not be the young.

Understanding the combination of online user behavior and the individual (one-to-one) customer's needs, and combining these with the business objectives of the company, is extremely powerful for real bottom-line results. Sites must contain elements that cater to each of these online interaction types to maximize their effect and achieve wider customer loyalty.

CONCLUSION

Have you ever wondered how Disney World achieves the seemingly impossible? They continuously draw millions of people from all over the world on an annual basis to the resort in Florida. And they do this while not being the cheapest holiday destination and by virtually no advertising or public awareness campaigns at all. They have never embarked on a client relationship management initiative. They have not gone through a business transformation or acquisition. Yet they do it! To find the answer to these questions, just talk to somebody who has been there. If you don't feel like going after that, then no amount of advertising would have gotten you there in the first place. Similarly, web sites need to provide a satisfying experience.

Online service providers in South Africa need to get Back to Basics (B2B) with fast, simple, available, secure, cheap sites, which seduce customers. They also need to get Back to Consumers (B2C). They need to learn about the consumers, understand them, listen to them, and put them at the center of the organization.

REFERENCES

Boer, S. (2001). Internet research methodologies & insights into South Africa Web usage. Lecture presented to Computer Society of South Africa, Cape Town.

Computing SA. (2001). Articles on online shopping in South Africa, April, 1,3.

Jarzebowski, K. (2001). MD of CareerJunction; an online recruitment and placing agency. Retrieved from the World Wide Web at: www.careerjunction.co.za.

Negroponte, N. Retrieved from the World Wide Web at:http://www.brainyquote.com/quotes/quotes/n/q130283.html, May 2002.

www.gigaweb.com. Retrieved from the World Wide Web, May 2001.

www.onlinebankingreport.com. Retrieved from the World Wide Web, March 2001.

www.southafrica.co.za/survey.South Africa Online web site. Retrieved from the World Wide Web, May 2001.

www.statssa.gov.za.South Africa Department of Statistics web site. Retrieved from the World Wide Web, June 2002.

www.webchek.co.za. Retrieved from the World Wide Web, 2002.

Chapter XVI

Explaining Information Systems Strategic Planning (ISSP) Behavior: An Empirical Study of the Effects of the Role of IS on ISSP

Jason F. Cohen
University of the Witwatersrand, South Africa

ABSTRACT

Contingency theory suggests that various environmental, organizational and managerial factors will influence an organization's approach to IT management. This chapter discusses the contingent nature of information systems strategic planning (ISSP) practices and presents the results of an empirical study of ISSP and the role of IS within 90 leading companies in South Africa. Results of a partial least squares analysis demonstrate the significant effect that perceptions of the future strategic role of IS within an organization have on ISSP behavior. Moreover, it was found that those organizations in the strategic quadrant of the McFarlan grid emphasized ISSP activities, committed more resources to the ISSP process and attributed greater importance to ISSP-business strategic planning integration mechanisms, than those organizations in the other quadrants of the grid. The relationship between ISSP and IS function performance was also significantly higher for firms in the strategic IS environment.

INTRODUCTION

Information systems strategic planning (ISSP), also referred to as strategic information systems planning (SISP), was born in response to concerns over the missed opportunities and wasted resources that result from lack of sufficient attention to long-term strategic IS plans (Edwards, Ward & Bytheway, 1991). Thus, by helping organizations avoid investments in IT systems that do not serve the business or its strategies, ISSP has become an important component of an organization's IS management agenda and is frequently described as a key IS management issue (Galliers, Merali & Spearing, 1994; Brancheau, Janz & Wetherbe, 1996; Watson, Kelly, Galliers & Brancheau, 1997; Gottschalk, 2000).

It is not surprising, therefore, that with a view to helping firms do more effective planning, most of the scholarly efforts in this area have focused on conceptualizing ISSP (McLean & Soden, 1977; King, 1978), discussing methodologies and frameworks for structuring the ISSP process (Hayward, 1987; Earl, 1989; Lederer & Gardiner, 1992; Min, Suh & Kim, 1999), examining factors critical to the success of ISSP efforts (Lederer & Sethi, 1991a; Ang & Teo, 1997), identifying planning problems (Lederer & Mendelow, 1987; Lederer & Sethi, 1992), and providing planning guidelines (Lederer & Sethi, 1991b; Lederer & Sethi, 1996). Limited attention, however, has been devoted to examining and understanding the extent to which ISSP process characteristics, design decisions and behavior conform to environmental and organizational contexts, or understanding the conditions under which various ISSP process characteristics are likely to emerge. Even most recent attention remains focused primarily on explaining planning success rather than planning behavior (Basu, Hartono, Lederer & Sethi, 2002).

This chapter addresses the above imbalance and, guided by the contingency perspective, seeks to examines whether ISSP behavior varies systematically with an important organizational factor, namely the role played by IS within an organization. Despite Weill and Olson's (1989) criticism, contingency theory remains the dominant epistemological leverage (Ansoff, 1984) in studies of management and information systems (IS) management. In the study of ISSP, contingency theory is particularly useful in understanding the various environmental, organizational and managerial factors that dictate the extent of IS planning taking place and the appropriateness of various IS planning systems (Cohen, 2001a). Although it is recognized that ISSP process characteristics will respond simultaneously to a number of contextual factors, it is not the objective of this chapter to identify a comprehensive set of contextual factors that may affect ISSP behavior. This chapter is, instead, illustrative of the contextual dependence of ISSP behavior.

BACKGROUND TO THE STUDY

The first and possibly most obvious ISSP contingency factor lies in the fact that information systems do not have the same strategic impact in every organization (McFarlan, 1984). Thus, prior studies on ISSP have predominantly focused on and suggested that organizational factors such as the role of IS in the organization were primary determinants of ISSP behavior (Raghunathan & Raghunathan, 1990; Premkumar & King, 1992; Premkumar & King, 1994; Tukana & Weber, 1996).

The study presented in this chapter continues the efforts of these prior works by empirically confirming the contingent nature of ISSP with respect to the role IS plays within an organization, and in particular confirms such theories in the context of a developing country, such as South Africa. While prior studies have focused mainly on planning differences between IS environments, this study, guided by the conceptual model presented in Figure 1, presents results of a partial least squares (PLS) structural model, testing the relationship existing between the role of IS and three important ISSP constructs that reflect the formulation of a comprehensive IS strategic plan aimed at aligning IS with business strategy. The effect of ISSP on IS function performance is also examined together with the moderating influence of the role of IS on this relationship. Results are important, as they point to the need to match the ISSP process with the role IS plays within the organization and will assist IS planners in determining the appropriateness of their planning systems.

Figure 1: Conceptual model

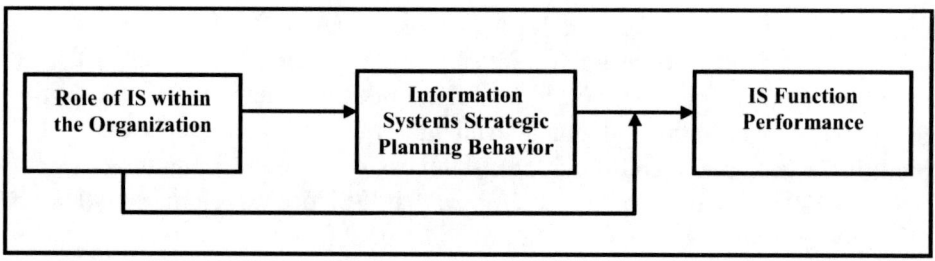

THE ROLE OF INFORMATION SYSTEMS

Despite the existence of alternative classifications (Earl, 1989), McFarlan, McKenney and Pyburn's (1983) strategic grid remains the most popular framework employed for studying the role of information systems within organizations. The strategic grid has received much attention in measurement research (Raghunathan, Raghunathan & Tu, 1999) and has also been operationalized in prior ISSP research (Raghunathan & Raghunathan, 1990; Premkumar & King, 1992; Kearns, 1997).

McFarlan et al. (1983) introduced their strategic grid in order to identify the different roles played by IS within organizations and thus to explain how and why different approaches to the management of IT within organizations was needed. The strategic grid (see Figure 2) identifies four different IS environments (strategic, turnaround, factory and support), depending on how critical current IT applications are to current business operations (current role) and depending on how important applications under development and future IT opportunities are to driving business strategy (future role). McFarlan et al. (1983) indicated that organizations in the support group should not expect senior management to devote the same amount of strategic thinking to IS as those organizations for which IS activities represent an area of greater strategic importance. Thus, the location of an organization within the strategic grid is likely to have implications for the design of its IS planning systems. The next section investigates this and the study's hypotheses are stated.

Figure 2: McFarlan's strategic grid (Adapted from McFarlan et al., 1983; Ward & Peppard, 2002)

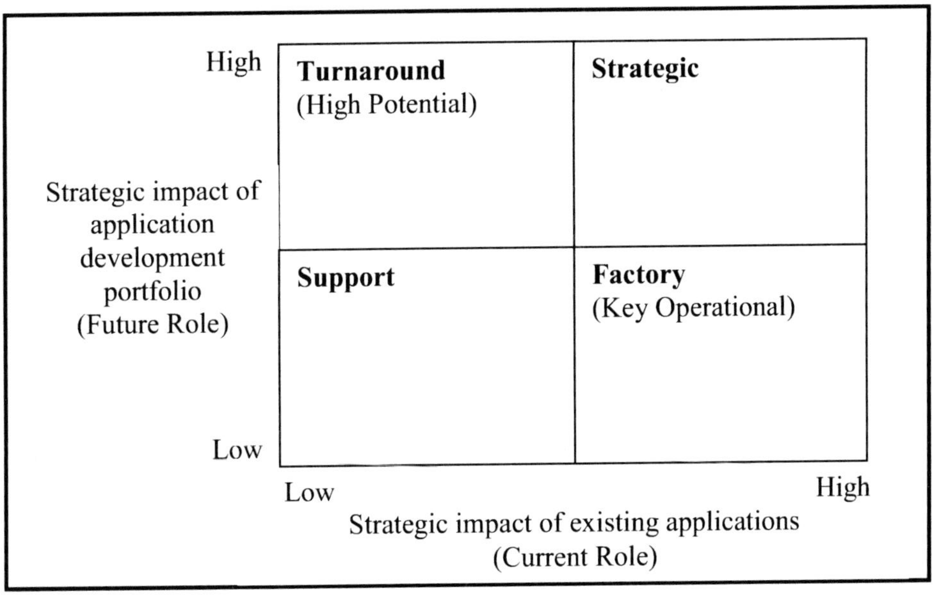

Strategic impact of application development portfolio (Future Role)	**Turnaround** (High Potential)	**Strategic**
	Support	**Factory** (Key Operational)

Strategic impact of existing applications (Current Role)

INFORMATION SYSTEMS STRATEGIC PLANNING

For firms in the strategic quadrant of McFarlan's grid, IT is viewed as essential for executing current strategies and, moreover, IT applications under development are crucial to future competitive success (Applegate, McFarlan & McKenney, 1999). For these firms, therefore, ad-hoc, incremental and disconnected (Ward & Griffiths, 1996) approaches to IS strategy formulation are simply not good enough given the opportunities that IT affords such organizations. Formal planning, carefully considered implementation and meticulous monitoring are required to ensure that strategic advantages from information systems are achieved (Lederer & Mendelow, 1986). The strategic management literature suggests that the benefits of planning are a product of the emphasis placed on various planning activities (Hopkins & Hopkins, 1997). Thus, for firms where IS plays a strategic role, emphasizing ISSP activities will be high on the IS management agenda. However, for organizations not currently dependent on IT, that can continue to operate in the event of major IT failure, and for which the strategic impact of IT applications under development is quite limited (Applegate et al., 1999), emphasizing ISSP activities is not likely to be a priority. It follows that the emphasis placed on planning activities is likely to be determined by the role and perceived importance of IS within an organization (Neumann et al., 1992). Hence:

Hypothesis 1: The greater the future role of IS within the organization, the higher the emphasis placed on ISSP activities.

Hypothesis 2: The greater the current role of IS within the organization, the higher the emphasis placed on ISSP activities.

In addition to the planning activities themselves, the provision of both tangible and intangible resources to the planning process are seen as necessary costs of doing effective and comprehensive planning and are representative of management's commitment to the planning concept (Ramanujam & Venkatraman, 1987). Commitment includes the allocation of tangible resources (time, money, people) to the ISSP process and intangible resources, such as the use of planning methodologies and the allocation of skilled and experienced planners. Yet, it has been argued that planning is often a drain on resources with little evident return and that the demands of daily operational issues afford managers little time or energy to devote to planning activities (Cohen, 2001b). These facts taken together with empirical evidence provided by Raghunathan and Raghunathan (1990) and Premkumar and King (1992) suggest that commitment to ISSP is likely to be higher for those firms with a more strategic role for IS. Hence:

Hypothesis 3: The greater the future role of IS within the organization, the greater the commitment to ISSP.

Hypothesis 4: The greater the current role of IS within the organization, the greater the commitment to ISSP.

In order to ensure that IT/IS investments are directed toward the achievement of both current and future business objectives, firms with a more strategic role for IT will need to ensure that IS planning is conducted within the context of business planning (Ward & Griffiths, 1996). Earl (1989), Remenyi (1993) and others have described this concept as planning integration, where fully integrated business strategic planning (BSP) and ISSP processes are necessary for those firms in which IS plays a major strategic role. Such integration is usually facilitated through the use of various integration mechanisms such as top management involvement in ISSP, IS management involvement in BSP, the use of steering committees where IS, users and management are represented (Premkumar & King, 1992), and by ensuring that the activities of ISSP dovetail in with BSP approaches and time tables (Teo & King, 1996). However, it has been suggested that in those firms where IS plays a non-critical role, planning systems tend to be reactive and the integration of IS and business planning processes is weak (Remenyi, 1993; Teo & King, 1996). Thus, it is hypothesized that:

Hypothesis 5: The greater the future role of IS within the organization, the greater the importance attributed to ISSP-BSP integration mechanisms.

Hypothesis 6: The greater the current role of IS within the organization, the greater the importance attributed to ISSP-BSP integration mechanisms.

In addition, Raghunathan and Raghunathan (1990) suggest that IS planning is more strongly associated with the future, rather than the current, role for IT within an organization. Thus, it is also hypothesized that:

Hypothesis 7: The future role of IS will have a significantly larger impact on the ISSP behavior than the current role.

Ward, in his textbooks (see Ward & Griffiths, 1996; Ward & Peppard, 2002), has mapped Earl's (1993) five planning approaches and Pyburn's (1983) three planning styles onto McFarlan's grid in order to illustrate the differing characteristics of planning processes in different IS environments. In addition, prior findings of Raghunathan and Raghunathan (1990) and Premkumar and King (1992) suggest that firms in different positions within the grid will approach planning differently. Thus, it is further hypothesized that:

Hypothesis 8: Emphasis placed on ISSP activities, commitment to ISSP, and importance attributed to ISSP-BSP integration mechanisms will differ depending on an organization's location within the McFarlan strategic grid, and will be greatest for organizations in the strategic quadrant of the grid.

A fit between the role of IS and the emphasis placed on planning activities, the firm's commitment to planning and the importance attributed to integration mechanisms should lead to improved IS performance. Premkumar and King (1992), however, did not find such a fit, between their planning variables and the role of IS, as having a significant effect on IS performance at the functional and organizational levels. Disappointed by that finding, this study revisits that concept of "fit" and hypothesizes that:

Hypothesis 9: Emphasis placed on ISSP activities, commitment to ISSP and importance attributed to ISSP-BSP integration mechanisms affect IS function performance more strongly in those organizations located in the strategic quadrant than in the support quadrant of the grid.

In addition, for firms in the strategic quadrant of the grid, a major objective of the ISSP process and an important IS performance criteria will be to improve the contribution of the IS function to the organization's strategic and competitive position. Thus, it is hypothesized that:

Hypothesis 10: The contribution of the IS function to the organization's strategic position will be higher in those organizations located in the strategic quadrant than in the support quadrant of the grid.

RESEARCH METHODOLOGY

Sample

A pilot-tested questionnaire was mailed to the directors of IT in over 450 companies listed on the Johannesburg Securities Exchange in South Africa. Data collection took place over a three month period and formed part of the refinement of measures and constructs for a larger doctoral study. One hundred completed questionnaires were returned, for a 22% response rate. Questionnaires with missing values were eliminated, yielding 90 useable responses. All respondents indicated that they were directly involved in their organization's ISSP process.

Measurement of the Study's Constructs

The role of IS was measured by asking respondents to indicate on a five-point scale the extent to which they agreed with five statements relating to the future and five statements relating to the current roles for IS within their organization (items adapted from Premkumar & King 1992). These perceptual measures of the role of IS were considered appropriate since managers' perceptions are an important component of the strategy-making process and enter into their strategy-making behavior (Bourgeois, 1980). Respondents were also asked to indicate, on five-points scales, the relative emphasis placed on 11 distinct ISSP activities over the last two years (very low emphasis to very high emphasis), and the extent of importance that had been attributed to four ISSP commitment measures and five ISSP-BSP integration mechanisms. These measures were all adapted from items found in the literature (see Table 1). Performance was measured by asking respondents to indicate the extent to which IS function performance had improved over the last two years with respect to four measures of the internal functioning of IS adapted from Nelson and Cooprider (1996). These items included the ability of the IS function to meet its organizational commitments, meet its goals, react quickly to organizational needs, and the quality of its work product. The contribution of the IS function to the organization's strategic position was measured by asking respondents to indicate the extent to which the IS function had improved over the last two years

Table 1: Measures of information systems strategic planning behavior

\multicolumn{2}{l}{Emphasis placed on ISSP activities (ISSP Emphasis) α = 0.93}
Activity1	Establishing IS mission and objectives
Activity2	Assessing the impact of future technologies on the organization
Activity3	Exploring opportunities for the competitive use of IT
Activity4	Analysis of the current IT environment within the organization
Activity5	Analysis of the external business environment and competitive trends relevant to IS
Activity6	Analysis of the organization's business strategy and the identification of opportunities for the use of IS to support that strategy
Activity7	Analysis of business processes that would benefit from IS
Activity8	Developing a set of programs and plans for managing the IS function
Activity9	Identifying and prioritizing projects
Activity10	Establishing policies and plans for IS development and/or procurement related to those projects
Activity11	Establishing policies and plans for infrastructure development
Integration Mechanisms (Integration) α = 0.90	
Integrate1	Use of a steering committee consisting of IS, user and senior management
Integrate2	Top management involvement in strategic IS planning
Integrate3	Participation of IS manager(s) in strategic business planning
Integrate4	Interaction between business and IS planners
Integrate5	IS planning linked to the approach, timetable and outcomes of strategic business planning
Commitment to ISSP (Commitment) α = 0.89	
Commit1	Inclusion of a proportionally high number of IS staff in the IS strategic planning team
Commit2	Use of IS planning methodologies
Commit3	Use of skilled IS planners
Commit4	Large commitment of time and money to IS strategic planning

in its contribution to business strategy formulation, implementation, the organization's ability to achieve its business objectives and a competitive advantage.

EMPIRICAL RESULTS

Reliability and Validity

Cronbach alpha was used to confirm the reliability of the scales. All alpha values exceeded the 0.60 cut off level and were considered acceptable. Factor analysis extracted single factors for all constructs except the future role construct. The analysis revealed that future role consisted of two dimensions that can be regarded as future strategic and future tactical roles respectively. The future strategic dimension consisted of items relating to the impact of future IS applications and technologies on the organization's long-term strategic objectives and business opportunities, while future tactical role items related to product improvements and cost reduction.

Analysis of Respondents

Consistent with Raghunathan and Raghunathan (1990), respondents were classified into four different groups corresponding to McFarlan's strategic, turnaround, factory and support IS environments. Twenty-nine firms were classified in the strategic grid, nine firms in the turnaround group, and 23 and 29 in the factory and support groups, respectively. This classification was based on respondent scores for the future strategic, tactical and current role dimensions, which were compared to the overall sample mean for each dimension, respectively. Table 2 presents results of the strategic grid classification together with corresponding industry classifications.

Table 2: Analysis of responses by industry and role of IS

Industry	Strategic	Turnaround	Factory	Support	Total
Manufacturing and Wholesale	2	0	4	14	20
Healthcare, Service, Hotels and Leisure, Transport	3	3	6	5	17
Financial services, Banking, Insurance and Assurance	5	1	4	5	15
Telecommunications, IT, Media	9	2	2	1	14
Retail	6	1	5	1	13
Non-mining, Chemicals, Oils and Construction	0	2	1	2	5
Other	4	0	1	1	6
Total	29	9	23	29	90

As expected, the majority of IT and telecommunications companies are located in the strategic grid. A large number of financial services, insurance companies, brokers and banks are located in the strategic and factory groups. This is consistent with Applegate et al.'s (1999: 444) description and the high information intensity of these firms. In addition, as indicated by Applegate et al. (1999), the movement of the retail industry into the strategic group is evident by nearly 50% of responding retailers positioned there. The majority of non-mining and construction companies are not currently dependent on IT applications. This is expected and is consistent with the low information intensity of these firms. Service companies are spread over the grid, possibly a result of aggregating potentially distinct groups, but—in the majority—IS is not currently perceived as playing an important future role for these companies. Interestingly, South African manufacturing and wholesale firms are in the majority using IS for support, rather than strategic purposes. This finding is consistent with Raghunathan and Raghunathan (1990) and Premkumar (1992), but is surprising given advances in computer-aided manufacturing, supply chain and logistics management that should see more of these organizations in the strategic and factory groups.

Partial Least Squares Analysis of Path Model

Results of a PLS analysis (see Figure 3), using PLS-Graph version 3.0, revealed that the future strategic role of IS strongly predicts the three planning constructs. The greater the importance of applications under development to future competitive success, the higher is the emphasis placed on ISSP activities, the importance attributed to integration mechanisms, and organizational commitment to planning, thus confirming the strong future orientation of ISSP. However, future tactical role did not influence planning activities, integration or commitment significantly, thus **hypotheses 1, 3 and 5 were only partially supported**. **Hypotheses 2, 4 and 6 are rejected**, as the path coefficients from current role of IS to the planning constructs were not found to be significant. The future strategic, rather than future tactical or current, roles of IS has the largest affect on the ISSP process, thus providing **support for hypothesis 7**. This finding is similar to the significance of the future role of IS reported in Premkumar and King (1994: 97). PLS analysis also reveals that the model explains 39% of the variance in the emphasis placed on ISSP activities, 29% of the variance in managerial commitment to planning, and 20% of the variance in the importance attributed to ISSP-BSP integration. These results provide support for the model's predictive and explanatory power, and confirm the important role that organizational factors play in determining ISSP process characteristics.

Figure 3: PLS model
** significant at the p<0.001 level   * significant at the p<0.01 level

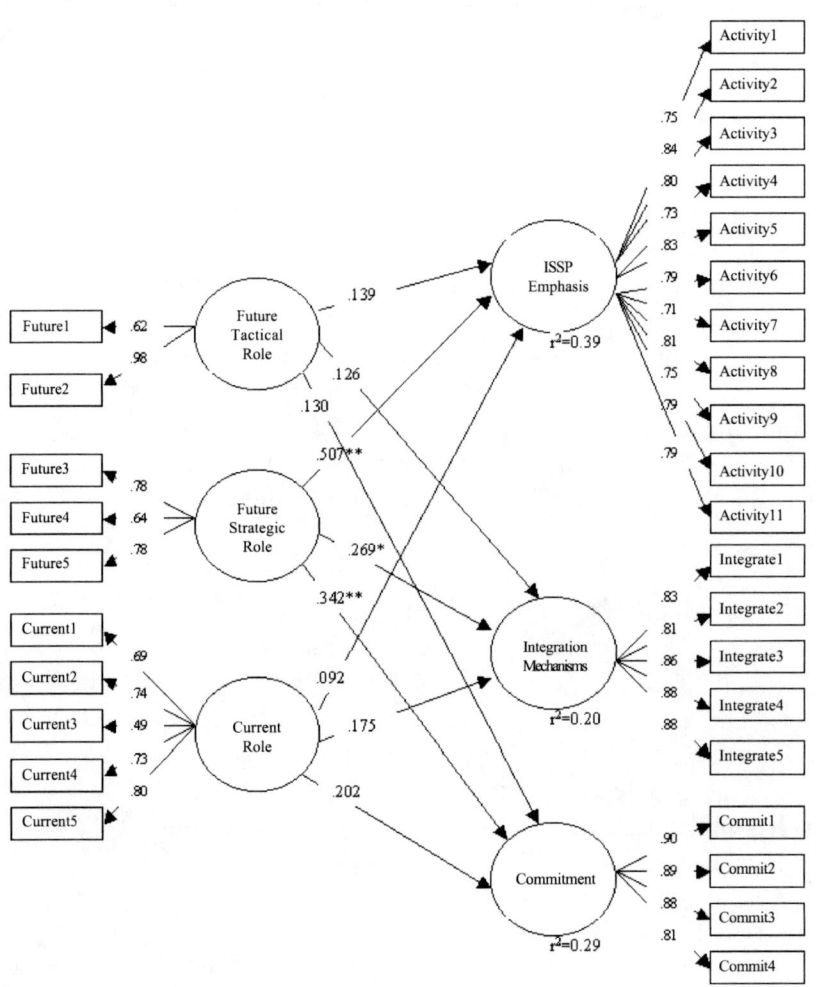

Differences Among the Four Groups

The mean of the 11 planning items, five integration mechanisms and four commitment measures were calculated in order to provide overall index values for the three constructs. These index values were then used for ANOVA testing.

Results revealed that the difference between the IS environments of the McFarlan grid is significant for emphasis placed on ISSP activities (F=10.506, p<0.001), integration mechanisms (F=4.995, p<0.01) and planning commitment (F=8.439, p<0.001). An analysis of means revealed that the emphasis placed on planning activities is, as expected, highest for firms in the strategic quadrant (4.2) and lowest for those in the support quadrant (3.3). Similarly, integration mechanisms and commitment were highest for firms in the strategic quadrant (4.3 and 3.6, respectively) and lowest for firms in the support quadrant (3.5 and 2.5, respectively). Thus, **hypothesis 8 was supported**.

Fit Between the Role of IS and ISSP

The concept of "fit" is integral, yet often misunderstood in contingency theory (Schoonhoven, 1981; Venkatraman, 1989) and it is important that the appropriate analytic scheme be employed to study "fit" (Venkatraman, 1989). The type of "fit" proposed in hypothesis 9 suggests that the role of IS moderates the strength and not the form of the relationship between planning and performance and, thus, calls for subgroup analysis. This was accomplished through regression analysis and the comparison of beta coefficients. Index values were relied upon as per above and were also calculated for the IS function performance construct.

The index values of the three ISSP constructs were regressed individually on performance for both the strategic and support groups. The statistical difference between the regression coefficients was calculated using a t-test. Results revealed that the differences between the regression coefficients were significant (see Table 3). This provides **support for hypothesis 9**, suggesting that planning has a stronger effect on performance for firms located in the strategic quadrant of the grid than it does for those in the support quadrant.

An index value for the contribution of the IS function to the organization's strategic position was calculated. ANOVA testing revealed that this value was significantly higher in the strategic group than in the support group ($F=9.693$ $p<0.01$), thus **supporting hypothesis 10**.

Table 3: Role of IS as a moderator of the strength of relationship between ISSP and performance

	ISSP Emphasis Beta Coefficients	Integration Beta Coefficients	Commitment Beta Coefficients
Strategic group	.529	.227	.519
Support group	.280	-.163	.022
t-value *	2.87	4.93	7.42
Diff. Significant	0.01 level	0.001 level	0.001 level

* $t = (b_1-b_2)/$pooled standard error; degrees of freedom $= (n_1-2)+(n_2-2) = 54$

MANAGERIAL IMPLICATIONS

While it is not the function of this chapter to provide prescriptive guidelines, certain important managerial implications emerging from the study are worthy of short discussion. Most importantly is that organizations wishing to move within the strategic grid (e.g., from support to turnaround) must recognize the need to also change their current IS management practices. In particular, is the need to place greater emphasis on certain ISSP activities (see Table 1), commit greater tangible and intangible resources to the ISSP process and ensure that ISSP is conducted within the context of business planning. This will help ensure future IS success. Secondly, is that those organizations wishing to improve their IS performance should ensure that their ISSP process is appropriate, i.e., matched to the expected role for IS within their organization. In those organizations for which IS represents an area of limited strategic concern, over-committing to an intense and costly ISSP process is unlikely to yield substantial performance improvements, while for those organizations in which IS plays an important future role, the performance consequences of inappropriate ISSP behavior can be significant.

CONCLUSION

A study of ISSP and the role of IS within 90 companies in South Africa was conducted and served to provide empirical support for contingency theories suggesting that organizational factors are important determinants of ISSP behavior. Results of a PLS analysis demonstrated the significant effect that perceptions of the future strategic role of IS within an organization have on the ISSP process. Moreover, it was found that those organizations in the strategic quadrant of the McFarlan grid emphasized ISSP activities, committed more resources to the ISSP process, and attributed greater importance to ISSP-BSP integration mechanisms than those organizations in the other quadrants of the grid. The relationship between planning and performance was also stronger for firms with a more strategic role for IS, suggesting that the role of IS within the organization moderates the strength of the relationship between planning and performance. Despite the promising results reported here, between 60% to 80% of the variance in ISSP is left unexplained. Future research would do well to continue identifying environmental, organizational and managerial factors, which explain greater amounts of variance in the ISSP behavior of firms.

REFERENCES

Ang, J., & Teo, T. S. H. (1997). CSFs and Sources of Assistance and Expertise in Strategic IS Planning: a Singapore Perspective. *European Journal of Information Systems*, 6(3), 164-171.

Ansoff, H. I. (1984). *Implanting Strategic Management*. New Jersey: Prentice Hall.

Applegate, L. M., McFarlan, F. W., & McKenney J. L. (1999). *Corporate Information Systems Management: Text and Cases* (5th ed.). Singapore: McGraw-Hill.

Basu, V., Hartono, E., Lederer, A. L., & Sethi, V. (2002). The Impact of Organizational Commitment, Senior Management Involvement, and Team Involvement on Strategic Information Systems Planning. *Information and Management*, 39(6), 513-524.

Bourgeois, L. J. (1980). Strategy and Environment: A Conceptual Integration. *Academy of Management Review*, 5(1), 25-39.

Brancheau, J. C., Janz, B. D., & Wetherbe, J. C. (1996). Key Issues in Information Systems Management: 1994-95 SIM Delphi Results. *MIS Quarterly*, 20(2), 225-242.

Cohen, J. F. (2001a). Exploring Information Systems Strategic Planning and Organisational Performance. *Proceedings of the South African Institute of Computer Scientists and Information Technologists Annual Postgraduate Research Symposium*, 30-40.

Cohen, J. F. (2001b). Environmental Uncertainty and Managerial Attitude: Effects on Strategic Planning, Non-Strategic Decision Making and Organisational Performance. *South African Journal of Business Management*, 32(3), 17-32.

Earl, M. J. (1989). *Management Strategies for Information Technology*. London: Prentice Hall.

Earl, M. J. (1993). Experiences in Strategic Information Systems Planning. *MIS Quarterly*, 17(1), 1-24.

Edwards, C., Ward, J., & Bytheway, A. (1991). *The Essence of Information Systems*. London: Prentice Hall.

Galliers, R. D., Merali, Y., & Spearing, L. (1994). Coping with Information Technology? How British Executives Perceive the Key Information Systems Management Issues in the Mid-1990s. *Journal of Information Technology*, 9(3), 223-238.

Gottschalk, P. (2000). Studies of Key Issues in IS Management Around the World. *International Journal of Information Management*, 20(3), 169-180.

Hayward, R. G. (1987). Developing an Information Systems Strategy. *Long Range Planning*, 20(2), 100-113.

Hopkins, W. E., & Hopkins, S. A. (1997). Strategic Planning-Financial Performance Relationships in Banks: A Causal Examination. *Strategic Management Journal*, 18(8), 635-652.

Kearns, G. S. (1997). Alignment of Information Systems Strategy with Business Strategy: Impact on the Use of IS for Competitive Advantage. *PhD Dissertation*, University of Kentucky.

King, W. R. (1978). Strategic Planning for Management Information Systems. *MIS Quarterly*, 2(1), 27-37.

Lederer, A. L., & Gardiner, V. (1992). Strategic Information Systems Planning: The Method/1 Approach. *Information Systems Management*, 9(2), 13-20.

Lederer, A. L., & Mendelow, A. L. (1986). Issues in Information Systems Management. *Information and Management*, 10(5), 245-254.

Lederer, A. L., & Mendelow, A. L. (1987). Information Resource Planning: Overcoming Difficulties in Identifying Top Management's Objectives. *MIS Quarterly*, 11(3), 389-399.

Lederer, A. L., & Sethi, V. (1991a). Critical Dimensions of Strategic Information Systems Planning. *Decision Sciences*, 22(1), 104-119.

Lederer, A. L., & Sethi, V. (1991b). Guidelines for Strategic Information Planning. *Journal of Business Strategy*, 12(6), 38-43.

Lederer, A. L., & Sethi, V. (1992). Root Causes of Strategic Information Systems Planning Implementation Problems. *Journal of Management Information Systems*, 9(1), 25-45.

Lederer, A. L., & Sethi, V. (1996). Key Prescriptions for Strategic Information Systems Planning. *Journal of Management Information Systems*, 13(1), 35-62.

McFarlan, F. W. (1984). Information Technology Changes the Way You Compete. *Harvard Business Review*, 62(3), 98-103.

McFarlan, F. W., McKenney, J. L., & Pyburn, P. (1983). The Information Archipelago – Plotting a Course. *Harvard Business Review*, 61(1), 145-156.

McLean, E. R., & Soden, J. V. (1977). *Strategic Planning for MIS*. New York: Wiley-Interscience.

Min, S. K., Suh, E. H., & Kim, S. Y. (1999). An Integrated Approach Toward Strategic Information Systems Planning. *Journal of Strategic Information Systems*, 8(4), 373-394.

Nelson, K. M., & Cooprider, J. G. (1996). The Contribution of Shared Knowledge to IS Group Performance. *MIS Quarterly*, 20(4), 409-432.

Neumann, S., Ahituv, N., & Zviran, M. (1992). A Measure for Determining the Strategic Relevance of IS to the Organization. *Information and Management*, 22(5), 281-299.

Premkumar, G. (1992). An Empirical Study of IS Planning Characteristics Among Industries. *Omega International Journal of Management Science*, 20(5/6), 611-629.

Premkumar, G., & King, W. R. (1992). An Empirical Assessment of Information Systems Planning and the Role of Information Systems in Organizations. *Journal of Management Information Systems*, 9(2), 99-125.

Premkumar, G., & King, W. R. (1994). Organizational Characteristics and Information Systems Planning: An Empirical Study. *Information Systems Research*, 5(2), 75-109.

Pyburn, P. J. (1983). Linking the MIS Plan with Corporate Strategy: an Exploratory Study. *MIS Quarterly*, 7(2), 1-14.

Raghunathan, B., & Raghunathan, T. S. (1990). Planning Implications of the Information Systems Strategic Grid: an Empirical Investigation. *Decision Sciences*, 21(2), 287-300.

Raghunathan, B., Raghunathan, T.S., & Tu, Q. (1999). Dimensionality of the Strategic Grid Framework: The Construct and its Measurement. *Information Systems Research*, 10(4), 343-355.

Ramanujam, V., & Venkatraman, N. (1987). Planning System Characteristics and Planning Effectiveness. *Strategic Management Journal*, 8(5), 453-468.

Remenyi, D. S. J. (1993). *Introducing Strategic Information Systems Planning*. Manchester: NCC Blackwell.

Schoonhoven, C. B. (1981). Problems with Contingency Theory: Testing Assumptions Hidden within the Language of Contingency Theory. *Administrative Science Quarterly*, 26(3), 349-377.

Teo, T. S. H., & King, W. R. (1996). Assessing the Impact of Integrating Business Planning and IS Planning. *Information and Management*, 30(6), 309-321.

Tukana, S., & Weber, R. (1996). An Empirical Test of the Strategic Grid Model of Information Systems Planning. *Decision Sciences*, 27(4), 735-765.

Venkatraman, N. (1989). The Concept of Fit in Strategy Research: Toward Verbal and Statistical Correspondence. *Academy of Management Review*, 14(3), 423-444.

Ward, J., & Griffiths, P. (1996). *Strategic Planning for Information Systems* (2nd ed.). Chichester: John Wiley.

Ward, J., & Peppard, J. (2002). *Strategic Planning for Information Systems*. (third edition). Chichester: John Wiley.

Watson, R. T., Kelly, G. G., Galliers, R. D., & Brancheau, J. C. (1997). Key Issues in Information Systems Management: An International Perspective. *Journal of Management Information Systems*, 13(4), 91-115.

Weill, P., & Olson, M. H. (1989). An Assessment of the Contingency Theory of Management Information Systems. *Journal of Management Information Systems*, 6(1), 59-85.

Chapter XVII

National Culture and the Meaning of Information Systems Success: A Framework for Research and its Implications for IS Standardization in Multinational Organizations

Hafid Agourram
Bishop's University, Canada

John Ingham
University of Sherbrooke, Canada

ABSTRACT

Information system (IS) success is still one of the most researched topics in the IS discipline, but most research on defining and measuring IS success was conducted in North America. As the world globalizes, multinational organizations consider information technology and IS as crucial and necessary tools to glue together all of their units. Moreover, IS standardization (i.e., the same IS implemented in all the units), particularly through enterprise systems (ERPs), has attracted these organizations because of the economic benefits standard applications can eventually yield to. However, researchers in the international management discipline have assessed that culture may be a major factor that influences organizational structure and management practices. Some researchers in the field of IS have also confirmed that national cultures do, indeed, have an impact on IS design and acceptance. As culture is defined as "a shared system of meaning," the success of IS should hold different meanings in different cultures. We found only sparse research work on how people from different national cultures perceive, define and operationalize IS success. The objective of this chapter is twofold: first, discuss why organizations that intend to standardize IS in different cultures should consider culture as an important factor in the achievement of success and second, propose a comprehensive framework for future cross-national research on IS success in multinational organizations. After the introductory section, the four main components of the proposed framework and their interrelations are presented: IS success, culture, IS standardization, and IS built-in success assumptions. The chapter concludes with the presentation of the new framework.

INTRODUCTION

From the most recent list of IS research mainstream, Markus et al. (2000) argues that one of the most enduring research topics in the field of information systems is information systems success. The urge to define, the dependent variable (IS success) was first called by Keen (1980) when he presented a list of five issues that IS researchers need to resolve (DeLone and McLean, 1992). DeLone and McLean (1992) argue that if information systems research is to make a contribution to the world of practice, a well-defined outcome measure is essential.

Today, managers are still frustrated because the question of IS success definition and measurement has no definite and clear answer (Myers et al., 1998). This problem of IS definition and measurement has largely been documented in North America, where most IS research has been conducted. The IS success problem becomes more complex for large multinational organizations, which conduct business activities in different parts of the globe, that is, in different contexts or cultures. This complexity is largely caused by the impact that different cultures may have on behavior, attitudes, and beliefs of individuals, which in turn influence the current managerial practices and the characteristics and type of use of the systems in place in a particular subsidiary. The complexity grows even more if a multinational organization seeks to standardize the IS in its foreign subsidiaries. A multinational organization that decides to standardize an

IS faces two major challenges. First, the system needs to be implemented successfully; that is, the system needs to successfully enter the operational phase of its cycle. Second, it later needs to actually produces its intended impacts. Those impacts must be measurable. Both challenges are within a particular context, the subsidiary context or culture.

North American researchers have developed some tentatively integrative IS success models (Delone and McLean, 1992; Seddon, 1997; Robey and Boudreau, 2000). However, these models are developed by people whose ideas and propositions reflect, in a way, what North Americans believe. Moreover, those models are generally tested with North American subjects. In other words, these researchers know something about the meaning system or constructs systems of people who belong to the North American culture. However, cross-cultural research has largely suggested that these made-in-the-USA models and theories cannot be transposed without precaution and further external validation to different contexts or cultures (Hofstede, 1980; Laurent, 1983; Maurice, 1979; Tayeb, 1994; Trompenaars, 1993). In reviewing the literature on cross-cultural IS, we could not find any study on how people in different cultures define, operationalize, or measure IS success. The intent of this chapter is to develop a framework IS researchers can use to try to fill in this gap.

Multinational organizations are good settings for conducting cross-cultural IS research. Until the headquarters of a multinational organization that seeks to standardize IS understands what a successful information system means for its managers and employees in a specific subsidiary located in a specific culture, and master the way these people operationalize it so that it can either adapt the new system to their beliefs and their values or take the challenge to act on their values and beliefs and adapt them to the way the corporate office define IS success, the IS implementation success and ongoing success are left to chance.

THE FRAMEWORK COMPONENTS
IS Success

The information systems success is the ultimate dependent variable of IS investments. A large volume of research has been conducted on the independent variables or what may cause the failure or the success of an IS: organization and IS unit size and structure; IS maturity, experience and resources; IS strategic planning and alignment; project management; IT characteristics; user's involvement and training; management support and intervention, to mention just a few. At the same time, a large but confusing volume of work has been done on the definition and the measurement of the dependent variable (Seddon, 1999). The confusing research findings on IS success has been justified by many factors. One of them is the mixture of the technical and the social aspects of an IS, as noted by Kanellis et al. (1998):

"...failure is the embodiment of a perceived situation (Lyytienen and Hirshhen, 1987). This highlights a fluidity and interpenetration between technological and social views, developed by the authors in another work (Kanellis et al., 1996), which leads us to argue: firstly, that plurality is unavoidable; and secondly, that success is a perspective that emerges from the social and technical interplay within organizations."

Alter (1999) also argues that information technology and work practices are now so much intertwined that it is difficult to identify their respective contribution to success.

Other researchers link the difficulty of defining IS success to the methodological aspects involved in measuring IS success: "Specifying a dependent variable is difficult because of the many theoretical and methodological issues involved in measuring IS success" (Garrity and Sanders, 1998). Seddon et al. (1999) present a recent and extensive literature review of IS success conceptualizations and measurements. They conclude that IS success is still a fuzzy concept contingent upon different stakeholders and different types of IT.

This complexity of IS success definition and measurement is at the origin of what is called the productivity paradox. Managers invest a lot of money on IS and IT and when it comes to the evaluation of the outcomes from the investment, they are faced with poor measurement instruments and, consequently, mostly base their evaluative judgment on intuition and personal perceptions. This has, of course, reduced the willingness of the CIO and CEO to put more money into IS and IT. These poorly demonstrated direct outcomes from huge investments in IS may not be a true finding, because it is not based on a strong and credible measurement. Ambiguity in measurement leads to low managerial trust and, therefore, low investment. On this aspect, Ballantine et al. (1998) wrote:

"The many well publicized information systems failures and the paradox of high investment and low productivity returns has brought issues of success causes and success measurement to the fore. Predicated upon success not being a random variable, a number of models which attempt to delineate success and success causes have been proposed."

IS managers are under increasing pressure to justify the value and contribution of IS expenditures to the productivity, quality and competitiveness of the organization (Myers et al., 1998). IS assessment is not well established and recent studies show that more research is needed (Clark, 1992; Delone and McLean, 1992; Dickson, Well and Wilkes, 1998; Saunders and Jones, 1992).

IS Success Models

The DeLone and McLean (1992) model of IS success is probably the most cited success model in the IS community. After an extensive literature review on IS success research work, the authors found that there was no clear agreement on what constitutes IS success. They claimed that researchers view the IS success concept in so many different ways and from so many perspectives that it was either impossible or very difficult to compare the findings. The authors finally proposed considering IS success as a process causally linking six variables: system quality, information quality, usage, user satisfaction, individual impact, and organizational impact. Three levels of IS success can be deduced from the model (Figure 1): the system itself (information quality and system quality), the individual level (use, satisfaction and individual impact), and the organizational level (organizational impact). The Delone and McLean model was recently successfully tested empirically (Rai et al., 2002). But, the Delone and McLean model is essentially a variance model (Seddon, 1997); variance at the system level deterministically produces variance at the individual level variables which, in turn, produces variance at the organizational level.

Robey and Boudreault (2000) propose also to study IS consequences at different levels, but from a process perspective. Two additional levels of impact (the group level and the inter-organizational level) are added to the original model to account for more recent developments in information technology (groupware, intranets, EDI, Internet), in management practices (team working) and in industrial organization (networks).

Figure 1: The original levels of IS success

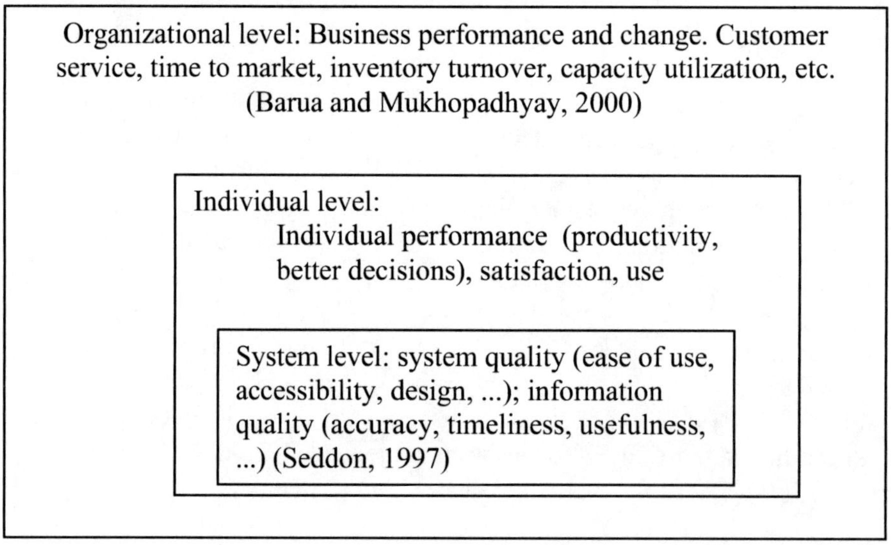

Organizational level: Business performance and change. Customer service, time to market, inventory turnover, capacity utilization, etc. (Barua and Mukhopadhyay, 2000)

Individual level:
Individual performance (productivity, better decisions), satisfaction, use

System level: system quality (ease of use, accessibility, design, ...); information quality (accuracy, timeliness, usefulness, ...) (Seddon, 1997)

Figure 2: A process view of IS consequences (Adapted from Robey and Boudreau, 2000)

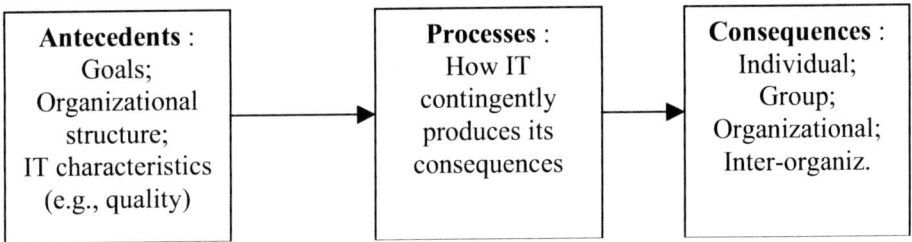

Recognizing that the consequences of the same IT may differ in comparable settings and that the consequences of IT differ within organizations, they also propose that IT success should be approached taking into account the contingent and uncertain processes by which IT produces its consequences (success or failure). This process view of IT impacts may be schematized as in Figure 2.

IS Success in a Multinational Context

The problem of IS success definition and measurement becomes even more difficult if we add the international dimension. As Ishman (1998) notes:

> "Few MIS instruments have been tested outside the homogeneous domestic environment in which they were developed. Yet, the variables such instruments attempt to measure are often operationalized in heterogeneous global environments. Information systems are very costly, especially those implemented globally. Accordingly, the development of a global research instrument that measures these variables that influence successful outcomes is important."

Garrity and Sanders (1998) propose, "that the field of information systems could certainly benefit from a generally agreed-upon measure of IS success." But, the researcher's and the user's basic values and perspectives of information systems modify their perceptions of IS success. The same authors further add that we do not all see things the same way. Just as people describing an accident often give different and contradictory stories or sequence of events based on their physical viewpoint relative to the incident, people likewise describe complex phenomena, like the success or failure of an information system, in different ways because of their differing viewpoints or philosophies which govern their perceptions.

In considering the international context perspective where cultural terms such as values and assumptions are used, and which may also be at the heart of the differing perceptions and interpretations, Shing-Kao (1997) argues that, "Research has shown that people notice, interpret and retain information based on their values, assumptions and expectations. Different assumptions and values lead to different ways of looking at the same thing."

This internationally differing perception of the meaning of a phenomenon is considered a hot topic in International Management or Cross-cultural Management disciplines. Do theories and concepts born in North America apply or have the same meaning elsewhere? Hofstede (1993), for example, after a large survey on work-related values in 60 countries, concluded that management theories and findings are not automatically transferable from one context to another.

> "There is something in all countries called management, but its meaning differs to a larger or smaller extent from one country to the other, and it takes considerable historical and cultural insights into local conditions to understand its processes, philosophies, and problems. If the world may already mean so many different things, how can we expect one country's theories of management to apply abroad?" (Hofstede, 1993)

The majority of theories of management have a western and, therefore, generally, a North American perspective which is based on the embedded values that influence the ways in which North Americans perceive and think about the world, as well as the way in which they behave within that world (Shing-Kao, 1997; Kedia and Bhagat, 1988; Robichaux et al., 1998). However, the majority of North American researchers do not explicitly state the context for which their proposed theory is built. They assume that their findings are culture-free (Kedia and Bhagat, 1988), which may not simply be taken for granted (Hofstede, 1993).

In research terms and from the systems perspective, Rosenzweig (1994) argues that a central concern in scientific research is external validity. That is the extent to which a theorized or observed relationship among variables can be generalized to other settings. The author does not mean external validity within a specific context or culture; rather, he questions the applicability of these relationships to other contexts and other cultures—that is the international dimension of the theory. The author based his argument on the basic definition of science which is "a systematic method of inquiry that consists of several stages, including: (1) the definition and operationalisation of variables; (2) the emerged relationship among variables; and (3) the measurement of variables to test hypotheses" (Rosenzweig, 1994). He further argues that the international generalization of management science research encounters obstacles at each of these stages of the scientific process.

At the definition stage of the research process, the universality of management science is impossible if terms used to define variables have different meanings around the world, especially when the conceptual equivalence of the variables is not met in different settings or cultures; that is, the variable may be translated literally, but fail to translate its meaning. At the operationalization level of variables, even if a variable can be translated with conceptual equivalence, it must also be operationalized in a way that leads to the valid interpretation of data. At the measurement of variables level, the author argues that there are two kinds of bias that occur in cross-cultural measurement of variables: respondent bias and observer bias. Finally, at the theorized relationship among variables level, the author argues that this relationship between variables often differs from one country to another. In part, these differences can be traced to value orientations that vary across cultures. In concluding, the author claims that the main question should not be: "Are management science theories that interest us valid elsewhere? But, how can we best understand management, as it exists around the world?" This is exactly the main purpose of this chapter where we seek to understand IS Success in different national cultures.

The above arguments imply then that the complex concept of IS success would have different meaning in other contexts than in the USA. This difference in meaning of any phenomenon in general, and IS success in particular, may find its origin in the concept of culture.

Culture

Culture is a term that was originally developed in the field of Anthropology and has recently become a prevalent research area in organizational studies. Unfortunately, a consistent definition of this ambiguous concept is extremely difficult to find. Lammers and Hickson (1979) summarize the problems, which have attended references to culture in the cross-national study of organizations:

1. Culture has rarely been well defined and even anthropologists, who have given more attention to the concept than other scholars, do not agree on the meaning of the term;
2. The boundaries of the cultural unit are difficult to define, particularly in light of the uncertainty about the meaning of the core concept itself;
3. The identification of variables as cultural is problematic in most studies, because there has been no explanation of their origins in the development of the society concerned;
4. Formidable problems exist in the measurement of cultural attributes; they are partly due to the lack of clarity in conceptual definition and partly of a purely operational nature.

Nevertheless, researchers need to deal with culture in cross-cultural studies. It is the only way to help understand how and why organizations are similar and different (Lammers and Hickson, 1979).

In 1952, the anthropologists Kroeber and Kluckholn claimed that there were more than 150 definitions of the concept of culture and proposed to define it as: "Culture consists of patterns, explicit and implicit of and for behavior acquired and transmitted by symbols constituting the distinctive achievement of human groups including their embodiment of artifacts." Baligh (1994) argues also that there are many ways to describe and define culture and that one may conceive of culture in terms of its parts and its components, and the two are related. According to Baligh (1994), the parts are: family, language and communication, religion, government and politics, education, transformation and technology, society, and economic structures and activities (business). Organizations, adds the author, are a part of a number of these, notably the last one. "A culture may be defined in terms of these parts." The components of culture are: truth, beliefs, values, logic, rules, and actions. The interaction of a part (e.g., business and economics) and a component (e.g., rules) may, for example, affect how an organization defines its customer orientation (e.g., customer comes first).

Schein (1990) links the cultural concept to the dual pressures upon human beings to face external adaptation and internal integration and proposes defining culture as: (1) a pattern of basic assumptions, (2) invented, discovered, or developed by a given group, (3) as it learns to cope with its problems of external adaptation and internal integration, (4) that has worked well enough to be considered valid and, therefore, (5) is to be taught to new members as (6) the correct way to perceive, think, and feel in relation to those problems. Culture then concerns a group of people who share a common understanding and meaning of things around them. It is a shared system of meaning (Trompenaars and Hampden-Turner, 1998) or the collective programming of the human mind that distinguishes members of one group from another (Hofstede, 1993). This programmed mind was well defined by Kolland (1990):

> What society has impressed upon a person forms the basis from which individual characteristics grow, which in turn make an individual unique among other members of society.

Figure 3: Trompenaars and Hampden-Turner (1998) cultural model

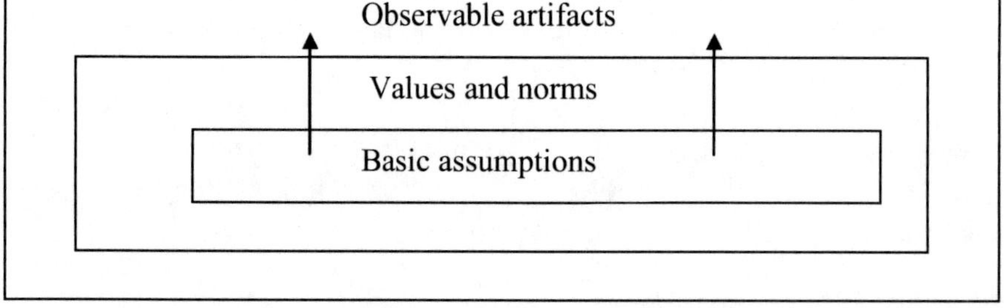

```
Observable artifacts
Values and norms
Basic assumptions
```

Trompenaars and Hampden-Turner (1998) propose framework in Figure 3 to understand culture.

The model indicates that the products of culture (observable artifacts) we see everywhere are symbols of the norms and values of the people living in that place which in turn are based on fundamental basic assumptions about human existence and life.

National Culture

The literature is rich with models that try to capture the concept of national culture. Morden (1999), for example, wrote a conceptual comparative paper in which he describes the different cultural models which can be based on either single or multiple dimensions. The following Table 1 summarizes some of the most popular models.

Hofstede (1980) proposes that national culture and values, as they affect the work environment and its management, could be categorized on the basis of four variables, namely: power distance; uncertainty avoidance; individualism-collectivism; masculinity-femininity.

With uncertainty avoidance, we are concerned with the extent to which people in a society avoid uncertainty and unclear situations. They control

Table 1: Popular models of national culture (Adapted from Morden, 1999)

Model	Source	Cultural dimensions
Single dimension	Hall, 1960	High context – Low context
	Lewis, 1992	Monochronic – Polychronic
Multiple dimensions	Hofstede, 1991	Power distance, Uncertainty avoidance, Individualism-Collectivism, Masculinity - femininity
	Trompenaars and Hampden-Turner, 1994	Universalism - particularism Analyzing - integrating Individualism - communitarianism Boundary management or inner-directed - outer-directed Time as sequence - time as synchronization Achieved status - ascribed status Equality - hierarchy

uncertainty by establishing and following rules and procedures. Personal ideas are not welcomed. Everyone needs to follow the procedures.

With individualism versus collectivism, we are concerned with the relationship between individuals on one hand and relationships between individuals and their organizations on the other hand. In individualistic societies, ties between individuals are loose. In the collectivist societies, ties between individuals are tight, and people believe in the between individuals relationships. That is, the group is more important than the individual.

With the dimension of power distance, we are concerned with the extent to which individuals accept the unequal distribution of power as a norm. Hofstede (1980) has shown that different cultures possess different distributions of power in their organizational and social hierarchies and that the power distance norm can be used as a criterion for characterizing societal cultures.

With the fourth dimension, masculinity versus femininity, we are concerned with the extent to which people put a lot of emphasis on status and achievement. Hofstede (1985) noted that in a masculine culture, the public hero is a successful achiever, an aggressive entrepreneur, and that "big is beautiful" (p. 85). In contrast, feminine societies emphasize quality of life, taking care of others, and preferring relationships than achievement. The emphasis is on "small is beautiful" (p. 85). Hofstede's model of national culture is based on work-related values and is one of the most widely used models in cross-cultural management. In addition, Hofstede's framework has been increasingly employed in information system research (Straub, 1994; Watson et al., 1994).

The values of people in a particular culture are the most widely used concept or variable in cross-cultural studies (Glenn and Glenn, 1981; Hofstede, 1980; Triandis et al., 1982). Hofstede's work on culture is based only on work-related values of people in different cultures. The reason behind the popularity of values as cross-cultural research variables is because at the deeper layers of culture, basic assumptions are preconscious (taken for granted) and are powerful because they are less debatable than espoused values (Lachman et al., 1994). The latter define values as the basis for the choice by a social group, of a particular end and particular means by which these ends are to be accomplished (Lachman et al., 1994). Hofstede (1985) provides a shorthand definition of value and defines it as "broad preferences for one state of affairs over others." Trompenaars and Hampden-Turner (1998) suggest differentiating between norms and values and claims that values direct our feelings of good and evil, and that norms are the basis by which a group of people judge something as right or wrong. Schein (1990) argues that basic assumptions are values that become stronger and are usually taken for granted.

Of the five dimensions, power distance and uncertainty avoidance are considered the most important in studying organizations in different national cultures (Hofstede, 1993). The combination of the extent of these dimensions yield to a four-quadrant framework, which represents organizational models. The framework is illustrated in the following figure.

To conclude, culture, a borrowed concept from the discipline of anthropology, is becoming an important issue in management and international management in general, and in information systems in particular (Ein Dor et al., 1992).

The importance of the concept in these new disciplines is basically linked to the emergence of globalization, which is due to a number of factors as stated by Burn and Cheung (1994):

> The world has experienced a shift in global alignment. The unification of the European Community market in 1992, the success of the democratic movement in Eastern Europe in the 1990s, the restructuring of the political and economic systems of the Soviet Union and its transformation into the Commonwealth of independent states and the opening of a vast China market to other countries, have combined to offer world-wide opportunities. The result has been a dramatic emergence of high-potential new markets to companies and a centered thrust toward international forums.

Figure 3: Four implicit models of organizations (Adapted from Hofstede, 1993)

HUA-LPD MACHINE Germany	HUA-HPD PYRAMIDE France
LUA-LPD MARKET Great-Britain	LUA-HPD FAMILY Hong-Kong

LPD: Low Power Distance; HPD: High Power Distance; LUA: Low Uncertainty Avoidance; HUA: High Uncertainty Avoidance.

We argue that national culture would have an impact on the meaning of IS success. To translate this proposition into practice, multinational organizations that wish to standardize IS in many different national cultures are faced with a major problem and challenge at the same time.

IS Standardization

Standards are defined as, "A set of rules or policies governing the characteristics of software and/or hardware that an organization may purchase or develop" (Gordon, 1992).

The benefits of IS standardization in multinational organization subsidiaries is the output of a complex equation which includes exogenous variables, such as the economical and socio-political environments of the subsidiaries and the cultural gap between the home country and the host country. The endogen variables include the company's structure, strategy, and the built-in assumptions of the information system to standardize. IS built-in assumptions are not well documented in the literature and are believed to be a critical barrier to IS transfer and implementation across cultures (Davenport, 1998).

IS Built-In-Assumptions

"Information systems have built-in values biases reflecting the value priorities of the culture in which they are developed" (Krumar and Bjoin-Anderson, 1990). This means that a cultural misfit is likely to occur if an information system or information technology developed in one culture is implemented in an organization in another culture (Leidner et al., 1999).

The outcomes and use of IS depend then on the degree of the "fit" between their built-in assumptions which are based on the designers' values (Krumar and Bjoin-Anderson, 1990; Watson et al., 1994) and the assumptions and the values of the adopting organization. Both implementation and success of a standard information system in different national cultures are targeted by the misfit problem. The problem comes from differences in meaning. Here we have two meanings: the shared system of meaning of people living in a particular national culture (e.g., their culture) and the built-in meaning of the system, that is, its built-in assumptions concerning the reason behind its development and the expected impact on its users. When the systems built-in assumptions do not fit the assumptions and the meaning given by its future users, then its built-in success assumptions are likely to differ from the meaning of its success from the perspective of these users. Two types of IS built-in success assumptions emerge then: IS built-in implementation success assumptions and IS built-in success assumptions. This classification is deduced from Markus et al., (2000) categories, IS implementation success and IS ongoing success, and adapted to IS built-in assumptions. The authors argue that IS success in general can be divided as

Copyright © 2003, Idea Group Inc. Copying or distributing in print or electronic forms without written permission of Idea Group Inc. is prohibited.

early success (implementation success) and later success (upward success) of the system and the two constructs are not closely related, that is, even if successfully implemented, the upward success is not guaranteed. Even if an adopting organization judges that both early and later successes are achieved in a particular culture, this is less likely to occur in the case of IS transfers from two different cultures, as stated by Leidner et al. (1999): "Even if successfully implemented, such systems may not yield the same benefits as they do in the culture from which the systems originally emerge." One probable cause for this is the misfit between IS built-in success assumptions and the meaning of IS success given by the adopting organization.

Multinational Corporations, which aim to standardize information systems in all of its subsidiaries usually face a challenging problem of both early and later successes (Robey and Rodriguez-Diaz, 1989).

Assuming that many corporate factors may lead to standard IS implementation success (early success), the meaning of the success of the standardized system in a particular subsidiary of the multinational organization, which is located in a different national culture, is likely to be different from the meaning given by the headquarters and the IS built-in success assumptions. This is mainly due to the existence of many shared systems of meanings and the meaning of the system itself.

National Culture and Information Systems

IT has the power to eliminate temporal and geographical barriers. This distinguishing aspect of IT, combined with the globalization of markets and economies, has encouraged IS researchers to investigate the impact of national culture on Information systems. Ein-Dor et al. (1992) conducted a literature review of IS research projects that dealt with national culture and IS. The findings of the analysis provide a list of cultural factors which are divided into organizational and national factors where each factor is further classified in terms of constant or changeable factor. The second result is the development of global information systems research model that put national culture variable as a key factor to take into account in cross cultural IS research. Robey et al. (1989) provide a conceptual framework for understanding cultural constraints on technology transfer. Again, their model incorporates national culture (societal culture in their words) as a key moderating variable in studying IT transfer. According to the authors, by considering organizational cultural differences to be a primary cause of implementation success and national culture to be a moderating influence, the model forces an examination of specific issues within the organizations engaged in a transaction. The table on the next page provides a sample of studies that dealt with national culture and IS.

Table 2: Selective studies on culture and IS

Authors	Objectives	Findings and results
Martinsons and Westwood, 1997	Examination of MIS in Chinese culture	Chinese managers make limited direct use of computer-based information systems. Management technology developed in one context cannot be readily transferred to another
Thanasankit and Corbitt, 1999	The impact of Thailand culture on the elicitation of requirements in IS development	Thai culture influences the elicitation of requirements in software development. Each country needs its own distinct methodology for information systems development
Robichaux and Cooper, 1998	Development of a model to identify effects of national culture on GSS participation	National culture variables (Hofstede) impact the ability of GSS to increase participation

National Culture and IS Success

The literature also provides some research on national culture and IS success. The majority of the authors conducted cross-cultural research between two or more culturally different countries and investigated whether or not existing theories or findings on IS success would hold in these cultures. Other researchers tested whether IS success variables would prove to hold in these cultures. To select their national cultures, the authors rely mainly on Hofstede's (1980) work-related national culture variables. Myers and Tan (2002) claimed that, "although there are many different definitions of national culture, most IS research has tended to rely almost solely on Hofstede's definition. This is perhaps not surprising given that Hofstede's typology of culture has been one of the most popular in many different fields." The following Table shows a sample of studies that were conducted on one or more issues of IS success and national culture using Hofstede's variables. However, we couldn't find a research work that develops IS success as it is perceived by people living in different national cultures.

Table 3: Selective studies on culture and IS success

Authors	Cultures	Findings	Variables
Straub, 1994	Japan, U.S.	U.S. companies exploit the advantage of IT, such as E-mail. Japanese firms do not, but they utilize more faxes.	Uncertainty avoidance
Hasan and Dista, 1997	West Africa, Middle East, Australia	Culture clashes whenever foreign technology is introduced. Each country must have a sensible IT policy that will choose the best technology for their culture.	Power distance Uncertainty avoidance Individualism-collectivism Time orientation Context Monochrony and polychrony
Martinons and Westwood, 1997	China, U.S.	The use of MIS in the Chinese management business culture has been and will continue to be shaped by factors such as paternalism, personalism and high-context communication.	Power distance Individualism Masculinity Uncertainty avoidance Confucian dynamism
Straub et al., 1997	U.S., Japan, Switzerland	Technology acceptance model may not predict technology use across all cultures.	Power distance Uncertainty avoidance Masculinity
Robey and Rodriguez-Diaz, 1989	Panama, Chile	In Panama, a standard accounting system was accepted. In Chile the same system was not accepted.	Culture in general
Leidner et al., 1999	Sweden, Mexico	Swedish managers perceived increased information availability the longer they had used EIS. Mexican managers perceived increased information availability the more frequently they had used the EIS. Swedish managers did not perceive increased information availability with frequent EIS use and Mexican managers did not perceive increased information availability with length of time of EIS use.	Power distance Individualism and collectivism Masculinity and Femininity
Tan et al., 1998	U.S., Singapore	Status influence was present in both Singapore groups and U.S. groups. In situations where status effects are harmful, Computer Mediated communications appears to be useful for reducing such harmful effects in both national cultures. Status influence was more sustainable and more strongly perceived in Singapore than in the U.S.	Power distance Individualism and collectivism
Simon, 2001	Asia, Europe, Latin America, North America	Perception and satisfaction of web sites' differences exist between the cultural clusters and gender groups with these cultures.	Power distance Individualism and collectivism Masculinity and femininity

THE RESEARCH FRAMEWORK.

The first three circles on the upper left side of the framework show the cultural layers of any subsidiary as proposed by Trompenaars and Hampden-Turner (1998). These are: basic assumptions, norms and values, and product layers. In the product layer, we choose the IS as a product. The arrow linking the three layers shows the dependency among them as proposed by Trompenaars and Hampden-Turner (1998) and described earlier in this document.

The second set of circles shows our proposed representation of IS success levels. It shows three levels of analyses of IS success: systems level, individual level, and organizational level. For the purpose of our research, the levels are used to show the meaning of IS success at each level.

We argue that the left set of circles (culture) influences the meaning of IS success at the systems level, the individual level and the organizational level. The

Figure 4: An integrated framework of cultural and IS success layers

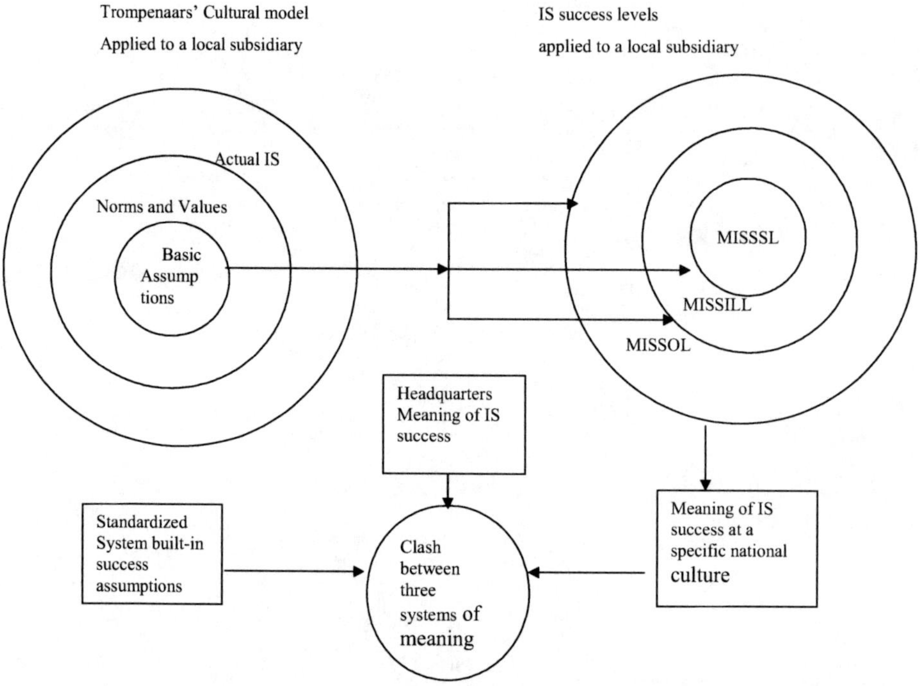

Legend:
MISSSL: Meaning of IS Success at the systems level
MISSIL: Meaning of IS success at the individual level
MISSOL: Meaning of IS success at the organizational level

model also shows the intersection of three systems of meanings: the meaning of IS success in a particular national culture, its meaning as defined by the headquarters office and the built-in success assumptions of the future standard system.

CONCLUSION

It has been argued that culture influences the outcomes and the type of many managerial practices. The implementation of a standard socio-technical system in different subsidiaries of a multinational corporation presents a great challenge. The most important goal of such an investment is to have a ROI as soon as possible. This means that the multinational corporation's employees in all subsidiaries need to understand the expected outcomes of such an investment. They also need to be aware of the impact of their culture on the implementation success of the systems, as well as the IS ongoing success. Furthermore, we are not proposing to force the system to fit their culture, nor are we proposing to change their culture to fit the system's built-in success. Rather, we propose that the alignment between the three systems of meaning as described in the framework is the best way to help to achieve a contribution to local subsidiaries and, therefore, a contribution to the overall performance of the multinational corporation.

REFERENCES

Alter, S. (1999) The Siamese Twin Problem: A Central Issue Ignored by Dimension of Information Effectiveness. *Communication of the Association for Information Systems*, Vol. 2, No. 20, 41-55.

Baligh, H. H. (1994). Components of Culture: Nature, Interconnections, and Relevance to the Decisions on the Organization Structure. *Management Science*, 40(1), 14-27.

Ballantine, J. A., Levy, M. S & Powell, P. (1996). Against Tailor-Made Solutions: Information Systems Strategy in a Learning Organization. *Proceedings of the SIGCPR/SIGMIS Conference*, Denver.

Barua, A. & Mukhopadhyay, T. (2000). Information Technology and Business Performance: Past, Present, and Future. In Zmud, R. (Ed.), *Framing the Domain of IT Management*.

Burn, J. M. & Cheung, H. K. (1994). Distributing Global Information Systems Resources in Multinational Companies—A Contingency Model. Proceedings of *IRMA Conference*.

Clark, T. D., Jr. (1992). Corporate Systems Management: An overview and Research Perspective. *Communications of the ACM*, 35(2).

Davenport, T. H. (1998). Putting the enterprise into the enterprise system. *Harvard Business Review*, 76(4).

DeLone, W. H. & McLean, E. R. (1992). Information Systems Success: The Quest for The Dependent Variable. *Information Systems Research*, 3(1), 60-95.

Dickson, G. W, Wells, C. E. & Wilkes, R. B. (1988). Toward a derived set of measures for assessing IS organizations. In Bjorn-Anderson and Davis, G. B. (Eds.), *Information Systems Assessment: Issues and Challenges*. North-Holland, NY: Elsevier Science.

Ein-Dor, P, Segev, E. & Orgad, M. (1992). The Effect of National Culture on IS: Implications for International Information Systems. *Journal of Global Information Management*, 1(1), 33-44.

Garrity, E. J. & Sanders, G. L. (1998). Introduction to Information Systems Success Measurement. *Information Systems Success Measurement*. Hershey, PA: Idea Group Publishing.

Glenn, E. S. & Glenn, C. G. (1981). *Man and Mankind: Conflict and Communication between Cultures*. Northwood, NJ: Ablex.

Gordon, S. R. (1992). Standardization of Information Systems and Technology at Multinational Companies. In *IRMA Conference Proceedings*, 274-278.

Hall, E. T. (1960). The silent Language of Overseas Business. *Harvard Business Review*, May-June.

Hasan, H. (1997). The Cultural Challenges of Adopting IT in Developing Countries: An Exploratory Study. *IRMA International Conference*.

Hickson, D. J. & McMillan, C. J. (1981). Organisations and nations., *The Oston Programme, IV*, Farnborough: Cower.

Hofstede, G. (1980) Motivation, Leadership and organization: do American theories apply abroad? *Organizational Dynamics*, 75, 42-63.

Hofstede, G. (1985). The Interaction between National and Organizational Value Systems. *Journal of Management Studies*, 22(4), 347-357.

Hofstede, G. (1993). *Cultures and organizations: software of the mind*. London: *McGraw-Hill*.

Ishman, M. (1998). Measuring Information Success at the Individual level in cross-cultural Environments. *Information Systems Success Measurement*. Hershey, PA: Idea Group Publishing.

Kanellis, P., Lycett, M. & Paul R. J. (1996). Failure, Identity Loss and Living Information Systems. *Journal of Strategic Information Systems*.

Kedia, B. L and Bhagat, R. S. (1988). Cultural Constraints on Transfer of Technology Across Nations: Implications for Research in International and Comparative Management. *Academy of Management Review*, 13(4), 559-571.

Keen, G. W. (1980). References Disciplines and a Cumulative Tradition. *Proceedings of the First International Conference on Information Systems*, December.

Kolland, A. (1990). National cultures and Technology transfer: The influence of the Mexican life style on technology adoption. *International Journal of Intercultural relations*, 14, 319-336.

Kroeber, A. & Kluckholn, C. (1952). Culture: A critical review of concepts and definitions. Cambridge, MA.

Krumar, K. & Bjorn-Andersen, L. A. (1990). Cross-Cultural Comparison of IS designer values. *Communications of the ACM*, 33(5), May, 528-538.

Lachman, R, Nedd, A. & Hinings, B. (1994). Analyzing Cross-national Management and Organizations: A Theoretical Framework. *Management Science*, 40(1), 40-55.

Lammers, C. J. & Hickson, D. J. (1979). *Organisations alike and unlike: Toward a Comparative sociology of organisations..* London: Routledge and Kegan Paul.

Laurent. A. (1983). The cultural diversity of western conceptions of management. *International Studies of Management and Organizations,* XIII (1-2), ME Shape, Inc., 75-96.

Leidner, D. E, Carlsson, S. & Corrales, M. (1999) Mexican and Swedish managers' perceptions of the impact of EIS on organizational intelligence, decision making and Structure. *Decision Sciences*, 30(3), 633-658.

Lewis, R.D. (1992). *Finland: Cultural Lone Wolf – Consequences in International Business*. Helsinki: Richard Lewis Communications.

Lucas, H. C. J. (1976). Performance and the Use of Information Systems. *Management Science*, 21(8).

Lyytienen, K., & Hirshhein, R. (1987). Information Systems Failures: A Survey and Classification of the Empirical Literature. *Oxford Surveys in Information Technology,* 4.

Markus, M. L, Axline, S., Petrie, D. & Tanis, C. (2000). Learning from adopters' experience with ERP: problems encountered and success achieved. *Journal of Information Technology*, 15, 245-265.

Martinssons, M. G. & Westwood, R. I. (1997). Management information systems in the Chinese business culture: An explanatory theory. *Information and Management*, 32, 215-228.

Maurice, M. (1979). For a study of the societal effect: the universality and specifity in organizational research. In Lammers, C. J. and Hickson, D. J. (Eds.), *Organizations alike and unlike.* London: Routledge and Kegan Paul.

Morden, T. (1999). Models of National Culture – A Management Review. *Cross Cultural Management,* 6(1).

Myers, B. L, Kappelman, L. A & Prybutok, V. R. (1998). *A Comprehensive Model for Assessing the Quality and Productivity of the Information Systems Function: Toward a Theory for Information Systems Assessment.* Hershey, PA: Idea Group Publishing.

Rai, A., Lang S. S. & Welker R. B. (2002) Assessing the Validity of IS Success Models: An Empirical Test and Theoritical Analysis. *Information Systems Research*, 13(1), 50-69.

Robey, D. & Boudreau M.C. (2000). Organizational Consequences of information Technology: Dealing with Diversity in Empirical Research. In Zmud, R. (Ed.), *Framing the Domain of IT Management*, Pinnaflex, 51-63.

Robey, D. & Rodriguez-Diaz, A. (1989). The Organizational and Cultural Context of System Implementation: Case Experience from Latin America. *Information and Management*, 17, 229-239.

Robichaux, B. P. & Cooper, R. B. (1998). GSS participation: A cultural examination. *Information and Management*, 33, 287-300.

Rosenzweig, P. M. (1994). When Can Management Science Research Be Generalized Internationally? *Management Science*, 40(1), 28-39.

Saunders, C. S. & Jones, J. W. (1992). Measuring the performance of the Information Systems function. *Journal of Management Information Systems*, 8(4).

Seddon, P. B. (1997). A Respecification and Extension of the Delone an McLean Model of IS Success. *Information Systems Research*, 8(3), 240-253.

Seddon, P. B., Staples, S., Patnayakuni, R. & Bowetell, M. (1999). Dimensions of Information Success. *Communication of the Association for Information Systems*, 2(20), 1-40.

Schein, E. H. (1990). Organizational Culture. *American Psychologist*, 45(2), 109-119.

Shing-Kao, L. (1997). A study of National Culture versus Corporate Culture in International Management. *PhD Dissertation*, Nova Southeastern University.

Simon, S. J. (2001). The Impact of Culture and Gender on Web Sites: An Empirical Study. *The Data Base for Advances in information systems*, 32(1).

Straub, D. W. (1994). The Effect of Culture on IT Diffusion: E-mail and Fax in Japan and the U.S.A. *Information Systems Research*, 5, 23-47.

Straub, D. W., Keil, M. & Brenner, W. (1997). Testing the technology acceptance model across cultures: A three country study. *Information and Management*, 33, 1-11.

Tan, B. C. Y., Wei, K. K., Watson, R. T. & Walczuch, R. M. (1998). Reducing status effects with computer-mediated communication: Evidence from two distinct national cultures. *Journal of Management Information Systems*, 15(1).

Tayeb, M. (1994). Organizations and national culture: Methodology considered. *Organizations Studies*, 15(3), 429-446.

Thanasankitt, T. & Corbitt, B. (1999). Cultural context and its impact on requirement elicitation in Thailand. *Paper* Toward an understanding of the impact of Thai culture on requirement elicitation *presented at the CITA 99 conference on computer and information technology in Asia.*

Triandis, H.C. McCusker, C., & Hui, C. H. (1982). Multi-method probes of Individualism and Collectivism. *Journal of Personality and Social Psychology.*

Trompenaars, F.T. (1993). *Riding the waves of culture: Understanding Cultural Diversity in Business.* London: Economics Books.

Trompenaars, F. T. & Hampden-Turner, C. H. (1998). *Riding The Waves of Culture – Understanding Diversity in Global Business.* McGraw-Hill.

Watson, R.T., Ho, T. H. & Raman, K. S. (1994). Culture: A fourth dimension of group support systems. *Communication of the ACM,* 37, 44-55.

About the Authors

Kalle Kangas is currently a professor of Information Systems Science at the Pori Unit of Turku School of Economics and Business Administration in Finland. He has extensive industrial experience in company-to-company sales and contracting in Finland and in the Middle East. His current research focuses on IT package implementation in conglomerates, information technology in global enterprises, information technology and economics in transitional countries, as well as economics of electronic business, and web-based learning and teaching. He has been the IRMA world representative for Finland since 1997, and vice president of the Global Information Technology Management Association (GITMA). He is also on the editorial review board of several leading IT journals, and general chair and member of the program committees for several acknowledged conferences in the field of Information Resources Management.

* * * * *

Hafid Agourram is a doctoral candidate in the department of Business Administration at the University of Sherbrooke, Quebec, Canada. He is also an assistant professor at Bishop's University, Quebec, Canada. His research interests focus on national culture and IS implementation and success in multinational organization.

Alan T. Burns is an assistant professor at the DePaul University's School (USA) of Computer Science, Telecommunications and Information Systems, where he teaches information systems and electronic commerce courses. His research interests include knowledge management within the realm of product development and technological solutions that can assist organizational knowledge transfer. He is completing his Ph.D. in MIS from Kent State University. Prior to his Ph.D. work, he worked in an engineering and management capacity in several functional areas of two organizations. He holds an M.B.A. from Kent State University and a B.S. in Mechanical Engineering from General Motors Institute.

Copyright © 2003, Idea Group Inc. Copying or distributing in print or electronic forms without written permission of Idea Group Inc. is prohibited.

About the Authors

Marly Monteiro de Carvalho holds a Production Engineering degree from the Engineering School of São Carlos-University of São Paulo, Brazil. She has an M.Sc. and Ph.D. in Production Engineering from the Federal University of Santa Catarina. Her research interests are project and technology management, quality and business strategies. For several years (1992-2000), she was a researcher for the Technological Research Institute of São Paulo State. Since 1992, she has been an assistant professor of the Department of Production Engineering at the Polytechnic School-University of São Paulo-EPUSP.

Jason F. Cohen is a lecturer in the School of Economic and Business Sciences at the University of the Witwatersrand, Johannesburg, South Africa, where he specializes in teaching strategic information systems management, and e-commerce to both undergraduate and postgraduate students. His research interests include strategic business and strategic IS management with a focus on strategy formulation, strategic planning and business performance. He is currently completing his Ph.D. in the area of information systems strategic planning.

Jakov (Yasha) Crnkovic is an associate professor of Management Science and Information Systems at the School of Business, University at Albany, New York, USA. After receiving his B.S. in Mathematics and Computer Science, he combined it with economics (M.S.) and computer information systems in business (Ph.D.) at the University at Belgrade, Yugoslavia. Before joining the University at Albany, he taught graduate and undergraduate courses at the University at Binghamton, College of Saint Rose, University at Belgrade, Yugoslavia, and University of Miami, Florida. His research is in the areas of decision support systems, management of information technology, system simulation, e-business and networking. He is the author or co-author for more than 10 textbooks and over 60 publications (in Serbian and English).

R. Brent Gallupe is a professor of Information Systems and director of the Centre for Knowledge Enterprises at Queen's Business School, Queen's University at Kingston, Canada. His current research interests are in computer support for groups and teams, global information systems, and knowledge management systems. His work has been published in such journals as *Management Science, MIS Quarterly, Academy of Management Journal, Sloan Management Review,* and the *Journal of Applied Psychology*. Dr. Gallupe advises both private- and public-sector organizations on the development and use of group support technologies for management teams. His clients include Canada Post, Health Insurance Division, Ontario Provincial Government, and the Canadian Urban Transit Association.

Babita Gupta is an associate professor of Management Information Systems in the School of Business at California State University Monterey Bay, USA. She obtained her Ph.D. in Business Administration from the University of Georgia. Her research interests are in the areas of electronic commerce, security and privacy, Web-design issues, customer relationship management, consumer behavior and global issues, intelligent agents, and knowledge management and parallel network optimization. Her research work has been published in the *Journal of Industrial Management and Data Systems,* the *Journal of Information Technology Cases and Applications,* the *Journal of Computing and Information Technology* and the *Journal of Scientific and Industrial Research.*

William K. Holstein (B.E., RPI, Troy, NY; M.S. and Ph.D., Purdue University, West Lafayette, IN) is currently a D. Hollins Ryan distinguished professor of Business Administration at The College of William and Mary, School of Business Administration, Williamsburg, VA, USA. Prior to that, he was an assistant and then an associate professor at Harvard University, Graduate School of Business, Boston, MA; professor, distinguished service professor and dean at the School of Business, University at Albany-SUNY, Albany, NY; visiting professor at IMEDE, Lausanne, Switzerland; and founding executive director at The Center for Private Enterprise Development in Hungary. Dr. Holstein has extensive consulting and project experience in the U.S., Europe, Southeast Asia, Central and South America and the Caribbean region. He is the author of three books and numerous articles on production planning and control, computer programming, management information systems and decision support systems.

John Ingham is a professor in the Faculty of Business Administration at the University of Sherbrooke, Quebec, Canada. He is also the head of the D.B.A. program at the same university. He holds a doctorate in applied economics from Université Catholique de Louvain, Belgium. His current research interests include virtual teams, electronic commerce management, information systems strategic planning and enterprise systems in a global context.

Lakshmi S. Iyer is an assistant professor in the Information Systems and Operations Management Department at the University of North Carolina at Greensboro, USA. She obtained her Ph.D. in Business Administration from the University of Georgia. Her research interests are in the areas of electronic commerce, intelligent agents, decision support systems, knowledge management, data mining, and cluster analysis. Her research work has been published in the *Annals of OR, Encyclopedia of ORMS, Decision Support Systems,* the *Journal of Information Technology and Management,* the *Journal of Scientific & Industrial Research,* the *Journal of Data Warehousing,* and *Industrial Management and Data Systems.*

Copyright © 2003, Idea Group Inc. Copying or distributing in print or electronic forms without written permission of Idea Group Inc. is prohibited.

Kevin Johnston was born in Umtata, Transkei, South Africa in 1953. He obtained a B.Sc. from Rhodes University, a B.Sc. (Hons) from the University of South Africa (UNISA), and an M.Com. from the University of Cape Town (UCT). He is married with two daughters. He also has over 20 years of experience in the IT industry in Southern Africa, working for companies such as De Beers, Liberty Life and BoE. He has spoken at IT conferences in Africa, Europe and the USA. He is currently a senior lecturer in Information Systems at UCT, South Africa.

Rajiv Kishore is an assistant professor of the School of Management at The State University of New York at Buffalo, USA. He received his Ph.D. in Computer Information Systems from Georgia State University. His current research interests include IT outsourcing, adoption of software process and emerging IT innovations, and software process improvement. His papers have appeared or will be appearing in *Information Systems Frontiers* and *Communications of the ACM*. He has consulted in these and related areas with a number of large companies, some of which include BellSouth, Blue Cross Blue Shield of Minnesota, Clearnet Communications (Canada), Dun and Bradstreet Software, IBM, and Pioneer Standard Electronics. He is also the recipient of a multi-year NSF research grant as a co-principal investigator for conducting research in the area of IS outsourcing.

Linda V. Knight is an associate dean of DePaul University's (USA) School of Computer Science, Telecommunications, and Information Systems. She is also the director of CTI's Center for the Strategic Application of Emerging Technologies. As co-developer of one of the largest e-commerce degree programs, she teaches and conducts research in the area of e-commerce business strategy, development, and implementation. She is an associate editor of the *Journal of IT Education*, and serves on the editorial review board of the *Information Resources Management Journal*. An entrepreneur and IT consultant, she has held industry positions in IT management and quality assurance management. She holds a Ph.D. in Computer Science from DePaul University.

Fernando José Barbin Laurindo holds a graduate, M.Sc. and Ph.D. degrees in Production Engineering from the Polytechnic School of University of São Paulo, Brazil. He is also a graduate of Law from the University of São Paulo, and created an extension course in Business Administration from the Fundação Getúlio Vargas. His research interests are information technology and business strategies, information technology planning and project management. During the past 15 years, he has worked for companies in the manufacturing, financial and service sectors. Since 1997, he has been an assistant professor of the Department of Production Engineering at the Polytechnic School - University of São Paulo-EPUSP.

Copyright © 2003, Idea Group Inc. Copying or distributing in print or electronic forms without written permission of Idea Group Inc. is prohibited.

Purnendu Mandal is an associate professor of MIS in the Department of Management and Marketing, Lewis College of Business, Marshall University, West Virginia, USA. His current teaching courses include principles of MIS, database management, electronic commerce and strategic MIS. He taught in England, India, Singapore, Australia and the U.S. He published over 100 refereed journal and conference papers. His works appeared in *EJOR, IJPOM, IJQRM, Industrial Management and Data Systems, Intelligent Automation and Soft Computing: An International Journal, Logistics Information Management,* etc. Dr. Mandal serves in a number of professional bodies and currently is on the editorial board of three international journals.

D. C. McDermid has over 10 years practical experience in the IT industry as well as many more years as an academic. His main research interests are in the area of systems modelling and systems thinking, particularly in how they can be applied to capturing information systems speacifications. He is also interested in how consultants and other senior IT professionals can assist the discipline in terms of adding value to IT business processes. He holds a bachelors degree with honours in Computing Science, an M.B.A. from the University of Glasgow, and a Ph.D. in Information Systems from Curtin University of Technology in Australia. He also has links and memberships with several professional bodies.

Andreas L. Opdahl is a professor of Information Systems Development at the Department of Information Science at the University of Bergen in Norway. His research interests include multi-perspective enterprise and IS modelling, IS-architecture management and requirements determination for IS. He is the author, co-author and co-editor of more than 40 journal articles, book chapters, refereed archival conference papers and books. Dr. Opdahl reviews papers for premier journals and serves regularly on the program and organization committees of renowned international conferences and workshops. He is a member of IFIP WG8.1 on Design and Evaluation of Information Systems.

Paul A. Pavlou is a Ph.D. candidate of Information Systems at the Marshall School of Business in the University of Southern California, USA. His research focuses on B2B and B2C electronic commerce, new product development, institutional trust, interactive marketing communications, and e-government. He has over twenty-five publications in journals, books, and refereed conference proceedings. His research has appeared (or scheduled to appear) in *MIS Quarterly, Electronic Markets, Journal of the Academy of Marketing Science, Journal of Strategic Information Systems, Journal of Logistics Information Management,* and *Journal of Interactive Advertising,* among others. He has recently won the Best Interactive Paper Award in the 2002 Academy of Management Conference.

Copyright © 2003, Idea Group Inc. Copying or distributing in print or electronic forms without written permission of Idea Group Inc. is prohibited.

Pauline Ratnasingam is an assistant professor of MIS at the University of Vermont (USA), School of Business Administration. She has lectured on the topics of project management, management of information systems and electronic commerce in Australia, New Zealand, Europe and America. She is an associate member of the Association of Information Systems, and is a member of the Information Resources Management Association and Academy of Management. Her research interests include business risk management, Internet-based business-to-business e-commerce, organizational behaviour, inter-organizational-relationships and trust. She has published several articles related to this area in national and international conferences and refereed journals. She has received a grant from the National Science Foundation to pursue her work on inter-organizational trust in business-to-business e-commerce.

Philip Seltsikas is a lecturer in Business Information Technology at the School of Management, University of Surrey, UK. He manages several research projects in Information Systems including a large European project on ASP. Before joining the University of Surrey, he held posts at Brunel University and at the Aston Business School where he lectured in business policy and strategic management. He holds a B.Sc. (Hons.) in Managerial and Administrative Studies from Aston University, an M.Sc. by research in Business Management from the Aston Business School and a Ph.D. in Management and Information Systems from the same institution. He has worked with senior management at Xerox Ltd. on business process and information management strategy for the Europe, Middle East and Africa region. He has also worked in the City of London on company take-overs and privatisations and as a systems analyst/programmer.

Tamio Shimizu earned his B.S. degree in Mathematics from the University of São Paulo, Brazil. He holds an M.Sc. from the Aeronautical Institute of Technology, São José dos Campos, and a Ph.D. in Production Engineering from the Polytechnic School of the University of São Paulo. His research interests are information technology, intelligent manufacturing systems and decision support systems. During the past several years, he was a professor of the Aeronautical Institute of Technology, São José dos Campos. Currently, he is a full professor and the current head of the Department of Production Engineering at the Polytechnic School-University of São Paulo-EPUSP.

Bongsik Shin is an associate professor at the Department of Information and Decision Systems at San Diego State University, USA. He earned a Ph.D. from the University of Arizona. His work has been published or accepted in *Communications of the ACM*, *IEEE Transactions on Systems, Man, and Cybernetics*, *IEEE Transaction on Engineering Management*, the *Journal of Data Warehousing*, the *Journal of Organizational Computing and Electronic*

Commerce, the *Journal of Systems Integration*, and the *Journal of Database Management*. His research interests are electronic commerce and telework.

Theresa A. Steinbach is an instructor at the DePaul University's School of Computer Science (USA), Telecommunications and Information Systems, and associate director of the CTI's Center for the Strategic Application of Emerging Technologies. She teaches Web-based scripting as well as teaching and conducting research in traditional and e-commerce systems analysis and design. Ms. Steinbach is the founder of the student-led DePaul Chapter of the Association for Computing Machinery-Women as well as its faculty sponsor. As owner of an IT consulting firm, she provided turnkey solutions for small- and medium-size enterprises. Ms. Steinbach is completing her Ph.D. in Computer Science from DePaul University. She holds a B.A. in Mathematics, an M.B.A in Quantitative Economics, and an M.S. in Information Systems from DePaul University.

Felix B. Tan serves as the editor-in-chief of the *Journal of Global Information Management*. He is also the vice president of Research for the Information Resources Management Association and the editor of the ISWorld Net's EndNote Resources page. Dr. Tan's current research interests are in electronic commerce, business-IT alignment, global IT, management of IT, cognitive mapping and narrative methodologies. His research has been published in *MIS Quarterly, Journal of Global Information Management, Journal of Information Technology* as well as other journals and refereed conference proceedings. Dr. Tan has over 20 years experience in IT management and consulting with large multinationals, as well as university teaching and research in Singapore, Canada and New Zealand. Dr. Tan is from The University of Auckland, New Zealand.

D. E. Sofiane Tebboune is a doctoral student at the Department of Information Systems and Computing, Brunel University, UK. He is also a member of the Centre for Strategic Information Systems (CSIS) at Brunel University. Mr. Tebboune holds an M.A. in Information Systems Management, and researches the area of IS Outsourcing, and collaborative strategies in the context of Application Service Provision. He has previously been involved in research on e-procurement and supply chain management.

Qiang Tu is an assistant professor of Management Information Systems at the College of Business of Rochester Institute of Technology, USA. He received his bachelor's degree in Management Engineering and a master's degree in Systems Engineering from Jiaotong University, China. He holds a Ph.D. from the College of Business Administration of University of Toledo. He has published in many prominent journals including *Information Systems Research,* the *Journal of Operations Management, OMEGA: The International Journal of Management Science,* the *Journal of Strategic Information Systems, Information Resources Management Journal,* the *Journal of Information Technology Management* and the *Computers and Industrial Engineering Journal.* His research interests include information systems strategy, manufacturing strategy, technology management, and behavioral issues in information systems and manufacturing management.

Wei Wang is a senior systems analyst and a data warehouse specialist at the Information Technology Services Department of Rochester Institute of Technology, USA. She holds a master's degree in Systems Engineering from Nanjing University of Science and Technology, China and an M.Sc. in Information Systems and Manufacturing Management from the University of Toledo. She has many years of IT consulting and training experience. She was a senior consultant with Keane Inc., one of the nation's top IT consulting firms. She has worked with a number of large manufacturing companies on their IT implementation projects, such as Champion International Paper and Maidenform Inc. Her current research interests include ERP implementation, data warehousing and business decision support systems.

James D. White is an instructor at the DePaul University's School of Computer Science (USA), Telecommunications and Information Systems. He teaches undergraduate and graduate Information Systems courses as well as conducts research in the strategic use of applications, and systems analysis and design. Prior to joining DePaul, Mr. White held the position of Vice President – Information Systems for the Chicago Board of Trade. He received a B.A. in Psychology from Northwestern University, an M.B.A. from the Dominican University and is completing his Ph.D. in Computer Science at DePaul University.

Index

A

action planning phase 89
action research study 88
action taking phase 89
administrative coordination 136
advanced manufacturing technologies (AMT) 16
alignment framework 28
American Hospital Supply Corporation's (AHSC) 102
analytic systems automatic purchasing (ASAP) 102
Application service providers (ASPs) 116, 160
ASP enablers 119
ASP organizing vision 163
ASP paradigm 162
authoritative communication 136
authorization mechanisms 204

B

Bain type competition model 132
balanced scorecard collaborative 175
behavioral theory of the firm 133
bilateral institutionalized practices 208
binary relationships 10
breadth in measurement 177
business intelligence 21
business metrics 175
business strategy 50
business to business (B2B) electronic commerce 200
business-IT alignment 50
business-to-business (B2B) 107
business-to-consumer (B2C) 106, 107

C

categorization 66
choosing mode 88, 94
CIM implementation 21
client-side know-what 162
cognitive categorization theory 66
cognitive mapping 64
cognitive theories 50
communication quality 9
comparing mode 88, 93
competence building 142
competence leveraging 142
competitive IT orientation 99
competitive locus 141
competitive marketplace 97
competitive strategies 109
competitive strategy 98
computer numerically-controlled (CNC) machines 16
computer-aided design and manufacturing (CAD/CAM) 16
computer-aided process planning (CAPP) 16
computer-integrated manufacturing (CIM) 16

consolidation 126
constructive alternativism 64
corollary 65
corporate span 141
cost reductions 152
critical decision areas 187
critical success factors (CSF) 187
CRM outsourcing 149
CRM outsourcing framework 153
CRM outsourcing success 154
CRM vendor 155
cross-cultural management disciplines 248
cross-functional integration 21
customer relationship management (CRM) 150

D

decision support systems (DSS) 170
design features of telework 2
designing mode 87
diagnosing step 89
direct participation 81
distributive project teams 2
dynamic double-loop learning 143
dynamic single loop learning 142

E

e-commerce 150
electricity sourcing 82
encryption mechanisms 204
energy trader specialists 81
enhanced competitive position 17
enterprise ASPs 119
enterprise resource planning (ERP) 16, 152, 194
evaluation phase 89

F

fit as covariation 5
fit as gestalts 5
fit as matching 4
fit as mediation 5
fit as profile deviation 6
fit concept 4
five dimensions of IT strategy 97

flexible manufacturing systems (FMS) 16
focused factory 18
framework 96
full service providers (FSP) 119
function-based systems structuring 29
fundamental postulate 65

G

gestalts 5

H

hierarchical level 32
horizontal ASPs 119

I

imitability 140
improved strategic flexibility 17
individuality corollary 65
industrial economics 133
industrial organization (IO) 134
information and communications technology (ICT) 74
Information Resources Management (IRM) 130
information system (IS) 16, 50, 242
information systems strategic planning (ISSP) 226
information technology (IT) 14, 50, 143, 186
information technology strategic alignment 186
institutional trust 200
integration mechanisms 231
intellective skills 20
international management 248
interorganizational trust 201
IS architecture 29
IS outsourcing 151
IS performance 232
IS-architecture alignment 31
IS-architecture work 29
ISSP-business strategic planning 226
IT architecture 74
IT governance 161
IT infrastructure perspective 191

IT investment metrics 171
IT organizational infrastructure perspective 191
IT outsourcing 161
IT strategic impacts 186

K

Kepner-Tregoe method 170
know-what uncertainties 162

L

learning-by-doing 141
Line service providers (LNSPs) 82
local productivity gains 19

M

management information systems (MIS) 15, 170
managerial cognition 50
manufacturing enterprise 14
manufacturing globalization 18
maximum enterprise integration 14
McFarlan's grid 230
meter providers (MP) 82
metering data agents (MDA) 82
metrics of business and management performance 173
micro-economic theory 131
multinational organizations 244

N

national electricity market (NEM) 81
national electricity marketing and management (NEMMCO) 82
neoclassical theory 132

O

office automation systems 15
online consumers 216
OPEN modelling language 35
operational benefits of IT 17
organisation units 38
organisational metatype 30
organisational structure 31

organization-unique motivation 3
organizational infrastructure perspective 191
organizational structure 19
organizational-level forces 2
organizations 2
organizing vision 163
outsourcing firm 149, 156

P

particular transaction 204
partnership quality 149
personal construct theory 64
petal 32
pilot-tested questionnaire 232
Poincaré's intuition 170
primary strategic resource 97
product development operational model (PDOM) 81
productivity paradox 187
profile 216
pure play ASPs 119

Q

quality of service 155

R

range corollary 65
rareness 140
representation framework 28
resource-based theory 129
resource-based view of the firm 136
resource-dependency theory 153
return on investment (ROI) 171
risk 96

S

shaping mode 87
situational normality 200
social cognitive theory 66
social exchange theory 153
South African online consumer 216
specific learning phase 89
strategic alignment model (SAM) 56, 189

strategic benefits of IT 17
strategic choice method 86
strategic grid 188, 229
strategic information systems (SIS) 16
strategic information systems planning (SISP) 227
strategic IT portfolios 96
strategic justification 19
strategic management 14
strategic mode 99, 110
strategic orientation 58, 110
strategic resource 109
strategic target 99, 110
strategy-making behavior 233
structural assurances 203
supply chain management (SCM) 15
supply chain operations reference (SCOR) 180
supportive organizational arrangements 140
systems development life cycle (SDLC) 81
systems integration 21

T

task-technology fit 8
technology trust 204, 207
telecommunications (TC) 143
telecommunications organization (TEL) 74, 79
telework effectiveness 2
temporal dominance 141
third-party Institutions 208
third-party technology Trust 208
total cost of ownership (TCO) 117
trading partner trust 207
transaction cost theory 135, 153

U

uncertainties in related decision fields (UR) 94
uncertainties in the working environment (UE) 93

V

value 140
vertical ASPs 119
verticalisation 126
virtual process 1
visual card sort technique 66

W

Webchek 217
work design 20
worker characteristics 2

InfoSci-Online Database

30-Day free trial!

www.infosci-online.com

Provide instant access to the latest offerings of Idea Group Inc. publications in the fields of INFORMATION SCIENCE, TECHNOLOGY and MANAGEMENT

During the past decade, with the advent of telecommunications and the availability of distance learning opportunities, more college and university libraries can now provide access to comprehensive collections of research literature through access to online databases.

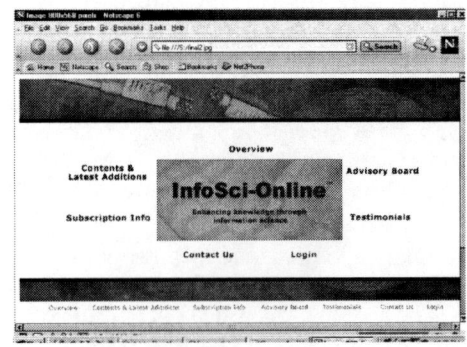

The InfoSci-Online database is the most comprehensive collection of *full-text* literature regarding research, trends, technologies, and challenges in the fields of information science, technology and management. This online database consists of over 3000 book chapters, 200+ journal articles, 200+ case studies and over 1,000+ conference proceedings papers from IGI's three imprints (Idea Group Publishing, Information Science Publishing and IRM Press) that can be accessed by users of this database through identifying areas of research interest and keywords.

Contents & Latest Additions:
Unlike the delay that readers face when waiting for the release of print publications, users will find this online database updated as soon as the material becomes available for distribution, providing instant access to the latest literature and research findings published by Idea Group Inc. in the field of information science and technology, in which emerging technologies and innovations are constantly taking place, and where time is of the essence.

The content within this database will be updated by IGI with 1300 new book chapters, 250+ journal articles and case studies and 250+ conference proceedings papers per year, all related to aspects of information, science, technology and management, published by Idea Group Inc. The updates will occur as soon as the material becomes available, even before the publications are sent to print.

InfoSci-Online pricing flexibility allows this database to be an excellent addition to your library, regardless of the size of your institution.

Contact: Ms. Carrie Skovrinskie, InfoSci-Online Project Coordinator, 717-533-8845 (Ext. 14), cskovrinskie@idea-group.com for a 30-day trial subscription to InfoSci-Online.

A product of:

INFORMATION SCIENCE PUBLISHING*
Enhancing Knowledge Through Information Science
http://www.info-sci-pub.com

*an imprint of Idea Group Inc.

Information Resources Management Journal (IRMJ)

An Official Publication of the Information Resources Management Association since 1988

Editor:
Mehdi Khosrow-Pour, D.B.A.
Information Resources Management
Association, USA

ISSN: 1040-1628; eISSN: 1533-7979
Subscription: Annual fee per volume (four issues): Individual US $85; Institutional US $265

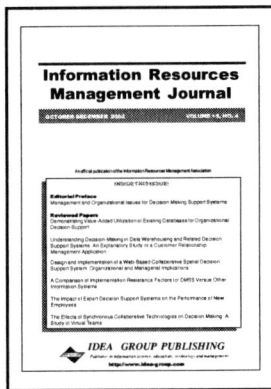

Mission

The *Information Resources Management Journal* (IRMJ) is a refereed, international publication featuring the latest research findings dealing with all aspects of information resources management, managerial and organizational applications, as well as implications of information technology organizations. It aims to be instrumental in the improvement and development of the theory and practice of information resources management, appealing to both practicing managers and academics. In addition, it educates organizations on how they can benefit from their information resources and all the tools needed to gather, process, disseminate and manage this valuable resource.

Coverage

IRMJ covers topics with a major emphasis on the managerial and organizational aspects of information resource and technology management. Some of the topics covered include: Executive information systems; Information technology security and ethics; Global information technology Management; Electronic commerce technologies and issues; Emerging technologies management; IT management in public organizations; Strategic IT management; Telecommunications and networking technologies; Database management technologies and issues; End user computing issues; Decision support & group decision support; Systems development and CASE; IT management research and practice; Multimedia computing technologies and issues; Object-oriented technologies and issues; Human and societal issues in IT management; IT education and training issues; Distance learning technologies and issues; Artificial intelligence & expert technologies; Information technology innovation & diffusion; and other issues relevant to IT management.

It's Easy to Order! Order online at www.idea-group.com or call our toll-free hotline at 1-800-345-4332!
Mon-Fri 8:30 am-5:00 pm (est) or fax 24 hours a day 717/533-8661

Idea Group Publishing
Hershey • London • Melbourne • Singapore • Beijing

An excellent addition to your library

A New **Title from IGP!**

Business to Business Electronic Commerce: Challenges & Solutions

Merrill Warkentin
Mississippi State University, USA

In the mid-1990s, the widespread adoption of the Web browser led to a rapid commercialization of the Internet. Initial success stories were reported from companies that learned how to create an effective direct marketing channel, selling tangible products to consumers directly over the World Wide Web. By the end of the 1990s, the next revolution began—business-to-business electronic commerce.

Business to Business Electronic Commerce: Challenges and Solutions *will provide researchers and practitioners with a source of knowledge related to this emerging area of business.*

ISBN 1-930708-09-2 (h/c); eISBN 1-591400-09-0 ; US$89.95; 308 pages • Copyright © 2002

Recommend IGP books to your library!

IDEA GROUP PUBLISHING

Hershey • London • Melbourne • Singapore • Beijing
701 E. Chocolate Avenue, Suite 200, Hershey, PA 17033-1117 USA
Tel: (800) 345-4332 • Fax: (717)533-8661 • cust@idea-group.com

See the complete catalog of IGP publications at http://www.idea-group.com